A Joyful Sound

Christian Hymnody

A Joyful Sound
Christian Hymnody

Second Edition

William Jensen Reynolds

*The Sunday School Board
of the Southern Baptist Convention*

Second Edition Prepared by

Milburn Price

Furman University

Holt, Rinehart and Winston

*New York   Chicago   San Francisco   Atlanta   Dallas
Montreal   Toronto   London   Sydney*

Library of Congress Cataloging in Publication Data

Reynolds, William Jensen.
A joyful sound.

First ed. published in 1963 under title: A survey
of Christian hymnody.
"Illustrative hymns and tunes": p.
Includes indexes.
1. Hymns—History and criticism.   2. Hymns,
English.   I. Price, Milburn.   II. Title.
ML3186.R5   1978   783.9'09   77–12048
ISBN: 0–03–040831–8

Preface to
the Second Edition

For the past fourteen years, William J. Reynolds's *A Survey of Christian Hymnody* has been widely used both as a text for the study of hymnology in colleges and seminaries throughout the country and as a source of enjoyable reading for those interested in the origins of congregational song and its use in Christian worship through the centuries. Its concise, yet incisive, coverage of the major historical developments that have led to the contemporary situation in English hymnody, its references to a wide variety of resources for supplementary study, and the section of illustrative hymn texts and tunes have been major factors in the book's appeal for both professional church musicians and the general public.

With the passing of time, there has developed a need for minor revisions of the *Survey*. From the creative side of hymnody have come new developments in text writing, tune composing, and hymnal compilation. From the scholarly pursuit of hymnology have come new insights into various aspects of the heritage of the past. When Dr. Reynolds's own demanding schedule as administrator, composer, editor, lecturer, and author prevented his preparing the revision, he kindly invited me to undertake the task, for which I am grateful. The second edition appears under a new title, *A Joyful Sound: Christian Hymnody,* which places renewed emphasis upon the role of congregational song as a vehicle for group expression of joyful praise.

In preparing the present edition, I have attempted to retain both the basic format and the concise approach to subject matter that characterized the original. The book therefore remains essentially as Dr. Reynolds described it in his preface to the first edition, which follows this preface.

There are four principal areas of change in the new edition:

1. Discussion of significant developments in text writing, tune composition, and hymnal compilation in England and the United States over the past fourteen years has been incorporated into the concluding sections of Chapters 5 and 7.
2. Treatment of a few key topics (the German chorale, metrical psalmody in Western Europe, American folk hymnody) has been modestly expanded.
3. An attempt has been made to make occasional minor revisions in the light of scholarly writings published in recent years that offer new in-

sight into historical developments. The suggestions for supplementary study have been expanded to make reference to many of the sources consulted.

4. There have been a few additions to the section of illustrative hymns and tunes (and a few necessary deletions in order to create space for the new material).

The increased importance given to the place and practice of hymnody in the worship of congregations representing a wide variety of denominations in recent years has made this project a timely one. The contributions and trends of the present, as well as the heritage of the past, have become matters of interest to many lay people, as well as to students, church musicians, and clergy. It is to this wide spectrum of both leaders and participants in congregational song that the present edition is directed.

There are a few individuals to whom specific words of appreciation must be directed: to William J. Reynolds, for reading and discussing all proposed revisions, offering thoughtful advice and suggestions, and writing the new material in Chapter 7 on "Expansion of Southern Shaped-Note Singing"; to Harry Eskew, for his numerous helpful suggestions regarding items to be given attention in this edition; and to my wife, Barbara, both for her encouragement throughout the project and for cheerfully serving as typist for the final manuscript.

Deep appreciation is also expressed to individuals and publishers who graciously granted permission for the use of copyrighted materials added to this edition.

M.P.

Greenville, South Carolina
January 1978

Preface to
the First Edition

One likes what has become familiar. Attitudes toward hymns and hymn singing are much influenced by subjective association. It does not follow that
hearty participation involves careful thought or conscious insight regarding
content or evaluation. For most of us the hymn has a sacred aura, and to
submit it to careful scrutiny sometimes causes inward resentment. But ministers as well as lay workers involved in programs of teaching and training have
a responsibility for selecting hymnic materials. If these leaders can be helped
to understand the values of hymn singing and the need for exercising careful
judgment in the choice of hymns, the intelligent appreciation of students and
the spiritual growth of congregations will be increased.

In the preparation of *A Survey of Christian Hymnody,* the author has endeavored to present a balanced systematic approach to the study of both traditional and modern hymn texts and tunes. The study of hymnody as an
academic pursuit is a relatively recent development; traditional guides found
in other areas are lacking. As a result, present courses vary widely in organization, importance, and merit.

Because the singing of hymns involves a musical experience, it is imperative
that attention be given to the intrinsic musical values of the hymn tune. Great
literary expressions cannot have fullest meaning when coupled with inferior
tunes. Because of their contribution, the appropriateness of text, melody,
harmony, and rhythm requires critical examination. From a musical
standpoint this is not to imply that complex and intricate tunes are the ideal,
for hymn tunes are the people's songs. But it does stress the fact that the
literary quality of the hymn and the musical worth of the tune merit careful
study and thoughtful appraisal.

In order to gain a perspective from which to understand hymns, it is imperative to have an awareness of the historical development of hymnody, a
knowledge of the broad scope of hymnic literature and of major trends in
religious thought. Prospective leaders need to understand the changing attitudes toward the use of hymns as church history unfolded and the motiva-
tions that caused writers to compose hymns and compilers to publish collections. Contemporary hymnody represents the accumulated inheritance of
centuries past. Each period has contributed to the present-day hymnal. The
materials presented here are designed to acquaint the student with the scope
of Christian hymnody, its historical patterns, the environment from which it
emerged, the contribution of significant individuals and specific collections of
hymns and tunes that furthered the ever-increasing stream of Christian song.

This presentation of hymnody is approached through five major areas: (1)
early church song; (2) the Lutheran chorale; (3) psalmody; (4) English hymnody; and (5) American hymnody. The first area deals with the period from
the pre-Christian Hebrew tradition through the Middle Ages. The second
area discusses the hymnody of the Protestant Reformation, centering around

the Lutheran tradition. The third deals with the rise of the metrical psalm in Geneva and its development and use in France, England, and Scotland. The fourth shows the transition from psalmody to hymnody in the seventeenth century in England and hymnic development to the present day. The fifth area, dealing with hymnody in America, begins with imported English psalmody, the transition to hymnody, and its development to the present. Supplementary reading from materials listed at the end of the final chapter will enrich the reader's experience and build an acquaintance with the finest books available in this field.

To illustrate historical development of our hymnody, a careful selection of hymns is provided representing the types and periods under consideration. These illustrative hymns are given in the form in which they appear in contemporary hymnals. Such presentation is more practical for critical study than the reproduction of the same material in its original form. The numbers in parentheses by hymn titles and tune names throughout each chapter refer to these illustrative hymns.

This selection is not to be regarded as an "abridged hymnal," but rather as a collection reflecting many facets of contributions to Christian hymnody. Both familiar and unfamiliar hymns will be found. The appearance of a familiar hymn set to an unfamiliar tune is not to imply preference for the unfamiliar over the familiar. Likewise, the absence of many hymns is not to imply that they are of lesser quality or value. The sole basis of selection has been the significance of each in historical development.

In the preparation of this material I acknowledge my indebtedness to such hymnologists as Julian, Benson, McCutchan, Ellinwood, Haeussler, and Routley. The contribution of the scholarly writings of these men has been a major factor in the present-day emphasis on the study of hymnody within the academic environment and has made the way brighter for all who follow.

Sincere appreciation is expressed to individuals and publishers who kindly granted permission for the use of their copyrighted materials. Every effort has been made to trace the ownership of all copyrighted items, although exact ownership is obscure in some instances. The kindness of The Pilgrim Press, publishers of *The Pilgrim Hymnal,* 1958, is particularly appreciated for granting their permission to use the format and many of the plates in their hymnal in making up the section of illustrative hymns included in *A Survey of Christian Hymnody.*

Deep gratitude goes to the late Robert Guy McCutchan who, in personal contact during the last decade of his life, and in the example of his own hymnological pursuits, provided irresistible inspiration and encouragement for research and study in this area; and to Irving Wolfe, out of whose concern for the appropriate recognition of hymnody in the church music curriculum came the initial suggestion for this undertaking. His wise counsel and guidance have been of invaluable assistance in the making of this book.

Nashville, Tennessee   W.J.R.
January 1963

Note to the Reader

Firsthand experience with the hymns themselves will prove of greatest value. Read each aloud to gain an appreciation of its literary significance as a religious and poetic expression. Sing the tune to gain an awareness of its musical characteristics and emotional impact. Doing both will give effective practice in good tempos and phrasing and furnish a means of realizing the full spirit of the hymn.

METRICAL FORMS OF HYMNS

Hymnic literature has made use of poetic meter and rhythm resulting in a system of symbols and terminology peculiar to this area of study. An examination of any hymnal will reveal a metrical form indicated for each hymn. Except for the three most frequently found meters—common, long, and short—these will be shown in a series of digits: 8.7.8.7; 12.11.12.11; 7.7.7.7.7; and so on. The number of digits shown indicates the number of lines per stanza, and each digit the number of syllables in each given line. For example, 7.7.7.7.7.7. indicates that each stanza has six lines, and each line seven syllables. The metrical form, 8.7.8.7., shows that each stanza has four lines, and that the first and third lines have eight syllables each, while the second and fourth lines have seven syllables each. The addition of D to these numbers, that is, 8.7.8.7 D., indicates that each stanza has eight lines, or a four-line stanza doubled. This could also be written 8.7.8.7.8.7.8.7.

Three metrical forms of hymns are usually indicated by initials rather than by digits: C.M. (common meter); S.M. (short meter); and L.M. (long meter).

Common Meter. Common meter (C.M.) is a four-line stanza made up of 8.6.8.6. syllables. This is the Old English ballad meter, originally two septenary lines each containing seven iambic feet, or fourteen syllables. This couplet, known as a "fourteener," breaks into four lines of four and three feet, or eight and six syllables. The rhyme is *abab:*

O God, our help in ages past,	(8)a
Our hope for years to come,	(6)b
Our shelter from the stormy blast	(8)a
And our eternal home.	(6)b
(Isaac Watts)	

or *abcb:*

In Christ there is no East or West	(8)a
In him no South or North,	(6)b

But one great fellowship of love   (8)c
Throughout the whole wide earth.   (6)b
(John Oxenham)

Short Meter. Short Meter (S.M.) is a four-line stanza made up of 6.6.8.6. syllables. It is a breakdown of the unequal couplet combining an Alexandrine and a septenary. This early Tudor meter was called "Poulter's Measure," because of the poulterers' custom of giving twelve for the first dozen and thirteen or fourteen for the second. The couplet of twelve and fourteen syllables breaks into a four-line stanza. Its rhyme is *abab:*

Blest be the tie that binds   (6)a
Our hearts in Christian love   (6)b
The fellowship of kindred minds   (8)a
Is like to that above.   (6)b
(John Fawcett)

or *abcb:*

I love thy kingdom, Lord,   (6)a
The house of thine abode,   (6)b
The church our blest Redeemer saved (8)c
With his own precious blood.   (6)b
(Timothy Dwight)

Long Meter. Long meter (L.M.) is a four-line stanza, each line containing eight syllables, 8.8.8.8. The form follows the iambic-dimeter pattern of the early Latin hymns of Ambrosian tradition. The rhyme is *abab:*

When I survey the wondrous cross   (8)a
On which the Prince of Glory died,   (8)b
My richest gain I count but loss,   (8)a
And pour contempt on all my pride.   (8)b
(Isaac Watts)

or *aabb:*

Lord of all being, throned afar,   (8)a
Thy glory flames from sun and star: (8)a
Center and soul of every sphere,   (8)b
Yet to each loving heart how near!   (8)b
(Oliver Wendell Holmes)

or *abba:*

Strong Son of God, immortal Love,   (8)a
Whom we, that have not seen thy face, (8)b
By faith, and faith alone, embrace,   (8)b
Believing where we cannot prove.   (8)a
(Alfred Tennyson)

Contents

5
English Hymnody, II 57

6
American Hymnody, I 71

7
American Hymnody, II 88

1
Early
Church Song

Behold, I bring you good tidings of great joy, which shall be to all people. For unto you is born this day in the city of David a Saviour, which is Christ the Lord.

LUKE 2:10-11

Christianity was born within a Jewish environment that existed in the midst of a widespread Greco-Roman culture. When the Christian era dawned, the religious activity of Judaism centered around the Temple and the synagogue. In the four hundred years that had elapsed between the return of the exiles from the Babylonian captivity to the advent of Christ, the Temple had developed an elaborate service of worship. Its ceremonies were under the careful administration of a priestly hierarchy. Obedience to Temple ordinances by the people and sacrificial worship by the priesthood for the people became basic functions. The synagogue seems to have developed during the Exile when the Jews were cut off from the Temple and its services. In the synagogue the scribes read from the Law and explained the Scriptures, and the people sang the psalms. After the synagogue was transplanted back to the Jewish homeland, it continued these practices and eventually rivaled the Temple.

Temple music was elaborate, that of the synagogue more simple. In the Temple, priests and choirs chanted the psalms and portions of the Pentateuch, but in the synagogue the people shared in the musical portion of the service. Instrumental music was employed in Temple worship, while in the synagogue singing was generally unaccompanied.

THE BOOK OF PSALMS

The Book of Psalms, found in the Old Testament, is thought to have been compiled during and after the Babylonian exile. On the basis of internal evidence, some of the psalms seem to indicate that they were used for public worship, some for private devotion, and some for the celebration of specific events. Singing of the psalms was usually done in a direct manner, but, on the basis of structure, some were obviously sung antiphonally. Scholars are not in agreement on whether or not the psalms were solely, or primarily, intended for use in Temple liturgy.

The Hebrew Psalter and the manner in which it was used provided the musical heritage of the early Christians. The texts reflected the basic concepts of God and his moral nature. They gave evidence of the personal element of religion—individual communion with God. The tunes were seemingly taught and preserved only in the oral tradition. With the psalms so positively associated with the vocal expression of religious experience, it is not surprising to find that, at the conclusion of the Last Supper, Christ and his disciples sang a hymn which historians believe to have been a portion of the Hallel, Psalms 113–118.

NEW TESTAMENT HYMNS

The early Christians sought to supplement their heritage of psalms with songs of their own Christian experience. They desired songs that would praise the name of Christ and tell of his gospel. Three lyric portions of the Nativity from Luke's Gospel were appropriated.

My soul doth magnify the Lord, and my spirit hath rejoiced in God my Saviour.

Luke 1:46

This song of Mary became known as the Magnificat and is found today as part of the Roman Catholic rites sung in the Office of Vespers. In the Anglican Service it is part of the Evening Prayer or Evensong.

Blessed be the Lord God of Israel; for he hath visited and redeemed his people.

Luke 1:68

This song, sung by Zacharias, become known as the Benedictus and is presently sung at Lauds in the Roman Catholic Church and at Morning Prayer in the Anglican Service.

Lord, now lettest thou thy servant depart in peace, according to thy word; for mine eyes have seen thy salvation, which thou hast prepared before the face of all people.

Luke 2:29–31

This song of Simeon became known as the Nunc Dimittis and is found today in the service of Compline in the Roman Catholic Church, in Evensong in the Anglican Service, and in the Lutheran Communion service.

In various places in the New Testament the hymnlike structure of the writing gives the implication that these scriptures were sung or chanted.

Awake thou that sleepest,
  And arise from the dead,
And Christ shall give thee light.
          Ephesians 5:14

Now unto the King eternal, immortal, invisible,
  The only wise God
Be honor and glory for ever and ever.
          I Timothy 1:17

Manifest in flesh,
Justified in spirit,
Visible to angels,
Preached among the nations,
Believed on in the world,
Taken up into glory.
          I Timothy 3:16

Thus, the body of Christian song began to take shape from the Scriptures and from the extemporized vocal expressions of the early Christians.

The practice of Christian song is well documented in the Scriptures. It is not known what songs or Scriptures were sung, but, for example, the account of the imprisonment of Paul and Silas relates:

And at midnight Paul and Silas prayed, and sang praises unto God: and the prisoners heard them.

                                        Acts 16:25

From the writings of Paul come further evidence of the significance of Christian song both as an instrument of praise to God and as a tool for teaching.

Be filled with the Spirit, speaking to yourselves in psalms and hymns and spiritual songs, singing and making melody in your heart to the Lord.

                                        Ephesians 5:18–19

Let the word of Christ dwell in you richly in all wisdom; teaching and admonishing one another in psalms and hymns and spiritual songs, singing with grace in your hearts to the Lord.

                                        Colossians 3:16

About the manner of performance, Paul writes:

I will sing with the spirit, and I will sing with the understanding also.

                                        I Corinthians 14:15

EARLY CHRISTIAN HYMNODY

After the destruction of the Temple in A.D. 70, there were significant developments that directly and indirectly exerted influence on Christian song. The persecution of believers increased, and meetings for praise and fellowship were held in secret. The Gospel spread beyond nationalistic bounds as Gentiles were converted to Christianity, but hostility grew between Christians and the Jews who did not accept Christ as the Messiah. In A.D. 70 and again in A.D. 132 the strength of Jewish nationalism was crushed by Roman conquests. The consequent overthrow of Jewish institutions loosened existing ties to the Jewish rituals and ceremonies. Christians therefore retained only those elements that they deemed appropriate to their needs during this formative period. In the early centuries, the distinction emerged between clergy and laity which later developed into a system of patriarchs, priests, bishops, and deacons. No longer were the clergy the servants or representatives of the people; instead they assumed a mediatorial function as the channels through which divine grace was transmitted to the faithful. In this position, the clergy assumed a greater responsibility for church worship, forming and shaping the liturgy and the music involved.

Hellenistic Influences   At the time of Christ, Hellenistic culture was the dominant influence throughout the Roman Empire. Greece had become a province of the Empire and as such was under political subjection to the Emperor, but the culture, philosophy, art, and language of the Greeks continued to be leading forces throughout the area under Roman rule. The Old Testament had been translated from Hebrew into Greek (this translation is known as the Septuagint), and the New Testament was written first in neither Latin nor Hebrew, but in Greek. It was the language of culture and the language of the church and remained such for three hundred years, even in Rome. Athens was the university city of the Roman world. Greek poetic forms—the epic, the comedy, the epigram, and the ode—were taken over by Roman writers.

Clement of Alexandria (c. 170–c. 220), the author of "Shepherd of eager youth" (148) and "Sunset to sunrise changes now" (124), has been called the father of Greek theology. As the head of the catechetical school at Alexandria, he was the first to approach Christian truth and teaching in the light of Greek thought and Gnostic speculation. His hymns reveal his efforts to combine the spirit of Greek poetry with Christian theology.

The Greek "Candlelighting Hymn" ("O gladsome light, O grace") (34), of unknown authorship, dates from the third century. This evening hymn from the pre-Constantinian period is still in use in the Greek church.

A strip of papyrus, discovered at Oxyrhynchos in Egypt in 1918, is the only evidence now available concerning the character of the music to which the early Christian hymns were sung. This fragment reveals the closing part of a hymn to the Holy Trinity. It was first published by A. S. Hunt in the fifteenth volume of the Oxyrhynchos Papyri, 1922. The work of an anonymous poet of the Alexandrian School, this "Oxyrhynchos hymn" dates from the end of the third century. In spite of its Greek notation, Wellesz points out that this hymn is not of Greek origin, but in all probability was patterned after an older song of praise of the Primitive Church.[1]

The ten hymns of Synesius of Cyrene (c. 375–c. 414) reveal evidences of Semitic influence on classic Greek poetry. The tenth hymn, "Lord Jesus, think on me" (38), is an epilogue to the first nine hymns.

Throughout the first four centuries the influence of Greek culture upon the early church declined. Beginning in the fourth century, Latin began to replace Greek as the language of the Western church, and this change was almost universal by the close of the sixth century. The Greek Septuagint was replaced by the Latin Vulgate.

Because of the difficulties with the northern barbaric tribes, Emperor Constantine moved the seat of government of the Roman Empire to Byzantium in A.D. 330, making it the capital of the empire and changing its name to Constantinople. A division of the Roman Empire into eastern and western areas resulted, and the departure of imperial power from Rome made possible the rise and spread of papal power. From the fifth century on, papal power gradually increased and imperial power decreased.

There was much activity in neighboring Syria as early Christians carried the Gospel beyond Palestine. In an effort to counteract the Arian heresy, the practice of antiphonal singing was introduced at Antioch early in the fourth century, and the chanting of the psalm verses became the responsibility of the congregation.

> Its members were divided into two semi-choruses, one of men, one of women and children, and the groups alternated with one another in the singing of the psalm-verses and combined in singing an Alleluia or, perhaps, some new refrain. The intercalating of passages of song between psalm-verses became, in the course of time, an organized practice and was destined to be imitated with telling effect in the West.[2]

In Syria, also, began the singing of hymns with texts in verse form. Ephraim (d. A.D. 373), the foremost Syrian hymn writer, employed the popular tunes of heretical groups and substituted orthodox texts for the people to sing.

Less than forty years after the founding of Constantinople, the Council of Laodicea, A.D. 367, prohibited the participation of the congregation and the use of instruments in the service. It further provided that only the Scriptures could be used for singing. With this restriction, hymn writers were limited to the canticles and the psalms, which accounts for the absence of hymns of personal experience during this period.

[1] Cf. Egon Wellesz, *A History of Byzantine Music and Hymnography*, 2d ed. (Oxford: Clarendon Press, 1961), pp. 152–156.

[2] Gustave Reese, *Music in the Middle Ages* (New York: W. W. Norton & Company, 1940), p. 68.

BYZANTINE HYMNODY

The greatest contribution of the Eastern church to Christian song was the Byzantine hymns. Influenced by Jewish tradition and Syrian practice, these hymns developed in the worship of the Eastern church as unaccompanied monophonic chant, mainly diatonic, lacking in strict meter, and closely following the rhythm of the text.

The earliest Byzantine hymns, appearing in the fourth and fifth centuries, were *troparia,* short prayers sung between the reading of the psalms. In the sixth century there developed the *kontakion,* consisting of a short introduction followed by eighteen to thirty stanzas of uniform structure and ending with a refrain. The stanzas were connected either alphabetically or by an acrostic. If the connection was alphabetical, the initial letter of each stanza followed the alphabet in usual order. If an acrostic was used, the initial letters of each stanza made a sentence that gave the title of the hymn and the name of the author. The outstanding writer of kontakion was Romanus (c. 500) whose identification in the acrostic was usually given as "the humble Romanus."

In the eighth century there appeared the canon (Greek *kanōn*), a long poem of nine odes (hymns), each originally consisting of from six to nine stanzas. The nine odes were based upon biblical canticles and were characteristically hymns of praise.[3] Within a single ode the same rhythmical form was used for each stanza. The chief writers of canon were Andrew of Crete (c. 650–730) (156) and John of Damascus (d.c. 780). "The day of resurrection" (70) is a translation of the first ode of the "Golden Canon" for Easter day, and "Come, ye faithful, raise the strain" (76) is a translation of the first ode of the canon for the first Sunday after Easter.

These three forms—troparion, kontakion, and canon—continued in use in the Eastern church. From the beginning of the ninth century the Studium monastery at Constantinople became the center of Byzantine hymnic activity. Among the monks associated with this monastery who wrote hymns were Anatolius and Theoctistus, the author of "Jesus, Name all names above" (150).

THE DEVELOPMENT OF LATIN HYMNODY

In the first three centuries, because of their persecution, Christians met in secret and, therefore, made limited use of singing. Following the Edict of Milan, A.D. 313, Christianity became the religion of the Empire, and the singing of Christians emerged as a joyful expression of their freedom. There was the singing of the psalms and the joyous *Alleluia* with its concluding

---

[3] Of the nine odes, most were based upon Old Testament canticles. The only New Testament canticle used as a source was the Magnificat.

jubilus, an extended musical phrase sung on the final *a* of the *Alleluia.* Responsorial singing, which employed an ornate solo followed by a refrain sung by the people, was widely used.

The person significant in first transferring hymnody based upon Greek models to the West seems to have been Hilary, Bishop of Poitiers (c. 310–366). During a four-year exile in Asia Minor, he became familiar with the hymnody of the Greek church. Upon his return to Poitiers, his hymns were intended to present Trinitarian doctrines to combat the Arian heresy.[4]

Ambrosian Hymnody   The practice of antiphonal singing in the Western church was adopted in the fourth century at Milan by Ambrose, Bishop of Milan (340–397). From Milan this practice spread to Rome where it was officially adopted during the papacy of Celestine I, 422–432. As has been previously noted, antiphonal singing had been used in the Eastern church, and the term originally meant "octave," such as the singing of boys and men together in octaves. Later, the term came to mean one group answering another group of singers.

Ambrose, like Hilary, realized the value of hymns in combating Arianism. More than a dozen hymns have been attributed to him, but only four are accepted as being authentic: *"Aeterna rerum Conditer"* ("Framer of the earth and sky"); *"Deus Creator omnium"* ("Maker of all things God most high"); *"Iam surgit hora tertia"* ("Now appears the third hour"); and *"Veni Redemptor gentium"* ("Come, thou Saviour of our race").[5] Another hymn traditionally attributed to Ambrosian authorship is *"Splendor paternae gloriae"* ("O splendor of God's glory bright") (1). These hymns deal with fundamental Christian teachings. The language is dignified, yet simple, making use of the expressions of the people for whom they were written. In contrast with the irregular, asymmetrical prose form of the psalms, these hymns appeared in a new symmetrical form. Each hymn was made up of a number of stanzas, usually eight, and each stanza contained four lines of iambic dimeter, a popular folklike rhythm rather than a classical metrical form. Here is the foundation for the long meter hymn form, which became, centuries later, one of the three basic hymn forms. The melodies were constructed usually with one note to each syllable.

The result was a plain, easily remembered tune, quite similar to the popular tunes of later antiquity. In short, the hymn may be called a spiritual folk song and the Ambrosian hymn became, a thousand years later, the model for the chorale of the Protestant Church.[6]

[4]Arius (c. 250–336), an influential leader in the church at Alexandria, proposed the theological doctrine that the Son was not equal to the Father, but was secondary to the Father. Though his views were condemned as heretical by both the Council of Alexandria (321) and the Council of Nicaea (325), the Arian doctrine was widely spread and popularized through the use of song.

[5] Reese, p. 104.

[6] Hugo Leichtentritt, *Music, History, and Ideas* (Cambridge: Harvard University Press, 1944), p. 31.

8   Thus, by the end of the fourth century, the pattern of Christian song had developed along three basic lines: responsorial psalm singing, antiphonal psalm singing, and the metrical hymn.

Office Hymns   The adaptation of existing Latin hymns to daily worship in monasteries resulted in the office hymns. By the fifth century, the services of canonical hours were established. They consisted of the nocturnal cursus: Vespers, Compline, Matins, Lauds, and the diurnal cursus: Prime, Tierce, Sext, and Nones. Through the influence of Benedict, hymns were introduced into use for all canonical hours, whereas the Ambrosian hymns had previously been used only for Matins, Lauds, and Vespers. An early collection of these sixth-century office hymns, known as the *Old Hymnal,* contained thirty-four hymns.[7]

Beginnings of the Roman Liturgy   During the early centuries the various parts of the Roman liturgy slowly began to take shape. By the time of Gregory, the *Kyrie eleison,* the *Gloria in excelsis,* and the *Sanctus* were sung by the congregation.[8] The *Kyrie* appeared in the Eastern church in the first century, and its Greek form was retained in the Latin Mass. The *Gloria,* known as the Greater Doxology, appeared in part in the second century in the Eastern church and in the sixth century was translated into Latin and adopted by the Western church. The *Sanctus,* which is of Hebrew origin, was used in Jewish worship before the Christian era.

The *Gloria Patri,* the Lesser Doxology, which has added to each psalm sung in the service, was known in its present form by the end of the fourth century in both Eastern and Western churches. The *Te Deum laudamus,* while similar in form to early Greek praises, seems to be wholly of Latin origin. The *Credo* (based on the Nicene Creed), first used in the Eastern church in the sixth century and later in the Western church, was introduced for congregational use to strengthen and confirm the faith of the people against the influence of Arianism. The *Agnus Dei* was adopted in the seventh century, and from this century the Ordinary of the Mass became gradually standardized. By the tenth century, Mass was sung by the choirs, congregational participation having been gradually abandoned. These early expressions of praise and worship remain today in the Roman Mass and also are found in the Anglican, Episcopal, and Lutheran liturgies.

Early Latin Hymn Writers   The hymns of Ambrose led to an increasing interest in the writing of hymns. The first significant successor to Ambrose was Aurelius Clemens Prudentius (348–413), a Spanish lawyer, judge, and poet. From his extended hymn cycles for the canonical hours and church festivals has come "Of the Father's love begotten" (4). Another hymn-writer of the same era was Caelius Sedulius (d.c. 450).

[7] Ruth Ellis Messenger, *The Medieval Latin Hymn* (Washington: Capital Press, 1953), p. 10.

[8] Winfred Douglas, *Church Music in History and Practice,* rev. ed. (New York: Charles Scribner's Sons, 1962), p. 37.

Other hymnists contributed to the growing body of hymn literature during the period labeled the Dark Ages. Venantius Fortunatus, Bishop of Poitiers (c. 530–609), was the author of "Welcome, happy morning, age to age shall say" (67). Diaconus, or "Paul the Deacon" (d. 799), wrote the hymn *"Ut queant laxis,"* which Guido d'Arezzo used in teaching solmization in the eleventh century. There is some evidence that the six syllables had been in use prior to Guido; nevertheless, he is credited with establishing the practical use of them in teaching music reading.

Two anonymous Latin hymns of the ninth century are "O Come, O Come, Emmanuel" (68) and "Come, Holy Ghost, our souls inspire" (6). The latter hymn has been attributed by several scholars to Rabanus Maurus (d. 856), who studied at the Benedictine Monastery in Fulda (Germany).

Gregorian Chant   At the beginning of the seventh century, the melodies of the Roman chant were gathered together in a recognized repertoire. While this codification had, no doubt, begun earlier, it is generally attributed to Pope Gregory I (590–604) and, throughout the centuries that followed to the present day, these chants bear his name. With few additions they remain the body of Roman plainsong today. Gregory is also credited with adding the four plagal modes to the already existing authentic modes. These chants are characterized as monophonic, unaccompanied, mainly diatonic, having an absence of strict meter, and freedom of rhythm to fit the rhythm of the text. Examples of these melodies found in present-day hymnals are: DIVINUM MYSTERIUM (4), SPLENDOR PATERNAE (1), DIES IRAE (3), and VENI CREATOR (6). The version of VENI CREATOR given here is from the Mechlin *Vesperale Romanum,* 1848, a collection of plainsong melodies designed to restore the use of plainsong in the Roman Catholic churches of France at a time when the practice of this ancient church song had been forgotten.

So strong was the influence of the Gregorian plainsong that it soon became the accepted pattern for Western churches. Before the end of the seventh century, it had reached England and was taken from England to Germany early in the eighth century. During the reign of Charlemagne, the Roman church prospered, and its influence increased. Churches, schools, convents, and monasteries were established throughout Europe, and the practice of Christian song was an integral part of this expansion. One of Charlemagne's counselors, Theodulph (c. 762–821), Bishop of Orleans, is the author of "All glory, laud, and honor" (16).

The Sequence   Mention has already been made of the *jubilus,* the extension of the final syllable of the *Alleluia.* Gradually the musical phrases of this extended melody were supplied with new text material. This new form, known as the *sequence,* first appeared in France, but its greatest development is attributed to Notker Balbulus (840–912) at the Benedictine monastery of St. Gall in Switzerland.

10

> In order to understand the extraordinary popularity and wide diffusion of the sequence it must be emphasized that it is not just another hymn, but an ornament to the mass, individually created for each and every festival with a particular theme in mind . . . The original Latin hymn was associated with daily secular worship and then with the canonical hours of the monastery. The sequence was associated with the celebration of the divine sacrifice.[9]

"Victimae paschali laudes" ("Christians, to the Paschal victim") (2), traditionally ascribed to Wipo of Burgundy (d.c. 1050) represents the development of the sequence in the eleventh century. The use of dialogue, as evidenced in this text, was a contributing factor in the development of the liturgical drama for Easter. Of further significance is the fact that the pre-Reformation chorale, *"Christ ist erstanden,"* and Luther's *"Christ lag in Todesbanden"* are patterned after this sequence.

The unrhymed style of the Notkerian sequence was gradually replaced by the rhymed metrical sequence of Adam of St. Victor in Northern France in the late twelfth century. The two best-known examples of the rhymed metrical sequence may be found in the *"Dies irae"* ("Day of wrath! O day of mourning" (3) and the *"Stabat mater"* ("At the cross her station keeping") (24). Both the *"Dies irae,"* whose opening line is taken verbatim from the Vulgate translation of Zephaniah 1:15, and the plainsong sequence given here date from the thirteenth century. The *"Stabat mater,"* originally a rhymed prayer intended for private devotions, is the work of an unknown Italian author of the thirteenth century. In the revised Roman Missal of 1570, made by the Council of Trent, all sequences were abolished except four: *"Victimae paschali"* for Easter; *"Veni Sancte Spiritus"* for Pentecost; *"Lauda Sion Salvatorem"* for Corpus Christi; and *"Dies irae, dies illa"* for Masses for the Dead. A fifth, *"Stabat mater dolorosa,"* was added in 1727 for Friday after Passion Sunday.

Latin Hymnody of the Middle Ages   Hymn singing gradually became a part of the service in many churches throughout the Empire. However, it was not until the twelfth century that Rome adopted this practice. The Council of Laodicea admitted only the Bible in the services, and nonbiblical texts had to wait six hundred years for acceptance in the Roman service.

Significant writers of Latin hymnic literature of this later period (the Middle Ages) are: Peter Abelard (1079–1142), author of "Alone thou goest forth, O Lord" (56); Bernard of Clairvaux (c. 1091–1153), author of "Jesus, the very thought of thee" (47) and "Jesus, thou joy of loving hearts" (78); Bernard of Cluny, twelfth century, author of "Jerusalem, the golden" (72); Francis of Assisi (c. 1181–1226), author of "All creatures of our God and King" (23); and St. Thomas Aquinas. "O Sacred Head! now wounded" (9) is sometimes ascribed to Bernard of Clairvaux, but is more probably the work of an unknown

---

[9] Messenger, p. 44.

writer of the fourteenth century. It is ironic that two of these leading medieval hymn writers—Abelard, a teacher and advocate of a reasoned, intellectual approach to Christian faith, and Bernard of Clairvaux, who espoused personal piety and devotion—engaged in extended, bitter debates with each other.

Laudi Spirituali   In the thirteenth and fourteenth centuries a body of nonliturgical music developed in Italy outside of the auspices of the Roman church. These *laudi spirituali* were religious songs of devotion and praise sung to simple melodies. The texts were not in Latin, but in the vernacular of the people, and their popularity was widespread. One of these texts from a fourteenth-century collection is *"Discendi, amor santo"* ("Come down, O love divine") (90).

Perhaps the most important writer of *laude*, as these vernacular songs of praise were also called, was Jacopone da Todi (1230–1306), who left a successful career as a lawyer at the age of forty to embark on a life of asceticism and eventually entered the Franciscan Order.

Attempts at Reform   The wide variance in the Gregorian melodies used in different parts of Europe, the infiltration of secular melodies into the liturgy, and the use of vernacular texts prompted the Council of Trent, 1545–1563, to initiate reforms. Official books were published—the Missal, Gradual, Antiphonary, Breviary and others—containing approved plainsong melodies for all churches to use. This attempt to purify the music of the Roman church and to restore the ancient monophonic song faced severe obstacles in the rising tide of polyphony and strong opposition to anything medieval in nature. In manuscript collections that followed, many variations appeared as well as new original melodies. The restoration of ancient plainsong awaited the work of the monks of the Abbey of Solesmes in the nineteenth century, which, with authentic texts, are now authorized for use by papal decree.

Later Developments in Latin Hymnody   The stream of Latin hymnody did not cease with the end of the Middle Ages. Illustrative of a continuing interest in the writing of hymns in Latin in succeeding centuries are *"O filii et filiae"* ("O sons and daughters, let us sing") by Jean Tisserand in the late fifteenth century and *"Adeste Fideles"* ("O come, all ye faithful") (111), written by John Francis Wade in the mid-eighteenth century. Also significant to the development of Latin hymnody was the series of revisions of the Breviary that occurred from the sixteenth through the eighteenth centuries.

2

The Lutheran Chorale

I am not at all of the opinion that the gospel should do away with art, as a few hyper-spiritual persons maintain; I would love to see all the arts, and especially music, in the service of Him who has given and created them.[1]

The sixteenth century saw the Renaissance at its height, and vocal polyphonic technique developed to its highest degree in what is recognized as the "golden age of polyphony." The five-line music staff has been established, but bar lines were not in common usage. Modality predominated, but major-minor tonality was emerging. The development of music printing was a great advance over the circulation of most literature by oral tradition and by laboriously copied manuscripts.

THE SIGNIFICANCE OF MARTIN LUTHER

At the time of Martin Luther (1483–1546), the practice of music in the Catholic church was dominated by the clergy, with the congregation as spectators and listeners rather than participants. The same conviction that motivated Luther's translation of the Bible into the vernacular of the people also produced the desire for congregational song in the language of the common man, so that all Christians might join in singing praises to God.

[1] Martin Luther, as quoted in John Spencer Curwen, *Studies in Worship Music*, 2d series (London: J. Curwen & Sons, 1885), p. 125.

12

Luther's Hymns It is extremely significant that Martin Luther, who led the Reformation, was also the first evangelical hymn writer. In addition to his interest in poetry, he was a musician and composed tunes to some of his own hymns. His hymn writing dates from 1523, shortly after he had completed his translation of the New Testament into the German language, and continued until two years before his death. Of his thirty-seven hymns, twenty-three were written during 1523–1524. Of these thirty-seven hymns, eleven were translations from Latin sources, four were revisions of pre-Reformation hymns, seven were versifications of psalms, six were paraphrases of other scripture selections, and nine are classed as original hymns. Luther possessed the ability to express profound scriptural teaching in a simple, straightforward manner. Yet in the simplicity of his hymns there is evidence of strength and courage.

Luther has been called the Ambrose of German hymnody, and his *"Ein' feste Burg ist unser Gott"* ("A mighty fortress is our God"), has been called the Marseillaise Hymn of the Reformation. His great hymn, a paraphrase of Psalm 46, apparently was written in 1529 for the Diet of Speyer, when the German princes made their formal protest against the revoking of their liberties, and thus received the name "protestants." An earlier hymn by Luther, a metrical paraphrase of Psalm 130, *"Aus tiefer Not schrei' ich zu dir"* ("Out of the depths I cry to thee") (7), written in 1523, was first published the following year in *Etlich Christlich Lieder*. At the time of the Diet of Augsburg, 1530, Luther remained in the Castle of Coburg. During these days of anxiety he would gather the servants of the castle about him and say: "Come, let us defy the devil, and praise God by singing the hymn, *'Aus tiefer Not schrei' ich zu dir.'*" In 1546, the people of Halle sang this hymn with tears in their eyes as they lined the streets when Luther's coffin passed through the city on its way from Eisleben to Wittenberg, its final resting place.

Early Lutheran Hymn Writers In the early years of the Reformation, Luther wrote to Nicholaus Haussman, pastor at Zwickau:

> I also wish that we had as many songs as possible in the vernacular which the people could sing during mass, . . . But poets are wanting among us, or not yet known, who could compose evangelical and spiritual songs, . . . worthy to be used in the church of God.[2]

In response to that plea came hymn texts and melodies from numerous German poets and musicians. Koch, in his *Geschichte des Kirchenlieds und Kirchengesänges,* cites fifty-one hymn-writers active during the years 1517–1560. A presumably exaggerated view of the extent of that response appears in the preface to a 1546 hymnal:

[2] Ulrich S. Leupold (ed.), *Liturgy and Hymns* (Vol. 53 of *Luther's Works*) (Philadelphia: Fortress Press, 1965), p. 36.

14   Throughout half of Germany there is scarcely a pastor or shoemaker who lacks
the skill to make a little song or tune to sing at church with his neighbors.[3]

Among the most important early contributors to chorale literature were
Justus Jonas (1493–1555), Hans Sachs (1494–1576), Paul Speratus (1484–
1551), Nicolaus Decius (c. 1458–c. 1546), Nicolaus Hermann (c. 1480–1561),
and Paul Eber (1511–1569). Some of these, like Luther, were poet-composers;
others made their primary contribution through either texts or melodies.

Sources of Early Texts and Tunes   Luther and his contemporaries drew
upon four principal sources for their texts and tunes:[4] (1) the liturgy, both
Mass and Office, of the Catholic Church, (2) pre-Reformation nonliturgical
vernacular and macaronic hymns, (3) secular folk song, and (4) works of
original creativity. The borrowed materials were treated in differing ways. In
some instances, text and melody were used, with textual alterations or paraphrases made in translating the Latin liturgical text into the vernacular. In
this manner, Decius transformed the *Gloria in excelsis* into *"Allein Gott in der
Höh sei Ehr"* ("All glory be to God on high") (8). The most literal translations of
this type took as their source the office hymns. For other adaptations, new
texts were provided for appealing melodies, and vice versa.

Musical Characteristics   Johannes Riedel, in his excellent monograph on
the Lutheran chorale, provides a concise description of the essential characteristics of the chorale melodies:

> The stately melodies of the chorale display economy of musical materials, and can
> often be reduced to a few primordial motives. Cadence formulae at the ends of the
> various phrases have a balance or relationship which stresses feeling for a certain
> key center or modal area. The rhythmic structure usually rests upon only one
> basic pattern.[5]

Structurally, the early chorale tunes displayed an indebtedness to the traditions of the German Meistersingers through the use of barform (AAB) and its
variants. Melodic contour of original tunes often also reflected a relationship
to the lied tradition through the use of a descending melodic passage span-
ning an octave.

One of Martin Luther's most significant musical contributions in the chorale
was the use of the Ionian mode, by which he moved beyond the traditional
church modes and anticipated the development of major tonality. Luther
utilized the Ionian mode particularly in his original works, such as "A mighty
fortress is our God" and "From Heaven above to earth I come."

---

[3] Quoted in Edwin Liemohn. *The Chorale: Through Four Hundred Years of Musical Development as a
Congregational Hymn* (Philadelphia: Muhlenberg Press, 1953), p. 12.

[4] For a more detailed study of this subject, see Johannes Riedel, *The Lutheran Chorale: Its Basic
Traditions* (Minneapolis: Augsburg Publishing House, 1967), pp. 15–31, and Friedrich Blume,
ed., *Protestant Church Music* (New York: W. W. Norton & Company, 1974), pp. 14–35.

[5] Riedel, pp. 9–10.

Rhythmic vitality was a distinctive trait of the early chorale, which differed substantially from the isometric chorale, with its characteristic movement in equal note values. The latter rhythmic style did not become standardized until the mid-seventeenth century. Sharply contrasted with the rhythmic flow of a typical chorale melody in a modern hymnal is the following example of *"Ein feste Burg"* as it appeared in 1544:

Ein fe - ste Burg ist un - ser Gott, ein gu - te
A might - y for - tress is our God, A bul - wark

Wehr und Waf - fen. Er hilft uns frei aus al - ler
nev - er fail - ing; Our help - er he a - mid the

Not, die uns jetzt hat be - trof - fen. Der alt bö - se
flood Of mor - tal ills pre - vail - ing. For still our an - cient

Feind, mit Ernst ers jetzt meint; gross Macht und viel, List
foe Doth seek to work us woe; His craft and power are great,

sein grau - sam Rüs - tung ist, auf Erd' ist nicht seins - glei - chen.
And armed with cru - el hate, On earth is not his e - qual

Early Lutheran Collections   In addition to his own writing, Luther secured the services of Johann Walther of Thuringia (1496–1570) and Conrad Rupff, both skillful musicians, whose services were invaluable in laying the foundations for Lutheran hymnody. Luther played a major role in selecting hymns and tunes and in guiding the publication of hymnal collections and their subsequent editions.

The first hymnals of Luther appeared in 1524. *Etlich Christliche Lieder,* known as the *Achtliederbuch,* contained eight hymns, four of them by Luther. Another collection was the *Erfurter Enchiridion,* which contained twenty-six hymns. The chorale melodies in these collections were unaccompanied. Both of them were for the congregation, to be used both at home and at church. In addition to his urging that these hymns be learned at home, Luther advocated the teaching of them to children in the parochial schools. Johann Walther's

16 *Gesangbüchlein,* also published in 1524, was the first collection of polyphonic settings of chorale tunes for choir use.

The popularity of these three early hymnals necessitated subsequent editions. The appearance of other hymnals without Luther's approval caused him to publish, in 1529, Joseph Klug's *Geistliche Lieder auff new gehessert,* which replaced the *Erfurter Enchiridion* as the basic hymnal for congregational usage. No copy of Klug's 1529 collection is known to exist today, but it was the first to include *"Ein' feste Burg ist unser Gott."* During the following sixteen years other hymnals appeared by Rauscher, 1531; Klug, 1535[6] and 1543; Schumann, 1539[7]; and Babst, 1545, but these were largely reprints of Klug's 1529 collection to which other hymns were added. Babst's collection of 1545, containing 120 hymns and 97 melodies, was the last publication Luther supervised.

Other Early Hymn Writers   The objective pattern of hymn writing set forth by Luther was carried on throughout the last half of the sixteenth century. Hymns of praise and adoration as well as hymns revealing an increased doctrinal emphasis came from other writers in the first century of the Reformation. Nicolaus Selnecker (1530–1592), Bartholomaeus Ringwaldt (1530–1598), Martin Moller (1567–1606), and Philipp Nicolai (1536–1608), carried on this early tradition. Some of these wrote melodies for their hymns, the most outstanding of which are Nicolai's *"Wachet auf! ruft uns die Stimme"* ("Wake, awake, for night is flying") (12) and *"Wie schön leuchtet der Morgenstern"* ("O morning star, how fair and bright") (10).

INCREASING POPULARITY OF CONGREGATIONAL SINGING

In spite of the great concern that Luther had for congregational song and his efforts in writing and publishing hymns, congregational singing developed slowly. The tradition of congregational participation in the church service did not develop immediately, and it was not until the last of the sixteenth century that hymn singing gained great prominence. The congregation continued to sing unaccompanied unison melodies, while the choir sang elaborate polyphonic settings of the tunes with the melody in the tenor voice.

The Influence of Homophonic Style   At the close of the sixteenth century there were evidences of revolt against polyphonic writing throughout the

---

[6] Luther's hymn text *"Von Himmel hoch, da komm' ich her"* ("From heaven above to earth I come") (74) first appeared in Klug's *Geistliche Lieder,* 1535.

[7] Schumann's *Geistliche Lieder,* Leipzig, 1539, marked the first appearance of the tune, VOM HIMMEL HOCH (74), sometimes attributed to Luther.

musical world in the dawn of the baroque. Polyphony continued, but homophonic writing took on new importance. Contrapuntal techniques gave way to harmonic ideas, and vertical chord structure and progressions received greater attention. About the time of the appearance of the "Camerata" in Italy, and prior to the development of the recitative in the operatic efforts of this group, Lukas Osiander published an unusual hymnal in Nürnberg in 1586. The tunes in this hymnal, *Fünfzig geistliche Lieder und Psalmen* (Fifty Spiritual Songs and Psalms), were written in four parts with the melody in the soprano voice harmonized with simple chords. This type of hymn tune could be sung in parts by the congregation. All previous hymnal publications had been designed for either the congregation or the choir, but not for both. Osiander brought the two forces together, each reinforcing the other. Hymn singing in the churches took on added strength and vitality through this new device. The technique of this simple four-part harmonization of the tunes was followed in Johannes Eccard's *Geistliche Lieder auff den Choral*, 1597; Bartholomaeus Gesius' *Geistliche deutsche Lieder*, 1601; Hans Hassler's *Kirchengesänge*, 1608; and Melchior Vulpius' *Gesangbuch*, 1609.[8]

In addition to Eccard, Gesius, Vulpius, and Hassler, composer of PASSION CHORALE (9), other significant names in the development of the chorale during this period were Melchior Teschner, composer of ST. THEODULPH (16), and Michael Praetorius. The latter published *Musae Sioniae*, 1605–1610, containing 1,244 settings of choral melodies, one of which is Es IST EIN' ROS' (17).

SEVENTEENTH-CENTURY DEVELOPMENTS

The Thirty Years' War, 1618–1648, had a significant influence on German hymnody. Beginning first as a Catholic-Protestant conflict, it spread rapidly until it became a political and religious struggle engaging, at one time or another, the entire continent. Silesia and Saxony, provinces of Germany, became the battlefields on which nations fought for three decades.

It was a time when men's hearts failed them for fear. State hurled itself at the head of state, army at the head of army, and those who fell not in battle perished before the still deadlier scourges of plague and famine. The very abomination of desolation seemed to be set up: raping and pillage, outrage and slaughter, reigned unchecked and unconfined. In vain, to all outward appearance, did the saints cry: How long? Yet of their cries and tears, and of the amazing tenacity of their faith, the hymns they have left us bear irrefragable witness.[9]

---

[8] Edwin Liemohn, *The Chorale* (Philadelphia: Muhlenberg Press, 1953), p. 40.
[9] Sydney H. Moore, *Sursum Corda* (London: Independent Press Ltd., 1956), p. 16.

Influence on Hymn Writing   The hymns written in the seventeenth century, during and following the strife and conflict, revealed a changing emphasis from the previous objective characteristics to a more subjective emphasis. The experience of the war which tested and tried Christian faith and courage resulted in a greater sense of dependency of the Christian on God's providence and care. Reliance on an omnipotent God for comfort and consolation was written into the hymns of this period, producing expressions of Christian devotion and individual self-consciousness.

> A study of hymn texts written during this period reveals man's quest for an intimate relationship between himself and God. Confronted with the horrible killing and pillaging of the Thirty Years War, the individual sought enlightenment, self-understanding, comfort, and consolation in a personal and subjective approach to God. . . . These texts, which centered more and more upon the needs of the individual, were not intended for congregational use but for private devotionals in the home.[10]

Important writers of this period were: Martin Rinkart (1586–1649), author of "Now thank we all our God," Paul Gerhardt (1607–1676), translator of "O Sacred Head! now wounded" (9), Johannes Olearius (1611–1684), "Comfort, comfort ye my people" (36), Johann Franck (1618–1677), author of "Jesu, priceless treasure" (18), Georg Neumark (1621–1681), author and composer of "If thou but suffer God to guide thee," NEUMARK (19), Johann Heerman (1585–1647), author of "Ah, holy Jesus" (20), and Johannes Rist (1607–1667).

Literary Refinement   There was a notable beginning of literary refinement during the seventeenth century, mainly through the efforts of Martin Opitz, (1597–1639), who founded the Silesian school of poets. Here was a systematic effort to reform the style and form of poetical writing with greater emphasis on the purity and quality of the language. The crudeness of the earlier hymns was gradually replaced by a more refined poetical expression and a smoother-flowing line in the hymn texts.

Johann Crüger's Collection   The outstanding hymnal of the seventeenth century was Johann Crüger's *Praxis Pietatis Melica* (The Practice of Piety Through Music), 1644. For forty years Crüger (1598–1662) served as cantor for St. Nicholas Church, Berlin, and his concern for congregational singing is evidenced by the great number of tunes he wrote and the five collections he published. Crüger was a skillful composer whose tunes are sturdy, simple, and syllabic, with firm metrical rhythm. They possess a distinctive lyric quality, which provides a fresh influence in chorale melody construction. Crüger's harmonic and rhythmic treatment of his melodies was influenced by the music of the French psalters, which he encountered through the influence of the Calvinistic movement in Berlin, where he was active as a composer and publisher.

[10] Riedel, p. 56.

Crüger provided new tunes for many of the hymns of Gerhardt, Franck, Heerman, Rinkart, and others. At the St. Nicholas Church, he worked closely with Gerhardt, whose texts appeared extensively in Crüger's publications.

His *Praxis Pietatis Melica* was the most influential and widely used collection of Lutheran tunes during the seventeenth century. By 1736, it had passed through forty-four editions. Two familiar tunes from this collection are: NUN DANKET ALLE GOTT and JESU MEINE FREUDE (18).

Two seventeenth-century German tunes which originated outside the bounds of the Lutheran tradition are STABAT MATER (MAINZ) (24) and LASST UNS ERFREUEN (23). These appeared in Roman Catholic collections primarily prepared for use in a local diocese. The first tune is an adaptation of a melody that was found in the Mainz *Gesangbuch,* 1661, and the second tune is from the Cologne *Ausserlesene Catholische Geistliche Kirchengesänge,* 1623.

PIETISM

The subjective religious thought that emerged during the Thirty Years' War developed during the seventeenth century and reached its culmination in Pietism in the latter part of the century. This Pietistic movement began with Jakob Spener, who founded the Collegium Pietatis in Halle in 1670 to encourage purer and more strict Christian living and personal devotion. Johann Jakob Schütz, author of "Sing praise to God who reigns above" (26), was an associate of Spener. Adam Drese, whose home in Jena was the meeting place for the Pietists, composed the tune SEELENBRÄUTIGAM (30). The outstanding Lutheran hymn writer in Denmark during this period was Thomas Hansen Kingo, 1634–1703, author of "Print thine image pure and holy" (37). Joachim Neander, author of "Praise to the Lord, the Almighty" (21) and composer of NEANDER (22), was a close friend of Spener and Schütz and actively supported the cause of Pietism. He was the foremost hymn writer of the German Reformed (Calvinist) Church, and has been called the "Paul Gerhardt of the Calvinists." Gerhard Tersteegen was the major hymn poet of the later years of the Pietistic movement.

The influence of Pietism produced hymns of greater subjectivity—more personal and passionate in character—than the earlier Lutheran hymns. Singular pronouns replaced the plural forms of the earlier hymns, and the intense personal quality of these hymns made them far more suitable for private devotion than for congregational use.

The subjective expression of these Pietistic hymns did not fit the virile Reformation melodies passed on by preceding generations. The new sentiment demanded new tunes or the adapting of old ones. The songlike lyric quality of Crüger's tunes soon reflected the melodic influence of the Italian operatic style. The grandeur and elaborate character of the baroque era, which began in Italy, spread throughout Europe, and the chorale melodies being written at this time did not escape its influence. The outstanding hymnal of this period and the first to challenge the prominence of Crüger's collection was Freylinghausen's *Gesangbuch*, 1704. Many of the melodies in Freylinghausen's collections appeared with a figured bass line, indicating the growing importance of *basso continuo* practices. The *Gesangbuch*, which was combined in 1741 with a second collection published in 1714, provided an extensive and comprehensive hymnal of 1,600 hymns and more than 600 melodies. One of these tunes was GOTT SEI DANK (25).

Benjamin Schmolck, a popular hymn writer of the early eighteenth century, was not of the Pietistic group. His hymns reveal the warmth of practical Christianity, but maintain a High Church spirit. He published more than a dozen collections, some of which ran into many editions and were widely used. Of his more than 900 hymns, two that remain in common usage are "My Jesus, as thou wilt," and "Open now thy gates of beauty" (22). Erdmann Neumeister, author of "Sinners Jesus will receive," followed the example of Schmolck in becoming an ardent champion of the older, conservative Lutheranism. He strongly opposed the influences of Halle and Herrnhut and used both pulpit and press to speak out against the "novelties" of the Pietists and the Moravians. Because of his publication of poetic paraphrases of Scripture appropriate for the various feasts of the church year, he is recognized as orginator of the church cantata.

Decline of Congregational Singing   Hymn singing by the congregation declined in the eighteenth century. Stalwart hymns of praise to God had given way to words of personal piety and individual expression. The organ became more and more prominent in the service as the facilities of the instrument and the skill of the organist increased. The use of ornamental interludes between stanzas and excessive alteration of the hymn tune, melodically and rhythmically, could only be detrimental to the singing of the congregation.

JOHANN SEBASTIAN BACH

The influence of Johann Sebastian Bach upon the development of congregational song was the least of his impact upon church music as a whole. The forces of the Pietistic movement and the rise of secular music had resulted in a general decline in church music. Spitta says that "Pietism had finished off good church music so that when Bach came he had little to work with."[11]

Apparently, Bach had only minor interest in chorale tunes as far as congregational singing was concerned, for his contribution primarily lies in his origi-

---

[11] J. A. Spitta, *Johann Sebastian Bach* (London: Novello & Co., 1899), II, 115.

nal songs and his chorale arrangement or harmonizations, neither of which were intended for the congregation.

Evidently, congregational singing in Bach's time had little importance, for the music of the service was largely provided by the choir and the organist. The immense output of organ and choral literature by Bach seems to bear this out.

> Not until the concert style of music was banished from the service, in the generation after Bach, and the town choirs that had been allotted to the churches ceased to exist did congregational singing become the characteristic and sole service music of the Protestant church.[12]

The Bach Chorales In spite of his seeming disinterest in congregational song, Bach employed the chorale melodies extensively in his writing. They were used frequently in his choral and organ compositions. The so-called Bach Chorales are those existing melodies that he arranged or harmonized in the contrapuntal style of the eighteenth century. These were collected and published in 1769 by C. P. E. Bach in the *Vierstimmige Choralegesänge*.

An interesting comparison may be made of the melodic, rhythmic, and harmonic characteristics of Nicolai's WACHET AUF (12) and Bach's adaptation of this tune (13). Here this sixteenth-century chorale melody is adorned with Bach's contrapuntal technique and structured within the confines of a steady rhythm of four beats to each measure. Bourgeois' PSALM 42 (36) received similar treatment from Bach (37). Here the flowing rhythm of this French psalm tune is reduced to Bach's four-square rhythm of equal quarter notes, and the rhythmic strength typical of Genevan style is lost. Criticism has been made of similar treatment these Genevan tunes received at the hands of English editors in adapting them to fit the meters of English psalmody. While the English adaptations and Bach's versions both show this reduction to notes of equal value, the distinguishing difference is Bach's great skill in contrapuntal writing.

The Decline of the Chorale In the last half of the eighteenth century, Pietism faded rapidly and was replaced by rationalism—the pursuit of truth for its own sake—which invaded religious thought. Excessive revising and editing of antiquated expressions in the older hymns resulted in the loss of much of their strength and virility. Alteration of the chorale melodies was confined to the removal of the melodic ornamentation, melodic innovations of Freylinghausen, and the changing of all notation to notes of equal value with a loss of the sturdy rhythmic movement so characteristic of early melodies.

---

[12] Albert Schweitzer, *J. S. Bach* (New York: Macmillan Co., 1950), I, 39.

HYMNODY OUTSIDE THE LUTHERAN TRADITION

Mention should be made of an extraordinary collection of Protestant hymns and carols compiled by Theodoric Petri, a young Finnish student at the University of Rostock. *Piae Cantiones,* published in Nyland in 1582,
is significant, not for the new tunes it contained, but for the old tunes, familiar
throughout Sweden, which were "revised and corrected" by Petri. Three
tunes familiar today are recorded in this collection: DIVINUM MYSTERIUM (4);
PUER NOBIS, (15); and TEMPUS ADEST FLORIDUM (14).

The Anabaptists   The Anabaptist movement, an expression of the Reformation spirit that emerged at approximately the same time as the Luther-led
movement in Germany, traces its origin to Ulrich Zwingli, a Catholic priest
who resigned his priesthood, married, and became an evangelical pastor in
Zurich, Switzerland. However, it was a group of young men who initially were
among Zwingli's followers, but rejected his leadership over the issue of infant
baptism, who became the early leaders of the Anabaptist movement. From its
early development in Zurich in the early 1520's,

> the movement spread into South Germany, the Tyrol, Austria, and Moravia.
> Before 1527 Anabaptists were found in the regions of the Upper Danube and the
> Upper Rhine valleys, and by 1530 their missionaries had swept northward into the
> Netherlands and Northwestern Germany, where numerous congregations had
> developed in nearly all large cities.[13]

The term Anabaptist ("re-baptizer") was not used by the members of the
movement, who called themselves Brethren, but was a term used derisively by
their enemies as a reference to Anabaptist insistence on baptism as a symbol of
a mature commitment to Christian discipleship. Hence, they were vigorously
opposed to infant baptism and insisted upon the re-baptism of those who
joined the movement. Because many of the Anabaptist doctrines were considered heretical by the established church, members of the sect were often
subjected to extreme persecution.

Like the Lutherans, the Anabaptists used vernacular hymns, generally sung
to familiar melodies. These hymns were used extensively for private and
family devotions, as well as for congregational singing. Because they were
viewed with suspicion and distrust by other religious groups, there was little
acceptance of Anabaptist hymnody outside of its own fellowship. Many of the

---

[13] Rosella Reimer Duerksen, "Anabaptist Hymnody of the Sixteenth Century" (unpublished
S.M.D. dissertation, Union Theological Seminary, New York, 1956), p. 7.

early Anabaptist hymns circulated for several decades in manuscript before being published in a hymnal.

The most significant collection of Anabaptist hymnody published in the sixteenth century was the *Ausbund,* which appeared c. 1565. The *Ausbund,* as it was published by Swiss Anabaptists in 1583, was in two distinct parts, the first including hymns written by and about several of the early martyrs of the group, among whom were Felix Manz, sentenced to death by drowning in 1527; Jörg Wagner and Michael Sattler, burned at the stake in 1527; Hans Schlaffer, beheaded in 1528; and Balthasar Hubmaier, burned at the stake in 1528. The second part, which had been published in 1564 under the title *Etlich Schöne Christliche Geseng,* contained hymns written by Swiss Anabaptists imprisoned in the castle of Passau. The two principal hymn writers of this group who have been identified were Hans Betz and Michel Schneider.

A predominant number of texts in both parts reflects the effect of constant persecution upon early Anabaptist thought. Several recount in great detail specific instances of martyrdoms of both individuals and groups. Because of the persecution directed toward Anabaptists and their sympathizers, editions of the *Ausbund* published in the sixteenth and early seventeenth centuries contained neither the name of the publisher nor the place of publication.

The first edition of the *Ausbund* contained only texts, but indicated underneath the number of each hymn the melody to which that hymn might be sung. These melodies were predominantly popular folk tunes, but Lutheran chorale melodies were also employed.[14] The *Ausbund,* in one of its later editions, is still used by the Old Order Amish in the United States, giving it the distinction of being the oldest hymnal still in use today.

Around the middle of the sixteenth century, the Anabaptists became known as Mennonites, the movement being named after Menno Simons. Simons, who left the Catholic priesthood to become an Anabaptist in 1536, became an influential leader in the development of the movement in the Netherlands and north Germany until his death in 1561.

Moravian Hymnody   A facet of German hymnody that paralleled the Lutheran tradition in the eighteenth century was the revival of Moravian activity. The Moravians, known earlier as the Hussites or Bohemian Brethren, had been the followers of John Hus of Bohemia, who was burned at the stake in 1415. In the congregations of the Bohemian Brethren, hymn singing seems to have been an accepted practice in the latter part of the fifteenth century, and their singing has continued to be characterized by great vitality and enthusiasm.

What seems to be the first collection of hymns published on the European continent, predating both Luther and Calvin, was brought out by this group in 1501. This hymnal, a copy of which is in the Bohemian Museum, Prague,

---

[14] Duerksen, p. 18.

contains eighty-seven texts. The most significant Moravian hymnist of the early sixteenth century was Michael Weisse, who was an acquaintance of Luther and whose texts were widely used in the Lutheran chorale tradition. Mɪᴛ Fʀᴇᴜᴅᴇɴ Zᴀʀᴛ (26) first appeared in the Bohemian Brethren's *Kirchengesänge*, published at Eibenschutz, Moravia, 1566.

Through more than three hundred years, this group, though small, had been frequently persecuted and ridiculed for its religious zeal and enthusiasm. The surge of evangelical revival, which affected its members in the eighteenth century, may be attributed to Count Zinzendorf, a man of noble birth possessing considerable wealth. Beginning in 1722, Moravian emigrants settled on his estate in Saxony, in the settlement called Herrnhut. Not the least of his significant contributions to this group were the hymns he wrote for their singing. His more than two thousand hymns reveal not only pietistic influence but also strong evangelical and missionary zeal. Many of them deal with the suffering and death of Christ and are lyric expressions of personal devotion.

The first hymnal published for the Herrnhut congregation was *Das Gesang-Buch der Gemeine in Herrnhut,* 1735. Among the 208 hymns by Zinzendorf found in the 999 hymns of this collection were "Jesus, lead the way" (30) and "Christian hearts, in love united" (27), both of which had appeared in an earlier collection by Zinzendorf. No tunes were included in this collection; however, a manuscript tune book was kept at Herrnhut and material appropriated from Lutheran chorale tunes and familiar German popular melodies was added to this growing body of Moravian tunes. Four that date from this time are: Cᴀssᴇʟʟ (27), Cᴏᴠᴇɴᴀɴᴛ (28), Hᴀʏɴ (29), and Sᴇᴇʟᴇɴʙʀäᴜᴛɪɢᴀᴍ (30).

The first tune book published by the Moravians in Europe was the *Choralbuch der evangelischen Brudergemeinen vom Jahr gehorige Melodien,* Leipzig, 1784. Christian Gregor, who compiled this collection for the 1778 hymnal, which he also supervised, was perhaps the outstanding leader among the Unitas Fratrum, or Moravian Brethren, during this period. His role of hymn writer, tune composer and arranger, and compiler was of extraordinary value in the development of Moravian hymnody during his lifetime.

REFORM AND RESEARCH

With the emerging evangelical spirit in the early nineteenth century came an awareness of the need for revitalization of congregational song. Reform and research attempted to restore hymn singing to its rightful place of prominence and effectiveness. Old hymns, long since lost, appeared in new collections. Altered and mutilated versions were dropped, and the originals were restored. Monumental works of research by Wackernagel, Winterfeld,

Zahn, and others have contributed significantly to our knowledge of the music of the Lutheran tradition.

Scholarly research produced valuable information, but it did not effect the reforms in actual practice as had been hoped. One of the results of the evangelical influence was the appearance of missionary hymns, such as "Spread, O spread thou mighty word" (25).

An effort was made by the Eisenach Conference of 1852 to set up a common hymnody for the Lutheran churches in Germany. A commission was appointed to select 150 hymns to be used as a basic core, and these were published as the *Eisenach Choralbuch.*

3

Psalmody

About the couch of David, according to Rabbinical tradition, there hung a harp. The midnight breeze, as it rippled over the strings, made such music that the poet-king was constrained to rise from his bed, and, till dawn flushed the eastern skies, he wedded words to the strains. [1]

Through the psalms of David and other writers the children of Israel found expression for religious experiences. Psalm singing was a vital part of the services of the Temple and the synagogue, and this practice was continued in the early Christian church. The psalms were sung in prose form, and the recitation melodies were known as psalm tones, one for each church mode.

INFLUENCE OF JOHN CALVIN

In the sixteenth century, the practice of singing metrical forms of the psalms assumed an important role in the form of worship developed by John Calvin in Geneva. Calvin recognized early the value of Christian song to nourish church piety and worship. His services were dignified yet simple and consisted of praying, preaching, and singing. Calvinistic theology and philosophy focused upon the Bible and centered upon the sovereignty of God. Calvin's firm conviction that congregational singing should employ only the psalms in the vernacular of the people excluded any hymns such as those that developed in the Lutheran traditions.

[1] Rowland E. Prothero, *The Psalms in Human Life* (London: Thomas Nelson & Sons, 1903), p. 13.

Calvin's philosophy of church music hinged upon two basic factors: simplicity and modesty. Since music was to be used by the people, it needed to be simple, and because it was used to worship a sovereign God, it needed to be modest. In singing, according to Calvin's viewpoint, these qualities were best achieved by the unaccompanied voice.[2]

Origins of Metrical Forms   The metrical structure of the psalms sung at Geneva followed the pattern of the popular songs of the day, many of which were inherited from the trouvères and troubadours of previous centuries. Several stanzas of four or more lines were sung to the same melody, and the singing was in unison without accompaniment.

Literary Work of Marot and Beza   Clement Marot began making metrical versions of the psalms a number of years before his first contact with Calvin. For at least fifteen years following about 1523, he was a favorite in the court of Francis I at Paris, and, following the same style of his translation of Latin and Greek poems, he turned his attention to the book of Psalms.

> History is full of strange ironies, but none more strange than the chain of circumstances which led to Metrical Psalmody beginning as the favourite recreation of a gay Catholic court and ending as the exclusive "hall-mark" of the severest form of Protestantism.[3]

Marot's publication of thirty metrical psalm translations in 1542 brought forth such opposition, including an indictment for heresy from church authorities, that he sought sanctuary in Geneva. Here he met Calvin, who enlisted his poetic ability for the preparation of additional metrical psalm versions. Calvin had undoubtedly been acquainted with Marot's work before that time, for included among the eighteen psalm versions appearing in a psalter issued in 1539 under Calvin's leadership during his brief sojourn in Strasbourg (generally known as the *Strasbourg Psalter*) were twelve by Marot, although these were printed in a version altered by Calvin from Marot's originals.

For about a year, Marot labored under Calvin's careful supervision and completed nineteen more psalm versifications. He left Geneva after that year of collaboration with Calvin and died soon afterward, in 1544. Following Marot's departure, Calvin unsuccessfully sought a successor to continue the work until the arrival in Geneva of Théodore de Bèze, or Beza (1519–1605), in 1548. By 1551 Beza had completed thirty-four psalms, and seven more were added by 1554. In succeeding years, Beza continued to produce psalm versifications until 1562, when the entire one hundred and fifty psalms were prepared for publication.

---

[2] Erik Routley, *The Church and Music* (London: Gerald Duckworth & Co., Ltd., 1950), p. 125.

[3] Richard R. Terry, *Calvin's First Psalter*, 1539 (London: Ernest Benn Limited, 1932), p. 111.

Musical Work of Bourgeois   About the same time that Calvin settled in Geneva, 1541, Louis Bourgeois, a noted composer, arrived in the same city. Calvin enlisted his assistance and, for more than a decade, he served as music editor for Calvin's psalters. His scrupulous setting of the tunes to fit the poetry of the text was done in a most skillful manner. The tunes, many of which were based at least in part upon secular chansons, were carefully designed for ease of singing by the congregation.

As cantor of St. Peter's Church in Geneva, 1545–1557, Bourgeois occupied a position of great influence, but it was his work as a composer and editor of psalm tunes that brought to him, more than to any other individual, recognition as the father of the modern hymn tune. Five of these tunes are: Old 100th (32), Old 134th[4] (33), Psalm 42 (36), Commandments (31) and Donne Secours (35).

The Genevan Psalter   The writing and publishing of metrical psalms in Geneva culminated in the *Genevan Psalter,* 1562. This monumental publication was made up of previously published psalters: the 1542 edition, having thirty psalms by Marot; the 1551 edition, including nineteen more by Marot and thirty-four by Beza; and the 1554 edition, including seven additional psalms by Beza. With these psalms were included metrical versions of the Ten Commandments and the Nunc Dimittis, with tunes provided for each.[5] The use of the Decalogue in this psalter seems somewhat strange, but the inclusion of the Nunc Dimittis can be accounted for by its regular use in the Genevan churches at the close of the Lord's Supper.

In this completed psalter of 1562, there were 125 tunes in 110 different meters. These tunes, almost entirely syllabic, had emerged under the careful editing of Bourgeois. Repetition of phrases, only one point of climax in each tune, and the frequent use of four-note motive, that is, the descending four-note pattern in the first phrase of Old 100th, are basic characteristics of these tunes. The presence of harmonic implications in the melodic lines of these tunes indicates a breaking away from modality.[6]

During the formative years of the French psalter, 1542–1562, more than thirty publications of words alone or words and tunes appeared. In 1562, the year in which the completed psalter appeared, more than twenty-five editions were issued. In the following thirty-eight years, more than eighty other editions were published, and during 1600–1685, at least ninety more editions appeared. From Geneva the *Genevan Psalter* spread through France and on throughout Christendom. Perhaps no other publication has so influenced Christian song. Within a few decades after its appearance, it was translated into more than twenty languages. Among these translations, the most widely

---

[4] This is the anglicized version of the original tune.

[5] The tune provided for the Nunc Dimittis is found today as Nunc Dimittis (34).

[6] For a comprehensive treatment of the music of this psalter, see Waldo Seldon Pratt, *The Music of the French Psalter of 1562* (New York: Columbia University Press, 1939).

used were the Dutch version by Peter Datheen published in 1566 and the translation into German by Ambrosius Lobwasser in 1573. A complete English translation with tunes appeared in 1592, but, because of the popularity of the work of Sternold and Hopkins, it had little influence in England.

Polyphonic Settings   In addition to his editing of unison psalm tunes for Calvin's psalters, Louis Bourgeois also composed polyphonic settings of the same tunes. Twenty-four harmonizations were published in 1547 at Lyons. In 1561, settings for four, five, and six voices of eighty-three of the Marot and Beza psalm versions were printed in Paris.

Two of France's finest musicians of the sixteenth century were fond of applying their skill at harmonization to the Genevan psalm tunes. Claude Goudimel (c. 1505–1572) published polyphonic settings of these tunes prior to his conversion to the Huguenot faith, for he published Catholic masses as late as 1558. He had written motet-like settings of some of the Genevan tunes as early as 1551. In 1565, Goudimel's harmonization of the entire psalter appeared, with a preface which indicated that it was intended to be used in the home rather than in the church service. Sometime after 1558, while living at Metz, Goudimel became a Huguenot. In 1572, as a victim of the St. Bartholomew's Day massacres, which spread throughout France in the wave of Roman Catholic persecution, he paid the supreme price for his faith.

Claude LeJeune (1528–1600) wrote settings of Genevan psalm tunes for three to seven voices. A collection for four and five voices was published posthumously in 1613 and widely used throughout France and Holland. The compositions of both Goudimel and LeJeune were published in Germany with translations of the psalms into German.

Among other significant composers to make polyphonic settings of the Genevan psalm tunes were Orlandus Lassus and Jan Sweelinck.

STERNHOLD AND HOPKINS

It is quite possible that the early work of Marot had reached England and had come to the attention of Thomas Sternhold, Groom of the Royal Wardrobe of Henry VIII and later of Edward VI. Sternhold experimented in making metrical psalm versions, at first without any thought of publication, in the hope that they might replace the currently popular bawdy, obscene songs of his fellow courtiers. Written primarily in ballad meter (forty-one of Sternhold's forty-four versifications were in this form), originally two lines of fourteen syllables, Sternhold's psalm versions were designed to be sung to familiar ballad tunes of his day. The first edition containing nineteen psalms, undated, appeared about 1547, with the title: *Certayne Psalmes chose out of the Psalter of David and drawe into English metre, by Thomas Sternhold, Grome of ye Kynges Maiesties roobes. Excudebat Londini Edvardus Whitchurche.*

A second edition, published posthumously in 1549, added eighteen more psalms by Sternhold. In 1557, a third edition appeared adding seven psalms by John Hopkins, a Suffolk clergyman and schoolteacher. From this point, the development of two important psalters became intertwined—the *Anglo-Genevan Psalter* (1561) and the *English Psalter* (1562).

The Anglo-Genevan Psalter   The persecution of Protestants by Queen Mary, 1553–1558, caused many to leave England and settle temporarily on the Continent. A large group settled at Frankfurt. However, dissension arose, and one group moved to Geneva where a church was established in 1555 with John Knox as its pastor.

A partial psalter for those displaced English Protestants appeared in 1556 in Geneva. Of the fifty-one psalms it contained, forty-four were by Sternhold and Hopkins, and seven by William Whittingham. Of the tunes included, two were from the French psalter, and the rest were of English origin. In 1558 another edition appeared containing sixty-two psalms, including nine new versions by Whittingham and two by John Pullain. The final edition of the *Anglo-Genevan Psalter* was published in 1561, and, in addition to the texts previously included, it contained twenty-five psalm versions by William Kethe. One of these, his version of Psalm 100, "All people that on earth do dwell" (32), is the earliest example of the metrical psalm still in common usage. Tunes for eighteen of Kethe's twenty-five psalms were borrowed from the *Genevan Psalter* tradition.

By 1560, after the death of Queen Mary, the refugees had returned home to England, taking with them the influence of Genevan psalm singing. Kethe remained in Geneva to complete the 1561 edition of the psalter.

The English Psalter, 1562   Beginning in 1560, a series of publications were issued under the editorship of John Day, culminating in 1562 in *The Whole Book of Psalms,* later to become known as the "Old Version" and also popularly called "Sternhold and Hopkins." A majority of the psalm versions in this completed *English Psalter* were by Thomas Sternhold and John Hopkins. However, the influence of the Anglo-Genevan developments is illustrated by the inclusion of fourteen psalms by Whittingham and seven by Kethe. Additionally, there appear a substantial number by Thomas Norton. Most of the texts in the *English Psalter* were in Common Meter, in contrast to the metrical diversity of the *Genevan Psalter,* published in the same year.

In 1563, Day published an edition of the *English Psalter* with sixty-five tunes set in four-part harmony, with melody in the treble. One of these was St. Flavian (39). The tunes were largely of English origin, but some of the texts were altered to fit the longer meters of the French melodies, and, in other instances, French melodies were altered to fit the shorter meters of the English texts. Each succeeding edition of the English psalter revealed an increasing influence of the French psalm tunes.

The Whole Book of Psalms became the accepted psalm book for English worship for almost a century and a half, until challenged by the "New Version" of Tate and Brady in 1696.

OTHER ENGLISH PSALTERS

In addition to the psalters already mentioned, several collections appeared in England that should be noted here.

Archbishop Parker's Psalter with Tallis' Tunes   Matthew Parker, who became Archbishop of Canterbury in 1559, published a metrical psalter about 1560. Nine tunes by Thomas Tallis were appended to this psalter, among which were TALLIS' ORDINAL (40), one of the earliest tunes in common meter, and TALLIS' CANON (41). The significance of this psalter lies only in the tunes of Tallis that it contained, and, other than the canon tune, these received little attention until the late nineteenth century.

Damon's Psalter   It is thought that common-meter hymn tunes were known and used before the Marian persecution, 1553–1558. However, the first collection of common-meter tunes is found in William Damon's *Psalter*, London, 1579, a collection of harmonized tunes. One of the short-meter tunes in this psalter was SOUTHWELL (38), one of the earliest tunes in this meter.

Este's Psalter   The early psalters of harmonized tunes were published in separate part books. Thomas Este's *Psalter*, 1592, was the first to provide four-part harmony for the tunes on opposite pages in one book. The tunes were harmonized by ten different composers, the most significant being John Dowland, John Farmer, Giles Farnaby, and George Kirbye. Of unusual significance is the fact that in this collection tunes were designated by specific names for the first time. This practice illustrated the emerging use of the "common tune," a tune that may be used with any psalm of appropriate metrical structure, in contrast to a "proper tune," which is identified with one particular psalm. The early tune names often designated the supposed place of the tune's origin. One of the tunes from Este's *Psalter* is WINCHESTER OLD (11), the harmonization of which is credited by Este to George Kirbye.

Ravenscroft's Psalter   Almost all the psalm tunes that had appeared in previous English psalters were included in Thomas Ravenscroft's *Psalter*, 1621, in four-part harmonizations. Tunes were drawn from the 1562 *English*

Psalter and its subsequent editions, from Scotland and Wales, and from other English sources. Those psalms that lacked proper tunes—tunes specifically assigned to certain psalms—were provided with other tunes. Six tunes were from the 1615 *Scottish Psalter*. The practice of naming tunes after places originated with Este, but it was Ravenscroft who systematically applied this usage and established this practice in England. Ravenscroft's *Psalter* was widely used and became a basic source book for tunes for all subsequent compilers.

Sandys's Psalms In 1637 George Sandys's *A Paraphrase upon the Divine Poems* was published. The psalms in this collection exhibited greater variety in metrical structure than those in the *English Psalter*. Tunes for twenty-four of Sandys's psalm versions were composed by Henry Lawes.

SCOTTISH PSALTERS

Psalmody developed along parallel lines in Scotland.[7] The *English Psalter* had been introduced by 1550, and later the *Anglo-Genevan Psalter* of 1558, with its tunes. John Knox had returned from Geneva in 1559 and provided leadership in the compilation of a psalter for Scotland. The texts of the resulting *Scottish Psalter,* 1564, were drawn primarily from the *Anglo-Genevan Psalter* of 1561 and the *English Psalter* of 1562, including psalm versions by Sternhold (39), Hopkins (37), Kethe (25), Whittingham (16), Norton (8), Pullain (2), and John Marckand (2). The remaining psalm versions were the contributions of Scottish writers John Craig (15) and John Pont (6), who probably collaborated with Knox in the publication of the *Scottish Psalter*. One hundred and five tunes were included from both the English and the French psalters. Musically, the Scottish psalter was superior to the English psalter because of its greater reliance on the French psalm tunes.

In addition to a group of proper tunes, the 1615 *Scottish Psalter* included twelve "common tunes," tunes not attached to any specific psalm, two of which were DUNDEE (42) and CAITHNESS (44). The *Scottish Psalter* of 1635, edited by Edward Millar, provided a harmonized version of the tunes, with the settings provided principally by Scottish musicians. LONDON NEW (43), one of the common tunes added to the 1635 edition, was used by John Playford in his *Psalms and Hymns in Solemn Music,* London, 1671, and came into English usage through this inclusion. Other tune-book compilers recognized the strength of these Scottish tunes and used them frequently in their collections.

It is interesting to note that in spite of the established tradition of a century of including the music in each psalter, the authorized 1650 *Scottish Psalter*

---

[7] A comprehensive study of Scottish psalmody may be found in Millar Patrick, *Four Centuries of Scottish Psalmody* (London: Oxford University Press, 1949).

contained no tunes at all. This 1650 edition marks the first appearance of the well-known version of Psalm 23, "The Lord's my shepherd, I'll not want" (83).

TATE AND BRADY'S "NEW VERSION"

In 1696 Nahum Tate and Nicholas Brady published *A New Version of the Psalms of David, Fitted to the Tunes Used in Churches,* London. Tate had been appointed poet laureate of England by William III, and this "New Version," as it came to be known as opposed to the "Old Version" of Sternhold and Hopkins, was faithfully dedicated to the king. This version was considered to be authorized or official to the extent that it was "allowed" by the king and the council and was "permitted to be used in all churches, as shall think fit to receive them."

There were no tunes in the 1696 edition, but a *Supplement* was published in 1708 which provided tunes. Among the new ones included were several by William Croft: HANOVER (45), and the familiar ST. ANNE usually ascribed to him.

As in every instance when an effort is made to change long-established church habits, the introduction of the New Version met strong opposition. Although the New Version was in use in the days of William and Mary, the Old Version was still being used when Queen Victoria was a girl. In all probability, the Old Version did not completely disappear from usage until the competition of these two versions had lasted for almost a century and a half, by which time the New Version itself was in rapid decline.

OTHER TUNE BOOKS

The publication of other tune books—Henry Playford's *Divine Companion,* London, 1701, and J. Bishop's *A Set of New Psalm-Tunes in Four Parts,* London, 1711—added to the tunes available for both new and old versions in the early eighteenth century. *Lyra Davidica,* London, 1708, the work of an unknown compiler, was largely a collection of translations of German and Latin hymns. The only surviving tune from this collection is EASTER HYMN (54).

William Tans'ur's *A Compleat Harmony of Syon,* London, 1734, described by Tans'ur on its publication as "the curiousest book ever published," included Tans'ur's tune BANGOR (56). The Scottish poet, Robert Burns, mentions this tune in his poem, *The Ordination,* indicating its popularity in the late eighteenth century.

> Mak' haste an' turn King David owre
> An' lilt wi' holy clangour;
> O' double verse come gie us four,
> An' skirl up the *Bangor*.

MUSICAL DEVELOPMENT IN PSALM TUNES

Both in England and in Scotland, psalm tunes had been syllabic, and while this made for ease of singing by the people, it greatly restricted musical interest. To tune composers and editors of collections, there were at least three possible ways to overcome this musical restriction: harmonic enrichment, rhythmic variation, and melodic embellishment. Bach's harmonizations of chorale melodies is the ultimate example of the first method. Variety in rhythm of the tune was most skillfully achieved by Bourgeois, but the English adapters of his tunes greatly weakened the strength of these melodies by reducing them to notes of equal value. OLD 100TH, as only one example, suffered in this respect.

Efforts at melodic embellishment began cautiously with the addition of an extra note—two notes per syllable—in a few places. Such an example is Croft's ST. MATTHEW (46), in the 1708 *Supplement.* Jeremiah Clark's KING'S NORTON (47), in Playford's *Divine Companion,* is one of the early attempts at breaking down the restriction that tunes should be written only in whole notes and half notes. This tune, made up of whole, half, quarter, and eighth notes, was, no doubt, most striking in its day, for it makes use of forty-four notes, with a range of an octave and a half, for a common meter stanza of twenty-eight syllables. Clark's tunes "are always perfectly regular in rhythm, and often have a very free and captivating melody."[8] Another example is his BISHOPTHORPE (49), which no doubt was written about the same time, although it first appeared in H. Gardner's *Select Portions of the Psalms of David,* c. 1780. It is interesting to compare the flowing movement of either of these tunes with Clark's ST. MAGNUS (48).

Many composers, imitating this melodic embellishment, overly indulged in this device, and ridiculous specimens resulted. Patrick describes the profuse introduction of

> roulades, runs, repeats, which made the tunes they were intended to adorn much more attractive to the singer than the steady-going syllabic tunes which had palled by incessant repetition and by the slow long-drawn-out dullness of the manner which was thought appropriate in singing them. Their spirited melodic style was at the other extreme from the dreary drawl to which generations had been accustomed.[9]

[8] Erik Routley, *The Music of Christian Hymnody* (London: Independent Press Limited, 1957), p. 87.

[9] Patrick, p. 185.

Following the work of Tate and Brady, other psalters appeared, but none of any significance. While the writing, publishing, and use of metrical psalm versions had been extremely popular throughout England, these poetic ventures were not immune to the scathing ridicule of critics and scholars who considered them largely sheer doggerel. The tunes did not escape scorn in this respect, for Queen Elizabeth was strongly opposed to these "Geneva jigs," and another critic wrote that "two hammerers on a smith's anvil would have made better music." On one occasion, the psalm singing in a certain church prompted the Earl of Rochester to pen these now famous lines:

> Sternhold and Hopkins had great qualms
> When they translated David's Psalms,
> To make the heart right glad;
> But had it been King David's fate
> To hear thee sing and them translate,
> By God! 'twould set him mad!

Throughout the eighteenth and nineteenth centuries, the metrical psalm gradually gave way to the hymn. At times it is difficult to separate their activity and development, for much mutual influence is evidenced, one on the other. Many tunes were used by both psalm and hymn singers. Here was common ground which proved to be distinctly advantageous to both. Existing psalm tunes were appropriated for the singing of the early hymns of Keach, Watts, and others, and they served adequately as a vehicle for hymn singing until the expansion of hymn meters by Charles Wesley. The fervor of the Evangelicals and the Wesleys, which resulted in a more vigorous tune for hymn singing, greatly encouraged those who desired similar tunes for psalm singing.

PSALMODY AND MUSIC EDUCATION

Beginning with Day's *Psalter,* 1562, and continuing into the nineteenth century, most of the psalters or tune books contained long introductions explaining the fundamentals of music. Only the imagination and initiative of the compiler limited the rules and studies designed to "enable most people to sing the psalm tunes correctly by notes according to the music, without the help of a master." An examination of these compilations reveals some of the interesting devices used to foster music reading. Motivation of the musical illiterate was sometime attempted by such doggerel as:

> Therefore unless
> Notes, Tunes and Rests
> Are perfect learn'd by Heart,

> None ever can
> With Pleasure scan
> True Tune in Music's Art.

In their efforts to improve psalm singing by teaching music reading, these compilers frequently produced elaborate "instructions" which, no doubt, often left the learner more confused than enlightened. Nonetheless, these ardent musicians—Thomas Este, Thomas Ravenscroft, John and Henry Playford, Christopher Simpson, William Tans'ur, Aaron Williams, and others of the seventeenth and eighteenth centuries—brought musical enlightenment through psalmody to the towns and villages of England. Of no little significance was their influence on New England psalmody in colonial America as their tunes were borrowed, their books reprinted, and their style of tune composition imitated by the early American compilers and composers.

4

English Hymnody, I

'Ere 'e comes, the 'oly 'umbug, 'umming 'is 'ymn! 'Ow I 'ate 'im![1]

The evolution of the English hymn as an expression of Christian song has its roots in the carol. This folk song, with stanza and refrain, was brought over from the Continent at an early date. By the thirteenth century, imported tunes began to give way to English alterations, which explains the English stanzas frequently followed by French or Latin refrains.[2]

The emergence of congregational song on the Continent predates both Luther and Calvin and seems to stem from the followers of John Hus in Bohemia, who produced their first hymn book in 1501.

The first English hymnal was Myles Coverdale's *Goostly Psalmes and Spirituall Songes drawen out of the holy Scripture.* This collection, issued about 1539, was the first attempt to introduce the use of the German chorale in England. Of the forty-one hymns, thirty-six were translations from German sources, one of which was the first English version of *"Ein' feste Burg."* Five hymns were originals, the last of which was a bitter tirade against Rome, entitled, "Let go the whore of Babilon." Coverdale's efforts to reproduce in England the chorale singing which had so impressed him on his visit to Germany were stymied by Henry VIII when this hymnal appeared on a list of prohibited works. An interval of almost two hundred years elapsed without any significant influence of the German chorale in English usage.

[1] Percy Dearmer, *Songs of Praise Discussed* (London: Oxford University Press, 1933), p. 123, quoting the Master of the Rolls, a learned lawyer, speaking of an eminent judge.

[2] One example in current usage is the French carol, "Angels we have heard on high," with its Latin refrain, *Gloria in excelsis Deo.*

38   As the Reformation spread from the Continent to England and Scotland, psalm singing became a vibrant part of the movement. Protestant forces in England in the sixteenth century chose to disregard Lutheran ideals and practices of hymnody and adopted Calvin's concept of congregational worship and praise, and psalm singing became the accepted practice.

The evolution of the hymn from the metrical psalm occurred, as Benson points out, along three lines: by way of an effort to improve the literary character of the authorized psalters; by accommodating the scriptural text to contemporary circumstances; and by the extension of the principle of scriptural paraphrase to cover the evangelical hymns and other parts of the Bible.[3]

METRICAL HYMNS ADDED TO THE PSALTERS

In spite of the dominating influence of psalmody, a small section of hymns appeared in English and Scottish psalters, a practice not found in any of the French psalters. Day's *Psalter*, 1562, contained a selection of nineteen hymns, eleven before the psalms and eight immediately following. Shortly afterward four other hymns were added in succeeding editions. Bassadine's edition of the Scottish psalter, *The CL Psalmes of David*, 1575, appended four hymns—metrical versions of the Lord's Prayer (Coxe), Whittingham's Ten Commandments with a responsory prayer, the first Lamentation, and the *Veni Creator* from the English Book of Common Prayer. This practice continued in other editions until by the 1635 edition thirteen hymns were included—eleven from the *English Psalter* and two by Scottish authors. The 1700 *Supplement* to Tate and Brady's New Version contained sixteen hymns, including Nahum Tate's "While shepherds watched their flocks by night" (11).

DEVOTIONAL LYRIC POETRY

Unfortunately, there was no Marot in England or Scotland to produce metrical versions of high quality, and the insistence of Puritan influence on pure, literal translations produced versions that were awkward and difficult to sing. During the reign of Queen Elizabeth, an abundance of lyric poetry was written. In this atmosphere of literary excellence, religious verse flourished. While these verses were often called hymns, they were in-

---

[3] Louis F. Benson, *The English Hymn* (New York: George H. Doran Company, 1915), p. 461.

tended neither to be sung nor to be used in the church services. In the latter part of the sixteenth century and the first half of the seventeenth, Robert Southwell, John Davies, John Donne, Thomas Campion, George Wither, Francis Quarles, Robert Herrick, and George Herbert (139) contributed to this body of devotional lyric poetry. "Jerusalem, my happy home" (120), a sacred ballad written in ballad meter consisting of twenty-six four-line stanzas, is the work of a anonymous English poet known only by the initials "F.B.P." and dates from the latter part of the sixteenth century.

George Wither published *The Hymnes and Songs of the Church,* 1623. While no hymn from this collection is in common usage today, this was a most extraordinary book for its day and time. Of greater significance than Wither's hymns were the tunes Orlando Gibbons prepared to accompany this collection of hymns. Fifteen tunes were provided for those hymns of Wither that did not fit existing psalm tunes. Two of these tunes are SONG 1 (50) and SONG 34 (ANGEL'S SONG) (51).

By the latter part of the seventeenth century, psalmody was on the wane. The popularity of the hymn was slowly gaining ground. Isaac Watts had not yet appeared, but those immediately preceding him laid some groundwork of significance. Some of the compilations of hymnic writing that appeared during this time were Samuel Crossman's *The Young Man's Monitor,* and *The Young Man's Meditation,*[4] 1664; John Austin's *Devotions in the Ancient Way of Offices Containing Exercises for every day in the week,* 1668; Thomas Ken's *A Manual of Prayers for the Use of the Scholars of Winchester College,*[5] 1674; Richard Baxter's *Poetical Fragments: Heart Imployment with God and Itself; the Concordant Discord of a Broken-healed Heart,* 1681; and John Mason's *Spiritual Songs; or, Songs of Praise to Almighty God upon several occasions,* 1683.

Here the evolution of the hymn from the metrical psalm was under way, moving from a

> close translation of canonical Scripture, to a free paraphrase first of Psalms then of other Scriptural songs, and up to the point where the purpose of turning Scriptural materials into metre met the impulse to give hymnic form to devotional poetry, and coincided in the production of hymns, freely composed and yet more or less based upon Scripture.[6]

In this evolution the major change was in subject matter, for the metrical form remained much the same. Since this was true, the same tunes could be used for both psalms and hymns alike. The writing and publishing of these seventeenth-century hymns was one thing, but introducing the singing of hymns in the churches was quite another.

---

[4] This included Crossman's "My song is love unknown" (138).

[5] This contained Ken's morning and evening hymns, "Awake, my soul, and with the sun" and "All praise to thee, my God, this night" (41), to each of which was appended his four-line doxology, "Praise God from whom all blessings flow."

[6] Benson, p. 73.

INITIAL EFFORTS AMONG ANGLICANS AND PRESBYTERIANS

Because of the decadence of psalm singing in the Anglican churches, John Playford, a London music publisher, sought to improve congregational singing by introducing some of the new hymns. To aid in the singing of the tunes, he published *Introduction to the Skill of Musick,* 1654, appending in the seventh and later editions instructions for "The Order of Performing the Cathedral Service." His *Psalms and Hymns in solemn musick of foure parts on the common tunes to the Psalms in metre,* 1671, interspersed the hymns between the psalms, placing them on an equal basis with the psalms. This was followed in 1677 by *The Whole Book of Psalms: with the usual Hymns and Spiritual Songs.*

Playford's son, Henry, published *The Divine Companion; or, David's Harp new tun'd,* 1701. The second edition of this collection, 1707, contained Jeremiah Clark's St. Magnus (48) and King's Norton (47). The partial success of these collections was due to the psalms they contained and the new tunes they included, but new hymns were not used. Playford's efforts to introduce them into the Anglican church services were unsuccessful.

The Presbyterian churches in England had great zeal for psalm singing and generally used the *Scottish Psalter,* 1650. However, Richard Baxter's *Paraphrase on Psalms of David in Metre with other hymns,* London, 1692; Joseph Boyse's *Sacramental Hymns,* Dublin, 1693; and Matthew Henry's *Family Hymns,* London, 1695, reveal the favor with which these eminent Presbyterian divines looked upon the "freely composed" hymn and their hopes for its use by their congregations.

BAPTISTS INITIATE CONGREGATIONAL HYMN SINGING

While the aforementioned activity was in progress in the Church of England and among the Presbyterians, controversy was stirring among the smaller dissenting groups. The problem among the General, or Armenian, Baptists was not whether to sing hymns or psalms, but whether there should be any congregational singing at all. In spite of the predominantly negative view among the General Baptists toward it, there are indications that some churches did employ congregational singing in their services in the mid-1860's.[7]

[7] For an informative study of early developments concerning congregational singing in Baptist churches in England, see Robert H. Young, "The History of Baptist Hymnody in England from 1612 to 1800" (unpublished D.M.A. dissertation, University of Southern California, 1959).

It was in the Particular, or Calvinistic, Baptist churches that congregational singing of hymns was used more extensively. Records of the Broadmead Church of Bristol indicate that congregational singing was regularly carried on from 1671 to 1685.[8]

Benjamin Keach   The recognition for leading the movement for hymn singing must go to Benjamin Keach, who became pastor of the Particular Baptist Church in Southwark in 1668. With the consent of his congregation, he began, about 1673, the practice of singing a hymn at the close of the Lord's Supper. About six years later, the church agreed to sing hymns on "public Thanksgiving days," and about 1691, hymn singing became a weekly practice of the congregation. Most of these hymns used at Southwark were written by Keach.

Controversy at Southwark   The opposition of a small minority of Keach's congregation, led by Isaac Marlow, produced bitter controversy in which both sides issued pamphlets representing their beliefs. The most significant of these writings was Keach's *The Breach Repaired in God's Worship; or, Singing of Psalms, Hymns and Spiritual Songs, proved to be an Holy Ordinance of Jesus Christ,* 1691. The issues in this controversy were: (1) whether or not the only vocal singing in the Apostolic Church was the exercise of an extraordinary gift of the Spirit; (2) whether the use of a set form of words in artificial rhyme was allowable; and (3) whether the minister sang alone, or together with a promiscuous assembly made up of the sanctified and profane, of men and of women (even though the latter were enjoined to keep silent in the churches). The advocates of hymn singing ultimately prevailed, and the practice became generally established among Particular Baptists by the end of the century. Keach had published some hymns as early as 1674 for use in his church, and, in 1691, he published *Spiritual Melody,* a collection of about three hundred original hymns.

Hymn Singing and the Lord's Supper   It is of particular interest that the introduction of hymn singing into church service occurred in connection with the Lord's Supper. There is indisputable scriptural evidence, for in the New Testament account it is stated, "And when they had sung an hymn, they went out into the Mount of Olives," Matthew 16:30. Another Baptist preacher, Joseph Stennett, pastor of the Seventh-Day Baptist Church, Devonshire Square, London, began, after 1690, to write hymns for use by his own congregation at the service called the Lord's Supper. A collection of thirty-seven hymns were published in 1697 as *Hymns in Commemoration of the Sufferings of Our Blessed Saviour Jesus Christ, compos'd for the celebration of his Holy Supper.*

[8] Benson, p. 96.

42 Stennett's collection went through three editions and was included as an appendix to a 1720 edition of Tate and Brady's "New Version," along with seventeen hymns by Isaac Watts.

John Bunyan   During the years when Keach and others were trying to persuade Baptist congregations to sing hymns, the pastor of the Baptist church in Bedford, John Bunyan, was having difficulties of his own. The powerful effect of Bunyan's sermons resulted in severe persecution and, for the crime of preaching, he was imprisoned for more than twelve years. Much of his time in jail was devoted to the writing of books, one of which was *Pilgrim's Progress.* His "He who would valiant be" (92) from the second part of *Pilgrim's Progress,* 1684, was added to hymnic compilations by nineteenth-century editors.

ISAAC WATTS

At the turn of the eighteenth century, the early ways of the dawn of English hymnody were already evident, but the first sunburst came with Isaac Watts, and a new epoch of Christian song began. Watts's basic philosophy was founded on the conviction that the song of the New Testament church should express the gospel of the New Testament, whether in psalm versions or in freely composed hymns. He was further persuaded that Christian song should not be forced to maintain the Calvinistic standards of strict adherence to literal Scripture, and he freely composed expressions of praise and devotion. Also, he held that Christian song should express the thoughts and feelings of those who sang, rather than merely relate the experiences and circumstances of the psalm writers of the Old Testament.

Watts's Collections of Hymns and Psalm Versions   The first published volume of the hymns of Watts was *Horae Lyricae,* 1705. This collection was in two sections: Book I, containing twenty-five hymns and four psalm versions; and Book II, containing odes and elegies in blank verse and meters.

Of much greater significance was his second publication, *Hymns and Spiritual Songs,* 1707. The hymns in this book were in three divisions: (1) hymns based on Scriptures; (2) hymns composed on divine subjects; and (3) hymns written for the Lord's Supper. There were 210 hymns, with an appended group of doxologies, all written in common, long, or short meter. "When I survey the wondrous cross" (115), "Alas! and did my Saviour bleed" (58), and "When I can read my title clear" (122) first appeared in this 1707 collection.

The writing of freely composed hymns did not lessen the interest and activity of Watts in making psalm versions. Four appeared in his 1705 book, and fourteen in 1707. Later he completed the entire book of Psalms, with the exception of twelve which he thought unsuitable for Christian usage. These 138 metrical versions were published in 1719 as *The Psalms of David imitated in the language of the New Testament, and apply'd to the Christian state and worship.* The title clearly reveals Watts's philosophy of Christian song. In the light of his psalmodic ideals, it is interesting to compare his metrical versions with the prose psalms of the Old Testament. His joyous hymn of Christ's birth, "Joy to the world! the Lord is come" (114), is based on Psalm 98. "Jesus shall reign where'er the sun" (60), perhaps the earliest missionary hymn, is based on Psalm 72. Psalm 90: 105 is the basis for his "Our God, our help in ages past," and "Before Jehovah's aweful throne" (52) is from Psalm 100.

Watts's two publications of 1707 and 1719 stand as monuments to the contribution of this dissenting preacher to Christian song. Many hymns herein contained are sung today by Christians throughout the world.

Though its contents have not had any significant impact on modern hymnals, Watts's *Divine Songs Attempted in Easy Language for the Use of Children,* published in 1715, was extremely popular in his own day. As the title suggests, the collection was intended for use in the religious instruction of children and was employed extensively for that purpose.

Tunes for Watts's Hymns   Since Watts wrote his hymns in the meters used for psalm versions, they could be sung to the psalm tunes the people knew. In addition to this small body of tunes, there appeared early in the eighteenth century several tune books that provided additional tunes for hymn singing as well as psalm singing. The most important of these tune books are three already mentioned: Playford's *Divine Companion,* 1701; the 1708 *Supplement* to Tate and Brady's New Version; and Bishop's *A Set of New Psalm-Tunes in Four Parts,* 1711.

The Significance of Watts   Watts is called the father of English hymnody not because he vastly improved or reformed the hymns that were already being written in his day, nor because of any radical change in form or structure. It is because he produced a "new song" based on the experiences, thoughts, feelings, and aspirations common to all Christians, expressed in what might be called classic objectivity.

METRICAL FORMS   With few exceptions he employed the three simplest metrical forms—common, long, and short—used by Sternhold and Hopkins 150 years earlier. When he deviated from these three meters, it was not to develop new forms, but merely to fit his hymn lines to a few well-known tunes of other metrical forms.

STYLE   Regarding the practical requirements of congregational song in the hymns of Watts, Benson points out his skill in

44 the adaptation of the opening line to make a quick appeal, the singleness of theme that holds the attention undivided, the brevity and compactness of structure and the progression of thought toward a climax, that gives the hymn a unity.[9]

APPROPRIATENESS TO THE SERMON One further aspect of Watts's writing should be noted here. Being of the dissenting tradition and outside the realm of the Church of England, the emphasis of his hymns was related to the sermon of the day rather than to the season of the year. This aspect of appropriateness led him to write hymns that would illustrate, reenforce, and climax the sermon from the pulpit. Perhaps one of the reasons for the enduring quality of so many of these hymns is the fact that they were written during the week in the quiet of his study as the sermon for the coming Lord's Day was taking shape in his mind. Sermon and hymn emerged together, but the hymn remains long after the sermon has been forgotten.[10]

INFLUENCE UPON HIS CONTEMPORARIES The influence of Watts upon his contemporaries can be noted in the hymns of Joseph Addison,[11] Philip Doddridge, Thomas Gibbons, Joseph Hart, and others. Some of these, though lacking Watts's genius and literary skill, were inspired by his work to write hymns. Doddridge, like Watts, was a Congregational minister and carried on the tradition of Watts in the Independent Church. While he wrote in the meters and style of Watts, he did not possess his poetic gift. His hymns are impersonal, yet have a greater awareness of the social message of the gospel than Watts's. His writings reveal the first missionary zeal in hymnic development, anticipating by more than half a century the missionary movement of the early nineteenth century. He wrote about 370 hymns which were published posthumously in 1755 by his devoted friend, Job Orton.

WESLEYAN HYMNODY

While Charles Wesley was the poet of Wesleyan hymnody, his older brother John must be given recognition as the founder of Methodist hymnody. As the driving force of the Wesleyan movement, he guided skillfully the planning, publishing, and promotion of this new stream of Christian song. He despised the prevalent manner in which the psalms were sung, and he ridiculed the psalmody of the Old Version. He felt keenly the need for revitalization and reform in the practice of congregational singing. As leaders in the Holy Club at Oxford, the Wesleys encouraged psalm and hymn singing.

[9] Benson, p. 208.

[10] "Am I a soldier of the cross?" (57) appeared in Watts's *Sermons*, 1721–1724, to conclude a sermon based on I Corinthians 16:13.

[11] See Addison's hymn, "When all thy mercies, O my God" (40).

Benson suggests that both the New Version of Tate and Brady as well as the psalms and hymns of Watts were used here.[12]

Visit to America   In 1735, John Wesley sailed for America to visit the British colony in Georgia. He was one of a group of thirteen members of the Oxford "Methodists," which also included his brother Charles. Among the several hymnals he took with him were the New Version and Watts's psalms and hymns. Of strange coincidence was the presence on board ship of twenty-six Moravians who were going to establish a colony in America. In the daily religious services during the voyage, Wesley's group became deeply interested in the enthusiastic singing of these Moravians, and, by the third day at sea, John Wesley had begun serious study of the German language. Soon he was reading and studying the Moravian *Gesangbuch,* and shortly he began to make translations of these German hymns for his use.

The Charlestown Collection   It is unique that the first Wesleyan hymnal was published on American soil, and the hymns written by Wesley for this collection seem to be the first hymns in English to be written in America. During this brief visit to Georgia, John Wesley published *A Collection of Psalms and Hymns* at Charlestown, 1737.[13] Seventy hymns taken from the hymnals and manuscripts that Wesley brought from England, plus the translations he had made from the Moravian hymnal, made up the contents of this collection. The hymns were arranged as a "Christian Week" rather than a Christian Year. They are divided into three sections: for Sunday, for Wednesday and Friday, and for Saturday. Wesley returned to England the following year and there produced his second hymnal, *A Collection of Psalms and Hymns,* London, 1738, which contained seventy-six hymns. As in the Charlestown Collection, about half of the hymns were from Watts, some of which were altered by Wesley (52).

Other Wesleyan Collections   The year 1739 marked the beginning of intense activity by both Wesleys, but particularly on the part of Charles. The use of hymn singing as an ally to their preaching became very much a trademark of the Wesleyan movement in this year. The third Wesleyan collection, *Hymns and Sacred Poems,* by John Wesley,[14] appeared in this year. It was the first collection to bear the same of either brother. Editions of previous collections and other small pamphlets of hymns followed, and these were largely designed for use in revival services and in the small "societies" that gathered in village and town.

[12] Benson, p. 223.

[13] For a detailed account of this Charlestown Collection, see Robert M. Stevenson, *Patterns of Protestant Church Music* (Durham, N.C.: Duke University Press, 1953), pp. 112–30.

[14] In this collection appeared Charles Wesley's "Christ the Lord is risen today" (54), "Hark, the herald angels sing" (73), and "O for a thousand tongues to sing" (130).

46   The first major hymnal designed for Sunday and weekday services was *A Collection of Psalms and Hymns,* London, 1741, containing 152 hymns. The concern of the Wesleys for hymn singing and the need for hymns is evidenced by the fact that they published fifty-six collections within a period of fifty-three years. The most comprehensive compilation of Wesley hymns was *A Collection of Hymns for the Use of the People called Methodists,* published in 1780.

Wesleyan Hymn Tunes   The wise judgment of John Wesley was evident in the tunes of the Wesleyan movement as well as in the hymns. While his technical knowledge of music was limited, his genius lay in practical sense and discernment. His basic concern was for tunes which all the people could sing, yet remain within the bounds of sobriety and reverence.

THE FOUNDERY COLLECTION   The first Wesleyan collection to contain tunes was *A Collection of Tunes, set to Music, as they are commonly sung at the Foundery,* 1742. The "Foundery" was the Wesleyan headquarters, located near Moorfields, a suburb of London. For a number of years it had been used by the government for the casting of cannon. However, in 1716 it was almost demolished and several workmen were killed by an explosion that occurred during the recasting of the guns captured by the Duke of Marlborough in his French wars. The site was abandoned, and it remained in ruins until 1739, when Wesley purchased it and turned it into the first Methodist meetinghouse in London.

The *Foundery Collection* contained forty-two tunes. Because of his dislike for the old psalm tunes, Wesley included only three: OLD 81ST, because of its popularity; OLD 112TH, a German chorale that he especially liked; and OLD 113TH, a favorite tune of his. Wesley was much more considerate of the newer psalm tunes that had appeared in the various editions and supplements of the "New Version," and included among these BURFORD, HANOVER (45) and ST. MATTHEW (46). There were eleven new tunes, perhaps the finest of which was ISLINGTON.

The influence of Handel is found here in JERICHO TUNE, an adaptation from the march of *Riccardo Primo,* an opera that Handel had written fifteen years earlier. Among the fourteen tunes of German origin were the first anglicized versions of WINCHESTER NEW (52), and AMSTERDAM (53).

Concerning the appearance of this tune book, Lightwood states:

> The *Foundery Tune-Book* was one of the worst printed books ever issued from the press; not only is the printing itself bad, but the work is full of the most extraordinary mistakes, such as wrong bars and notes and impossible musical phrases, while in the tune from Handel's opera the editor has simply transcribed the first violin part from the score.[15]

[15] James Lightwood, *Hymn-Tunes and Their Story* (London: The Epworth Press, 1923), p. 122.

OTHER TUNE COLLECTIONS   One of the two non-Wesleyan tune books used by the Methodists was J. F. Lampe's *Hymns on the Great Festivals, and Other Occasions,* 1746. Lampe, a bassoonist at Covent Garden where Handel's operas were performed, met John Wesley in 1745 and the year following published this collection of twenty-four hymn tunes at his own expense. Perhaps the outstanding collection of this era was *Harmonia Sacra,* 1753, compiled by Thomas Butts, a close friend and companion of the Wesleys. It contained all the Methodist tunes in use at that time and became the source book for all subsequent compilations.

In time, John Wesley became dissatisfied with Butts's collection, and, in 1761, published his second tune book under the title, *Select Hymns with Tunes Annext.* The "tunes annext" had a separate title page, *Sacred Melody,* by which title this collection of tunes is known. It contained melodies only. A harmonized version of the 1761 tune book appeared in 1781, entitled *Sacred Harmony.* Here the tunes were arranged for two and three voices, and the hymns for each tune were provided. Wesley's *Pocket Hymn-book for the use of Christians of all Denominations,* 1785, marked the first hymnal inclusion of Thomas Oliver's "The God of Abraham praise" (55).

The character and quality of the Methodist tunes of the late eighteenth century declined. Trivial tunes became widely used and the overly florid style that became so popular greatly weakened the strength of Methodist hymn singing as the nineteenth century approached.

Significant Contributions of the Wesleys   Christian song was never the same after the impact of the Wesleys. Charles, the poet, added some 6,500 hymns to the growing treasure of hymnody. Among the nine hymns given here are some of the finest examples of his writing.

"Blow ye the trumpet, blow" (105)
"Christ the Lord is risen today" (54)
"Christ, whose glory filled the skies" (81)
"Forth in thy name, O Lord, I go" (51)
"Hark, the herald angels sing" (73)
"Jesus, lover of my soul" (86)
"Love divine, all loves excelling" (125)
"O for a thousand tongues to sing" (130)
"Ye servants of God, your Master proclaim" (45)

John Wesley contributed only about twenty-seven hymns and translations,[16] but his role of leader, administrator, teacher, publisher, admonisher, and counselor far exceeded his own literary efforts.

Even more than any quantitative measure of significance is the consideration of what the Wesleyan movement did to the hymn itself. It was changed, both in a literary and in a spiritual sense.

[16] See John Wesley's translation, "Now I have found the ground wherein" (66).

EVANGELICAL EMPHASIS   Here was a new evangelical element being sung. The unlimited atonement of Christ which they preached was sung from the pages of their hymnals. The scriptural teaching that Christ died for all mankind and that all mankind must give an account unto God was a basic tenet of their faith. The word "all" must have had a special place in Charles Wesley's vocabulary, for it appears so frequently in his hymnic writing. These were strange sayings in a day when the Calvinistic belief in a limited atonement— that Christ died to save only the "elect"—was widely held.

HYMNS OF CHRISTIAN EXPERIENCE   In addition to these hymns of the free gospel—free to all men—were hymns of Christian experience. Charles Wesley's writings ran the gamut of Christian experiences—in public worship as well as in private devotion. For a comparison of the objective writing of Watts with the subjective character of Charles Wesley, it is interesting to contrast "Jesus shall reign where'er the sun" (60) with "O for a thousand tongues to sing" (130). Both hymns follow the same theme—the praise and adoration of Christ. Watts writes impersonally, viewing the worldwide sweep of Christian praise, as

> People and realms of every tongue
> Dwell on His love with sweetest song.

Wesley, on the other hand, writes of his own personal experience of salvation and the joy that overflows from his conversion.

> His blood can make the foulest clean,
> His blood availed for me.

Both the Wesleys had great reverence for the Lord's Supper, and constantly admonished their followers regarding the importance of its regular observance. The one hundred and sixty-six hymns included in *Hymns for the Lord's Supper,* published by the Wesleys in 1745, reveal their concern for this ordinance of the church.

LITERARY IMPROVEMENTS   Not only were spiritual changes made, but literary improvements also are evident. The Wesleys contended for lyric quality and poetical beauty in their hymns. Great care was exercised to create hymnic literature of the highest and noblest quality.

METRICAL EXPANSION   Watts confined his hymn writing largely to three meters, but Charles Wesley experimented freely, using thirty different metrical forms. Possibly because the old psalm versions employed iambic meters extensively, he seemed to prefer trochaic meters, for he used them with greater frequency than iambic.

Concern for the Manner of Singing   In addition to the evidence of critical judgment in the writing, publishing, and selection of tunes for their hymns, there was great concern about the manner in which they were sung. In the preface to *Sacred Melody*, 1761, John Wesley gave the following instructions for congregational singing.

I. Learn these *tunes* before you learn any others; afterwards learn as many as you please.

II. Sing them exactly as they are printed here, without altering or mending them at all; and if you have learned to sing them otherwise, unlearn it as soon as you can.

III. Sing *All*. See that you join with the congregation as frequently as you can. Let not a slight degree of weakness or weariness hinder you. If it is a cross to you, take it up, and you will find it a blessing.

IV. Sing *lustily* and with a good courage. Beware of singing as if you were half dead, or half asleep, but lift up your voice with strength. Be no more afraid of your voice now, nor more ashamed of its being heard, than when you sung the songs of Satan.

V. Sing *modestly*. Do not bawl, so as to be heard above or distinct from the rest of the congregation, that you may not destroy the harmony, but strive to unite your voices together, so as to make one clear melodious sound.

VI. Sing *in time*. Whatever time is sung be sure to keep with it. Do not run before nor stay behind it; but attend close to the leading voices, and move therewith as exactly as you can; and take care not to sing *too slow*. This drawling way naturally steals on all who are lazy; and it is high time to drive it out from among us, and sing all our tunes just as quick as we did at first.

VII. Above all sing *spiritually*. Have an eye to God in every word you sing. Aim at pleasing *Him* more than yourself, or any other creature. In order to do this attend strictly to the sense of what you sing, and see that your *Heart* is not carried away with the sound, but offered to God continually; so shall your singing be such as the Lord will approve of here, and reward you when He cometh in the clouds of heaven.[17]

Instrumental Accompaniment for Hymn Singing Almost all Wesleyan hymn singing was without any instrumental accompaniment. In the great services they conducted out of doors, any accompanying instrument would have been completely drowned out by the sound of the singing, and very few of the small chapels had sufficient funds to provide for organ installations. During Wesley's lifetime, not more than three chapels introduced organs into the services.[18]

Excerpts from Conference Minutes Several rather interesting comments have been found by Curwen[19] in the Minutes of the Conferences, which shed additional light upon eighteenth-century Wesleyan hymnody.

[17] Cited in Lightwood, pp. xix–xx.

[18] W. J. Townsend (ed.), *A New History of Methodism* (London: Hodder and Stoughton, 1909), I, 515.

[19] John Spencer Curwen, *Studies in Worship-Music* (London: J. Curwen & Sons, 1880), p. 12.

From the Minutes of 1763:

What can be done to make the people sing true? 1. Learn to sing true your-selves. 2. Recommend the tunes everywhere. 3. If a preacher cannot sing himself, let him choose two or three persons in every place to pitch the tunes for him.

From the Minutes of 1765:

Teach them to sing by note, and to sing our tunes first; take care they do not sing too slow. Exhort all that can in every congregation to sing. Set them right that sing wrong. Be patient herein.

From the *Minutes* of 1768:

Beware of formality in singing, or it will creep upon us unawares. "Is it not creeping in already," said they, "by these complex tunes which it is scarcely possi-ble to sing with devotion?" Such is "Praise the Lord, ye blessed ones;" such the long quavering hallelujah annexed to the morning song tune, which I defy any man living to sing devoutly. The repeating the same word so often, as it shocks all common sense, so it necessarily brings in dead formality, and has no more religion in it than a Lancashire hornpipe. Besides that, it is a flat contradiction to our Lord's command, "Use not vain repetitions." For what is vain repetition, if this is not? What end of devotion does it serve? Again, do not suffer the people to sing too slow. This naturally tends to formality, and is brought in by those who have very strong or very weak voices. Is it not possible that all the Methodists in the nation should sing equally quick?

HYMNODY OF THE EVANGELICAL REVIVAL

Before proceeding to the nineteenth century, it is necessary to return to 1741 and pick up the stream of the Evangelical Revival which, at the time, may have been of greater influence in the spread and popularizing of hymn singing than the Methodist or Wesleyan movement.

George Whitefield   George Whitefield had been a co-laborer with the Wes-leys, but broke away in 1741 because of doctrinal differences. An immensely popular person and a preacher of rare talent, Whitefield had a large following of faithful believers. His popularity brought him both fame and strong oppo-sition. Complaints about his preaching were taken to King George II, who replied that the best way to silence him would be to make him a bishop.

Whitefield attempted no organizational structure of his forces paralleling the Wesleyan "methods" from which they received their name. From his association with the Wesleys, Whitefield knew the value of hymn singing and continued it in all of his services. Great crowds thronged to hear him, and wherever he preached, there was vigorous hymn singing. Gadsby states that "nearly twenty thousand" made up his audiences in the mining area of Bristol, and the responsiveness of these miners to Whitefield's preaching was evidenced by the "white gutters made by their tears, which plentifully fell down their black cheeks, as they came out of their coal-pits."[20]

In spite of their fervent hymn singing, the Evangelicals lacked the leadership of John Wesley and the poetic genius of Charles Wesley in the development of their hymnody. Nevertheless, some of Whitefield's associates successfully engaged in the writing and publishing of hymns.

Evangelical Collections John Cennick, who was associated with the Wesleys but separated from them with Whitefield after John Wesley's sermon was published against the Calvinistic doctrine of election, published *Sacred Hymns for the Children of God,* London, 1741–1744, in which appeared "Children of the heavenly King" (112); and *Sacred Hymns for the Use of Religious Societies,* Bristol, 1743.

Another associate, Robert Seagrave, published *Hymns for Christian Worship: partly composed and partly collected from various authors,* London, 1742, in which appeared "Rise, my soul, and stretch thy wings" (53). Designed for use by his congregation at Loriner's Hall, London, this latter collection was quite widely used.

When Whitefield opened his new Tabernacle at Moorfields in 1753, he published his own *Hymns for social worship, collected from various authors, and more particularly design'd for the use of the Tabernacle Congregation in London.* The following year he published a companion tune book, *The Divine Musical Miscellany.* In this collection Whitefield endeavored to combine the doctrinal and stately style of Watts with the evangelical fervor of Charles Wesley, Cennick, and Seagrave. The liberties he took in making textual changes in the Wesleyan hymns were bitterly resented by the Wesleys. Immensely popular and widely used, Whitefield's *Hymns* ran through thirty-six editions between 1753 and 1796.

Lady Huntingdon A striking and extraordinary person associated with the Evangelical Revival was the Countess of Huntingdon. She had a close association with Whitefield, whom she appointed as her chaplain, and at the same time she was an intimate friend of the Wesleys. In addition to the group of Evangelical hymn writers, she was a friend of Watts and Doddridge and of Toplady, who remained in the Established Church, and also of William Williams, the great Welsh hymnist. Her wide circle of acquaintances included many outstanding musicians, such as Handel and Giardini. While she wrote no hymns, she was a constant source of encouragement to her many hymn-writing friends and was directly or indirectly responsible for the publication of at least a dozen collections.

Edward Perronet, the author of "All hail the power of Jesus' name" (59),

[20] John Gadsby, *Memoirs of the Principal Hymn-Writers and Compilers of the 17th, 18th, and 19th Centuries* (London: John Gadsby, 1861), p. 144.

which appeared in 1779, had left the Wesleys eight years before the writing of this hymn and had become associated with Lady Huntingdon. MILES LANE (59), the tune which was published with Perronet's hymn, was written by William Shrubsole. Because of his sympathetic attitude toward the Evangelical and Methodist movements, he was relieved of his post as organist of the Bangor Cathedral in 1784. He spent the remaining twenty-two years of his life as organist of Spa Fields Chapel, one of the chapels established by Lady Huntingdon.

Because of her great wealth and position, Lady Huntingdon was of invaluable assistance to both Evangelicals and Methodists. She was able, through her political influence, to intervene in times of persecution and opposition. After a long and fruitful Christian life, she died in 1791, at the age of eighty-four. Gadsby, writing seventy years later, says:

> I do not know that she ever wrote any hymns, but she compiled a selection which was once or twice enlarged, for the use of her connexion. Her "collegians" have discarded her book, as well as her doctrines, though they stick tenaciously to her endowment.[21]

INDEPENDENTS, PRESBYTERIANS, AND BAPTISTS

Congregational singing among the nonconformist groups in the eighteenth century shows the dominating influence of the psalms and hymns of Watts. As the popularity of Watts spread, numerous collections were published using either the entire Watts or a large selection from Watts, to which were appended a selection of hymns from other sources—the Wesleys, Toplady, Whitefield, and others. Not infrequently such a publication was motivated by the compiler's desire to attach his own original hymns to the popular hymns of Watts. Simon Browne, Thomas Gibbons, William Jay, and George Burder provided collections designed as an "appendix to Dr. Watts" for use in the Independent churches.

Michaijah Towgood, Michael Pope, and William Enfield were among those who published Presbyterian collections of this type. In the latter part of the eighteenth century, Presbyterianism experienced the influence of Unitarian thought and a concern for liturgical worship, both of which came from the Church of England. These factors are reflected in Presbyterian hymnody in the altering of existing texts to conform to Arian theology, and in the appending of these altered hymns and psalms to a liturgical "form of prayer." Several collections of this type were published for local use. The most widely accepted

---

[21] Gadsby, p. 81.

was Kippis's collection of 1795, which largely left the impression of cold and external piety. "The avoidance of personal Christian experience," says Benson, "seems to leave the worshipper a spectator at Bethlehem and Calvary rather than a participant in redemption."[22]

Those Baptist congregations which overcame the lingering opposition to congregational singing welcomed the psalms and hymns of Watts. By far the most popular collection among the Baptist churches was John Rippon's *A Selection of Hymns from the best authors, intended to be an appendix to Dr. Watts's Psalms and Hymns,* 1787, which marked the first appearance of "How firm a foundation, ye saints of the Lord" (118). Rippon's editorial judgment in appending to Watts the finest hymns of the Wesleyan and Evangelical writers made this collection and its subsequent editions of real significance, and it became the standard of Baptist hymnody well into the nineteenth century. It was used in Spurgeon's Tabernacle, London, until 1866, when it was replaced by Spurgeon's *Our Own Hymnbook.* Rippon's *Selection of Psalm and Hymn Tunes,* published in 1791, provided an important collection of more than two hundred fifty tunes which had far-reaching significance. The influence of Watts and Rippon touched other collections as it became a source book for many compilers both in England and in America.

MORAVIAN HYMNODY IN ENGLAND

The Moravian hymnody, which so impressed the Wesleys on their voyage to America, was brought from Herrnhut to England by Moravian missionaries about 1735. Following his return from Georgia, John Wesley associated himself for a while with this small group of Moravians in London and became more closely acquainted with their hymns and tunes. A small collection of English translations of the Herrnhut hymns was published in London in 1742. The lack of literary skill on the part of the Moravian translators and their insistence upon fitting the English versions to the unusual meters of the Herrnhut melodies often resulted in literary awkwardness. Later retranslations and alterations greatly improved the earlier translations.

Together with original Moravian hymns in English, these translations have remained the peculiar property of Moravian congregations both in England and America and are seldom found in the broad stream of English hymnody. Three hymns of this eighteenth-century activity in England are: "Christian hearts, in love united" (27), "Gracious Lord, our shepherd and salvation" (28), and "Jesus makes my heart rejoice" (29).

[22] Benson, p. 135.

HYMN SINGING IN THE CHURCH OF ENGLAND

Throughout the eighteenth century, hymn singing was unauthorized in the Church of England. While this was the official rule, there were many exceptions. Watts's psalm versions were introduced into the service and, in some instances, gradually replaced the New Version, as the literal psalter versions gave way to Watts's versions in the "language of the New Testament." Furthermore, there was the impact of the Wesleyan movement, for most of the leaders of this movement remained ordained ministers of the Established Church. Finally, religious services outside the realm of the regular stated worship services became increasingly popular. It was in such meetings as these—prayer and devotional services—that evangelical power grew within the Church of England, and for these meetings many hymnal collections were compiled and used.

Publications of Madan, Conyers, and Toplady In 1760, Martin Madan published *A Collection of Psalms and Hymns,* London, which contained 170 hymns. While he borrowed many of Whitefield's textual alterations, Madan extensively tampered with many hymn texts, the results of which have been widely copied by subsequent compilers. In 1769, Madan published a tune book for his hymnal, *A Collection of Psalms and Hymn Tunes, never published before.*

Richard Conyer's *A Collection of Psalms and Hymns from various authors: for the use of serious and devout Christians of every denomination,* London, 1767, and Augustus M. Toplady's *Psalms and Hymns for public and private worship,* London, 1776, are collections of somewhat greater significance. Conyers relied heavily on Madan, appropriating approximately two-thirds of his 1760 hymnal. This collection was widely used, especially in northern England, and, as the title indicates, was designed to appeal beyond the limitations of any specific denominational group. Toplady's collection, which included his "Rock of ages, cleft for me" (116), was predominantly Calvinistic. Because of this fact, and Toplady's violent doctrinal disagreement with John Wesley, it is surprising to find several of the Wesleyan hymns included.

All of the aforementioned "unofficial" hymnals of the Church of England have much in common. There was a common urgency to promote and encourage hymn singing and to provide suitable hymns to be sung. They all drew their material from the same sources. Most predominant were the hymns of Watts, plus those of Wesley, Hart, Doddridge, and others. The first works of Newton and Cowper are found here. While most of the titles of these collections included the words, "psalms and hymns," there is little evidence of concern for the metrical psalms. Of the group, only Madan, who provided a book of tunes, indicated any interest in the musical aspect of hymn singing.

During the last half of the eighteenth century, the tunes that were used in this transitional period from psalmody to hymnody appeared in numerous collections. In addition to those collections already mentioned, other significant items seem to be: Caleb Ashworth's *A Collection of Tunes,* Manchester, 1760; William Riley's *Parochial Harmony,* London, 1762; Aaron Williams's *The Universal Psalmodist,* London, 1763; Isaac Smith's *A Collection of Psalm Tunes in Three Parts,* London, c. 1770; Stephen Addington's *A Collection of Psalm Tunes,* London, 1780; Ralph Harrison's *Sacred Harmony,* London, 1784; James Leach's *A New Sett of Hymn and Psalm-Tunes,* London, 1784; Henry Boyd's *Select Collection of Psalm and Hymn Tunes,* Glasgow, 1793.

The Olney Hymns   By far the most important and influential Evangelical hymnal was John Newton and William Cowper's *Olney Hymns,* published in 1779. This collection, containing 280 hymns by Newton and 68 by Cowper, was prepared for the use of the congregation at Olney, where Newton served as curate, 1764–1780.

> The people of Olney were lacemakers, working by hand in their damp, ill-lit hovels; they were poor and they were ignorant, and suffered a great deal of hardship. Newton loved them and looked after them, even at the expense of the few wealthy members of his congregation who were by no means pleased to see their church filled up with noisy, uncouth villagers.[23]

A large empty mansion, which stood near the church, was used by Newton for special services, classes for children, prayer meetings, and weekday preaching services. Because of the popularity of these meetings, "The Great House" became the social center of the village in a day when

> there were no traveling facilities for the poor, few schools, no free libraries, and no village forums; to say nothing of popular newspapers, theaters, or broadcasting.[24]

It was in this atmosphere of an attempt at religious education that the hymns of Olney collection were published and used. Five hymns from this collection found in most present-day hymnals are Cowper's "O for a closer walk with God" (44), and "God moves in a mysterious way" (42); and Newton's "How sweet the name of Jesus sounds" (77) "Glorious things of thee are spoken" (62) and "Amazing grace! how sweet the sound" (117).[25]

The Olney Hymns marked a point of transition in the introduction of hymnody in the Church of England. It was the last of a group of hymnals which sought to bring Evangelical hymnody within the Church of England without any effort at accommodation to the *Book of Common Prayer.*

[23] John Henry Johansen, "The Olney Hymns," *The Papers of The Hymn Society,* XX (New York: The Hymn Society of America, 1956), p. 7.

[24] Johansen, p. 7.

[25] Cf. Hugh Martin, *They Wrote Our Hymns* (Naperville, Ill.: Alec R. Allenson, Inc., 1961), pp. 57 80.

56   **Official Approval of Cotterill's Collection**   Other evangelical books followed, and in their persistence to gain acceptance for hymn singing, efforts
were made to adjust and adapt the hymns and hymnals to fit the traditional
customs and practices of the Church. After much controversy, Thomas Cotterill's *A Selection of Psalms and Hymns for Public Worship,* ninth edition, London,
1820, received the approval of Archbishop Harcourt, Archbishop of York.
With this long awaited acceptance of hymn singing into the liturgical services
of the Anglican Church, the development of hymn writing and the publication of hymnals increased greatly to meet the opportunities thus afforded.
Julian lists forty-two hymnals which were published during the first two decades of the nineteenth century for use in the Church of England.[26]

TRANSITIONAL WRITERS: MONTGOMERY AND KELLY

          In the controversy over his hymnal, Cotterill had the stalwart
support of James Montgomery, editor of the Sheffield *Iris,* a radical political
publication. Montgomery's hymn, "Angels from the realms of glory" (82), first
appeared in an issue of this paper. The Cotterill controversy turned
Montgomery's literary talents to hymn writing, and he published two collections: *Songs of Zion,* 1822, and *Christian Psalmist,* 1825. This latter collection
contained an introduction which was the first English work on hymnology.
     The fervent evangelical preaching of Thomas Kelly, the son of an Irish
judge, brought him into disfavor with the archbishop, who restrained him
from preaching in Dublin. He withdrew from the Church and established
places of worship throughout Ireland. He published *A Collection of Psalms and
Hymns,* Dublin, 1802, and *Hymns on Various Passages of Scripture,* Dublin, 1804.
In these two collections and their subsequent editions appeared his 765
hymns.
     Montgomery and Kelly stand between the eighteenth and nineteenth cen-
turies. These two represent the transitional period between the Wesleyan and
the Evangelical hymnody of the eighteenth century and the rising tide of
Anglican hymnody of the nineteenth century. Routley[27] refers to Montgomery as "the typical English hymn writer," and to Kelly's hymn, "The
head that once was crowned with thorns" (48), as "the greatest English hymn."

[26] John Julian, *A Dictionary of Hymnology.* (London: John Murray, 1915), p. 333.
[27] Erik Routley, *Hymns and Human Life* (New York: Philosophical Library, 1952), pp. 125, 146.

5

English Hymnody, II

THE NINETEENTH CENTURY

The rise of the romantic movement during the last of the eighteenth century reached its full flowering in the nineteenth century. This romantic spirit was a revolt against classical restriction. It was a triumph of subjectivity over objectivity, of emotion and imagination over the intellect and judgment. Literature, art, music, and philosophy were all affected by this change in intellectual life. Creative writing immediately took on an emotional and imaginative quality.

Literary Emphasis in Hymnic Writing   The poetic ideals and literary style of the time were reflected in the appearance of hymnic literature which revealed a higher poetical quality than had been evident before. Hymns of didactic design and utilitarian purpose gave way to hymns of poetic feeling and literary art. Reginald Heber is apparent as the most significant hymnist of this period.

In a letter to a friend, John Thornton, dated February 15, 1809, Heber refers to the singing in his church at Hodnet.

> My psalm-singing continues bad. Can you tell me where I can purchase Cowper's *Olney Hymns,* with the music, and in a smaller size, without the music to put in the seats? Some of them I admire much, and any novelty is likely to become a favorite, and draw more people to join in the singing.[1]

[1] Amelia Shipley Heber, *Memoirs of Reginald Heber, D.D., Bishop of Calcutta* (Boston: John P. Jewett and Company, 1856), p. 50.

From this interest in using *Olney Hymns* to increase the attendance in his services, Heber began to write hymns and proposed to compile a hymnal, which he referred to as a collection of religious poetry. For this collection he solicited hymns from his literary friends, among whom were Scott, Southey, and Milman. Only Milman submitted any hymnic writings.

In 1823, Heber sailed for India, where he served for three short years as Bishop of Calcutta until his death in 1826. The posthumous publication of his collection appeared the following year, entitled, *Hymns, written and adapted to the weekly church service of the year.* It contained fifty-seven hymns by Heber, one of which was the familiar "Holy, holy, holy! Lord God Almighty!"

The significance of Heber's *Hymns* lay not only in its literary expression and lyric quality but in the accommodation of these hymns to the liturgical church year. Each Sunday and most Holy Days of the Anglican Church were provided with appropriate hymns, based generally on the teaching of the day as given by the Epistle or Gospel. The inclusion of several earlier translations of Latin hymns was a prelude to the emphasis of the forthcoming Tractarian Movement.

Other hymn writers of the early nineteenth century, whose hymns reflect the romantic spirit in hymnody, with one of their more familiar hymns, are: John Bowring, "In the cross of Christ I glory"; Charlotte Elliott, "Just as I am, without one plea"; Robert Grant, "O worship the King" (63); Henry Francis Lyte, "Abide with me"; and Hugh Stowell, "From every stormy wind that blows."

Musical Developments   New trends in the music of Christian hymnody emerged in the nineteenth century. Tune books were published with greater ease and facility than earlier compilers had experienced. The surge of interest in the teaching of sight singing and the conflict of the "fixed do" method of Wilhem, imported from France, as against the "movable do" method, or tonic sol-fa system developed by Curwen, resulted in the widespread popularity of singing classes. Professional music teachers, such as Joseph Mainzer and John Hullah, became the urban counterpart of the itinerant singing-school teachers of the previous century.

The desire for hymn tunes in the romantic idiom reflected the romantic movement in secular music. Tunes with harmonic enrichment in this style became more and more in demand than the classical style of the previous period. Both the psalm tunes and the evangelical hymn tunes continued into the nineteenth century, but during the century the characteristics of each became less distinctive. The evangelical tunes lost some of their fervor and became more restrained, while the tunes of the Anglican service revealed more freedom in style.

Samuel Stanley's *Twenty-Four Tunes in four parts,* Birmingham, and Edward Miller's *Sacred Music,* London, both published in 1802, were tune collections of some significance. Miller's collection marked the first English use of Aus-

TRIAN HYMN (62). The two volumes of William Gardiner's *Sacred Melodies,* London, were published in 1812 and 1815. The latter volume included GERMANY (61) and LYONS (63). Gardiner's collections introduced the use of adaptations of melodies lifted from the classic works of Haydn, Mozart, Beethoven, and others. The appropriating of these melodies with the necessary alterations to hymn-tune requirements became a fashionable enterprise, and, no doubt, the compilers who indulged in this practice felt that the appearance of the names of outstanding musicians in their collections added greatly to their prestige.

Vincent Novello's *The Psalmist,* published in four volumes, 1833–1843; John Hullah's *Psalter,* 1843, and Henry J. Gauntlett's *Comprehensive Tune Book,* 1846, and *Hallelujah,* 1849, all had as a common objective the improvement of the musical quality of the tunes and the elevation of public taste in this regard. Here was an attempt at renaissance—to restore ancient psalm tunes and popularize the chorale melodies of the Lutheran tradition. Since the emphasis was on the tunes, usually no texts were included. Novello's four volumes, each containing one hundred tunes, were by far the most comprehensive and were very popular. However, few of the tunes which he introduced found a permanent place in English usage.

Tunes of the Methodist tradition from the previous period continued in the early nineteenth century and were used by the Independents and Baptists, as well as the Methodists. More popular than the early Wesleyan tunes, these were more restrained than the inferior florid tunes of the late eighteenth century. Many of these new tunes were written by village musicians, some of which were published for local use, while others, such as DIADEM (65), were not published until many years after they had become well known in many towns and villages. William Matthews, composer of MADRID (66), was a stocking maker by trade, who became a popular village choirmaster and music teacher. These two tunes, DIADEM and MADRID, both having wide melodic range, are typical of this period, and are now known as the "old Methodist tunes."

THE OXFORD MOVEMENT

The third decade of the nineteenth century witnessed the beginning of the Oxford, or Tractarian, Movement which had widespread influence on nineteenth-century English hymnody. This movement was originally known as the Tractarian Movement because of the pamphlets, *Tracts for the Times,* 1833–1841, written by John Henry Newman, John Keble, and E. B. Pusey. Keble, who had published *The Christian Year* in 1827, is credited with initiating this movement by his "Assize Sermon," preached on July 14, 1833,

60   which dealt with the subject of national apostasy. Printed and widely distributed, this sermon marked the beginning of this movement, and the pamphlets of Newman, Keble, and Pusey, covering the fields of church history and
doctrine, fanned the flame of Tractarianism throughout England.

Dedicated to this new cause, these men looked with alarm upon the
influence of the sweeping evangelical revivals of the previous generations and
the increasing strength of evangelicals within the Church of England. They
were further concerned with Anglican apostasy and were bold in their efforts
at reform. In their attempt to revitalize the Anglican Church through a purification of its service, great interest was aroused in the revival of the practices
and ideals of the pre-Reformation Catholic Church.

Influence of the Oxford Movement   The influence of the Oxford Movement affected the clergy, the sacraments, and the liturgy. A renewal of con-
ventual life emerged in the concern for personal piety and asceticism on the
part of the clergy. Colorful clerical garb, the practice of auricular confession,
and the use of the name "Father" reflected the clergy's changing role. Greater
respect and importance was placed upon the sacraments of the Church. Re-
appraisal of the *Book of Common Prayer* in the light of Tractarian ideals resulted
in changes in the Anglican liturgy reflecting the influence of the Roman
Breviary.

The great emphasis placed upon the Roman Breviary resulted in the liturgical hymn in the Anglican service. As the liturgy was modeled after the
worship of medieval Catholic practice, the content of the hymn was affected,
and it was accorded a new place and purpose in the service. In contrasting this
new liturgical aspect with the evangelical hymn, Benson states:

> The Evangelical Hymn is inevitably the voice of the believer; the Liturgical
> Hymn is the voice of the worshipping church. The Evangelical Hymn deals
> primarily with inward experience; the Liturgical Hymn, even though expressive
> of common experience, relates it objectively to the hour of worship, the church
> season or occasion, the ordinance and sacrament. The Evangelical Hymn is free;
> the Liturgical Hymn, closely articulated liturgical order, having its fixed place
> which determines its content.[2]

Translations of Greek, Latin, and German Hymns   The awakened interest in the piety and practice of the early church resulted in the appearance of
translations of early Greek and Latin hymns, as well as those from German
sources. The early Oxford leaders wrote few original hymns, and many of the
translations they made were simply literary adventures not intended for hymnic use. Of the many translations made during this period, the following are
found among those in common usage today:

[2] Louis F. Benson, *The English Hymn* (New York: George H. Doran Company, 1915), p. 498.

Edward Caswall:
  "At the cross her station keeping" (24)
  "Jesus, the very thought of thee" (47)
Frances E. Cox:
  "Sing praise to God who reigns above" (26)
John Ellerton:
  " 'Welcome, happy morning!' age to age shall say" (67)
John Mason Neale:
  "All glory, laud, and honor" (16)
  "Come, ye faithful, raise the strain" (76)
  "Jerusalem, the golden" (72)
  "O come, O come, Emmanuel" (68)
  "Of the Father's love begotten" (4)
  "The day of resurrection" (70)
Philip Pusey:
  "Lord of our life, and God of our salvation" (69)
Catherine Winkworth:
  "All glory be to God on high" (8)
  "Comfort, comfort ye my people" (36)
  "From heaven above to earth I come" (74)
  "If thou but suffer God to guide thee" (19)
  "Jesus, priceless treasure" (18)
  "Now thank we all our God"
  "O Morning Star, how fair and bright" (10)
  "Open now thy gates of beauty" (22)
  "Out of the depths I cry to thee" (7)
  "Praise to the Lord, the almighty" (21)
  "Spread, O spread, thou mighty word" (25)
  "Wake, awake, for night is flying" (12)

Many of these English versions first appeared in volumes of translations by individual writers. A large number of John Mason Neale's translations appeared in his *Translations of Medieval Hymns and Sequences* and became known to Anglican churches through their inclusion in *The Hymnal Noted*, which first was issued in 1851. Edward Caswall published his translations in *Lyra Catholica* (1849), and those of Catherine Winkworth appeared in *Lyra Germanica* (1855).

Of this group of translators, perhaps the most significant is John Mason Neale, a devout Anglican clergyman who spent most of his ministry as the warden of Sackville College, East Grinstead, a home for the indigent.[3] His strong attachment to the old Breviary hymns caused him to urge the omission of the Protestant hymns from the Anglican service in favor of the translations of medieval hymns. The work of the translators restored to the stream of hymnody a rich heritage long forgotten and provided an enrichment of last-

[3] See the account of Neale given in Robert M. Stevenson, *Patterns of Protestant Church Music* (Durham, N.C.: Duke University Press, 1953), pp. 139–50. Also see J. Vincent Higginson, "John Mason Neale and 19th-Century Hymnody: His Work and Influence," *The Hymn*, Vol 16, No. 4 (October, 1965), pp. 101–17.

62   ing value in the spirit of medieval thought couched in nineteenth-century vocabulary.

Original Hymnody from the Oxford Movement   Although the principal contribution to hymnody of the men associated with the Oxford Movement was the rediscovery of the rich treasury of hymn materials from Greek, Latin, and German sources and the consequent translation of a large number of these hymns into English, some important contributions were also made through original text writing. Before the beginning of the Oxford Movement, John Keble had published a collection of hymns for the liturgical year under the title *Christian Year*. Included in this hymnal was "Sun of my soul, thou Saviour dear." Also prior to the movement, John Henry Newman wrote the autobiographical "Lead, kindly Light" (95).

Other lasting hymn contributions from the Tractarians are Frederick William Faber's "Faith of our fathers, living still" and Matthew Bridges's "Crown Him with many crowns."

HYMNS ANCIENT AND MODERN

In respect to English hymnody, the surging sweep of the Oxford Movement and its resultant influences culminated in *Hymns Ancient and Modern*. The title was in itself a confession of faith in the new movement. Of the 273 hymns in this collection, 131 were of English origin, 132 were Latin translations, and 10 were German translations. Only 12 of the English hymns were new, 119 having been already in use. Provision was made for appropriate hymns for days of the week, feasts, fasts, and services of the *Book of Common Prayer*, occasions and saints' days, including the Annunciation and Purification of The Blessed Virgin Mary.

Forces at work for several decades had prepared the way for this significant compilation. New concepts of worship called for new hymns. Those hymns produced by the Tractarian writers—both originals and translations—were already being used. In the atmosphere of reforming Tractarian influence, this hymnal of High Church spirit appeared and is recognized as a monumental bench mark in the unfolding story of English hymnody.

Francis H. Murray, rector of Chislehurst, Kent, only one of many compilers of Anglican hymnals, was one of the first to express a willingness to discontinue his own publication, if others would do likewise, in order that a new representative collection might be compiled and published. In September, 1858, the initial meeting was held in London, and the October 20, 1858, issue of the Church of England *Guardian* carried an advertisement soliciting contributions for this proposed new hymnal. More than two hundred suggestions were received by Henry Williams Baker, secretary of the committee. After a trial pamphlet of thirty-six pages, containing fifty hymns, was circulated in May, 1859, and a larger trial edition of 108 pages in November, the first edition was published by Novello late in 1860.

The first music edition, with W. H. Monk as musical editor, was published in 1861. Adaptations of German chorales and plainsong melodies to English meters had appeared in W. H. Havergal's *Old Church Psalmody,* 1847, and Thomas Helmore's *Hymnal Noted,* 1852. Monk and those who assisted him drew upon these resources, carefully avoiding those tunes of eighteenth-century evangelical origin. Of the new tunes, Monk contributed seventeen, John B. Dykes, seven, and F. A. G. Ouseley, five.

Hymns Ancient and Modern became a national institution in England and exerted extraordinary influence throughout the English-speaking world. Sales figures of all editions have reached astronomical proportions.

> The total sales since 1860 cannot be ascertained, for the publishers' records were destroyed in the war of 1939–1945, but the hundred million mark was passed many years ago. If we say 150,000,000, we shall not be far wrong.[4]

In spite of its popularity, this hymnal did not become the official hymnal of the Church of England, for no hymnal has ever received such recognition. However, since its appearance one hundred years ago, its imprint is evident in the development of Christian hymnody. All subsequent hymnal compilers are debtors to this hymnal, for they have reprinted its liturgical hymns, copied its format, and maintained the marriages of many texts and tunes which appeared here for the first time together.[5]

VICTORIAN HYMNS AND TUNES

As the nineteenth century progressed, new hymns reflected new concepts of liturgical emphasis, devotional piety, humanitarian interests, as well as hymns of personal Christian experience. Never had hymnic writing encompassed such a wide range of Christian expression. In addition to the translations already mentioned, such original hymns as William W. How's "For all the saints" (91), Claudia Hernaman's "Lord, who throughout these forty days" (39), John Ellerton's "The day thou gavest, Lord, is ended" (31), Edward H. Plumptre's "Thine arm, O Lord, in days of old" (46), William Chatterton Dix's "As with gladness men of old" (84), Henry Alford's "Come,

[4] W. K. Lowther Clarke, *A Hundred Years of "Hymns Ancient and Modern"* (London: William Clowes & Sons, Ltd., 1960), p. 88.

[5] Cf. Erik Routley, *The Music of Christian Hymnody* (London: Independent Press Limited, 1957), pp. 119–21.

64 ye thankful people, come" (75), Samuel John Stone's "The church's one foundation" (71), and Frances Ridley Havergal's "Take my life and let it be" illustrate the scope of hymnic material produced in England during these years.

New hymns demanded new tunes, and these new tunes played a large role in the acceptance of this new hymnic material. Reflecting secular-music influences, these tunes followed the patterns of contemporary part songs. Their appeal often relied more on rich-sounding harmonies than on sturdy melodic lines. As in previous periods, many inferior tunes appeared, but the composers of Victorian hymn tunes gave a new impetus to congregational song as they spoke in the musical language of the day in which they lived. Dyke's NICAEA and ST. AGNES (79), Smart's REGENT SQUARE (82) and LANCA-SHIRE (70), Sullivan's ST. KEVIN (76) and FORTUNATUS (67), Elvey's ST. GEORGE's WINDSOR (75), Wesley's AURELIA (71), Smith's MARYTON (80), Monk's EVENTIDE, and Baker's QUEBEC (78), rank among the most familiar of these Victorian hymn tunes now in common usage.

Among the collections that added to the repertoire of hymn tunes were the 1868, 1875, and 1889 editions of *Hymns Ancient and Modern;* Henry Smart's *Psalms and Hymns for Divine Worship,* 1867; Arthur S. Sullivan's *The Hymnary,* 1872; Samuel S. Wesley's *The European Psalmist,* 1872; and John Stainer's *The Church Hymnary,* 1898.

NON-ANGLICAN HYMNODY

With few exceptions, little significance is found in the hymnals and tune books published by the dissenting church groups—Congregationalists, Baptists, and Methodists—during the last half of the nineteenth century. A great many collections appeared that reprinted hymns in current use, but added little of value beyond that previously mentioned of the Anglican hymnody. A great furor arose among the Congregationalists over a small collection of hymns, *The Rivulet,* published by Thomas T. Lynch in 1855. Known as the "Rivulet Controversy," this difficulty centered around the hymns of Lynch, which dealt with the goodness of God as seen in nature (147). Strong opposition within the church denounced Lynch's *Rivulet* as an "unspiritual publication," and, as Routley comments, "it was over a handful of hymns that the Congregational Union very nearly floundered."

Hymn singing gained new vitality because of the evangelical revival spirit that appeared about 1858. The fires of evangelism burned brightly through England, Northern Ireland, Wales, and Scotland. While activity was greatest among the Methodists, Baptists, Congregationalists, and Presbyterians, the Anglican Church, in spite of strong opposition by High Church leaders, did not completely escape the influence of this evangelical fervor. First beginning in the larger cities, this movement spread to every village and hamlet. One of the many outgrowths was the establishment of the Salvation Army. Vigorous hymn singing accompanied these revivals, and the hymns of the eighteenth-century Evangelical writers enjoyed a fresh popularity. Hymns of Watts, Wesley, Newton, and others were sung with a new meaning by Christians, who had discovered a new joy in their Christian life, and new converts in their conversion experience.

By the 1870's this evangelistic zeal had prepared the way for Dwight L. Moody, the American evangelist, and his musical associate, Ira D. Sankey, who were outstanding personalities in English evangelical activity for more than two decades. The story of Sankey and the gospel hymn will be dealt with in the development of hymnody in America. It is sufficient to say that the use of "Sankey's songs" among evangelical congregations in England today bespeaks the influence of the "gospel hymn" imported from America.

Hymnic interest awakened late among the psalm-singing Presbyterians in Scotland. The writing of devotional hymns reveals the influence of the Evangelical Awakening that first began in Wales and also a breaking away from the metrical psalms. George Matheson's "O love that wilt not let me go," Elizabeth Clephane's "Beneath the cross of Jesus," and Horatius Bonar's "No, not despairingly" are illustrative of this era. These hymns supplemented the use of the *Scottish Psalter,* and other psalters, with some new tunes, appeared. *The Northern Psalter,* Aberdeen, 1872, marked the first appearance of CRIMOND (83). In the last half of the century, the influence of Anglican hymnody in Scotland increased, and these efforts culminated in the Scottish *Church Hymnary,* 1898, with John Stainer serving as musical editor.

The hymnody of the Wesleyan and Evangelical Movements had found fertile soil in Wales in the eighteenth century, and the Second Evangelical Awakening in the middle nineteenth century added an increased vigor to Welsh hymn singing. Many tunes from a folk-like tradition emerged, and the melodic strength of these Welsh tunes, together with the virile manner in which they were sung, produced a hymn tune of unusual, distinctive flavor. Early in the twentieth century some of these tunes came into usage in England and America and have added greatly to the repertoire of hymn tunes. LLANGLOFFAN (85), LLEDRED (98), and Joseph Parry's ABERYSTWYTH (86), illustrate the sturdy vitality so characteristic of these Welsh tunes. John Hughes' CWM RHONDDA (87), written shortly after the turn of the twentieth century, has become widely known.

Near the close of the nineteenth century, John Julian, England's greatest hymnological scholar, produced his *Dictionary of Hymnology,* London, 1892. It is most appropriate that this monumental work should climax a century of almost unbelievable development in congregational song. Between Edward Miller's *Sacred Music,* 1802, and Robert Bridges's *Yattendon Hymnal,* 1899, hymnody had undergone tremendous change, and, strangely enough, both of

66   these collections were efforts at reform. Both were produced by men who were greatly dissatisfied—Miller, with the dullness of psalmody, and Bridges, with the trite conventionality of the Victorian hymnody. The prolific output of hymns and the expansive development of hymnal publications throughout the century produced kaleidoscopic changes in congregational song. Bridges stood at the threshold of a new century and with his *Yattendon Hymnal* opened the door for those who were bold enough to follow. Among the excellent translations of his own which Bridges included in the *Yattendon Hymnal* was "Ah, holy Jesus" (20), his translation of Nicholas Heerman's *"Herzliebster Jesu."*

THE TWENTIETH CENTURY

The emphasis of hymn singing in the chapel services of the public schools in England resulted in an unusual development in English hymnody that should be noted here. Beginning in the middle of the nineteenth century, hymnals were published for specific use in these schools—Rugby, Harrow, Marlborough, Repton, Willington, Clifton, Sherburne, and others. Latin translations and hymns of literary excellence found in these collections reveal the strong influence of the Oxford Movement. Tunes in the earlier collections were borrowed from those in common usage. However, toward the end of the century there began to emerge a distinctive "public-school hymn tune" that featured a broad melodic line for unison singing, supported by warm, rich harmonies in the organ accompaniment. Hearing these tunes sung by several hundred boys in a school chapel can be an impressive experience. However, the extremely wide compass of these melodies greatly restricts their usage with the ordinary church congregation. An example of the development of twentieth-century public-school tunes may be seen in W. H. Ferguson's LADYWELL (94), which appeared in the *Public School Hymn Book*, London, 1919. P. H. B. Lyon's "Lift up your voice, ye Christian folk" (94) was written for the *Rugby School Hymn Book*, 1932.

The hymns and tunes of the early twentieth century indicated a new awakening in English hymnody. Such hymns as G. K. Chesterton's "O God of earth and altar" (85) and John Oxenham's "In Christ there is no east or west" (143), and "Peace in our time, O Lord" (146) gave evidence of growing social consciousness and the revolt against the hymnic ideals of the previous period. A new musical vocabulary appeared through the efforts of Parry, Stanford, Davies, and Vaughan Williams in the growing dissatisfaction with the Victorian tunes of Dykes, Barnby, Wesley, and Stainer. The extreme efforts—both literary and musical—of the compilers of the 1904 edition of *Hymns Ancient and Modern*[6] produced strong opposition and resulted in its failure.

[6] One of the new tunes included here was Parry's INTERCESSOR (89).

Major Twentieth-Century Hymnals *Worship Song,* 1905, *The English Hymnal,* 1906, and *Songs of Praise,* 1925, are three outstanding hymnals of the early part of the century. The first of these, the work of Garrett Horder, reveals the fullest expression of the literary hymn since the efforts of Heber.

The English Hymnal, because of its wide variety of material, is one of the most catholic of English hymnals. Under the literary editorship of Percy Dearmer, new hymns and new translations of ancient hymns were added, with a strong emphasis upon high scholarly standards. The refusal of the proprietors of *Hymns Ancient and Modern* to grant permission for the use of forty-four copyrighted tunes (the proprietors were exceedingly wary regarding possible rivals of their hymnal), caused Ralph Vaughan Williams, music editor of *The English Hymnal,* to seek other tunes. Fortunately, he turned to folk melodies, and perhaps the outstanding contribution of this hymnal was the popularizing of the use of folk material for hymn tunes. Two of Vaughan Williams's folk-tune arrangements are KINGSFOLD (93) and MONKS GATE (92). Among his original tunes appearing in this hymnal are SINE NOMINE (91) and DOWN AMPNEY (90). Also included are a number of French church melodies, such as ISTE CONFESSOR (69). These measured tunes came into use in the cathedrals at Chartres, Rouen, Angers, and other centers of church music in France, replacing the older unmeasured plainsong melodies. One of the outstanding collections of these adapted plainsong melodies in measured form was *Méthode du plainchant,* compiled in 1745 by François de la Feillée, a priest of Chartres. The 1782 and 1808 editions of this collection became primary sources of these French church melodies for subsequent English collections. The musical vocabulary of Christian song was greatly enlarged by *The English Hymnal,* and it has exerted a profound influence upon later hymnals, both in England and America.

Percy Dearmer's *Songs of Praise* (1925) followed the pattern of *The English Hymnal,* yet was more liberal in thought and more daring and adventurous musically. Two brothers, Martin and Geoffrey Shaw, exerted great influence in this collection and made it the most advanced hymnal of its time with regard to its tunes. W. H. Harris' ALBERTA (95), is from the *Enlarged Songs of Praise,* 1932.

The third complete revision of *Hymns Ancient and Modern,* begun in 1939, was published in 1950. One of the new tunes that appeared here is Cyril V. Taylor's ABBOT'S LEIGH (97). The following year the Congregational Union published *Congregational Praise,* replacing the 1916 *Hymnary.* Eric H. Thiman served as chairman of the Musical Advisory Committee and contributed a number of fine tunes. The *BBC Hymnal,* 1951, was prepared as a source book for the hymns used in the religious broadcasts of the British Broadcasting Corporation. The compilers sought to prepare a "popular" hymnal of highest quality without any evidence of denominational restriction. The tunes combine the traditions of the cathedral, the parish church, and the public school. One of the new tunes included is Herbert Murrill's CAROLYN (96).

The Baptist Hymn Book was published late in 1961 and released to the churches in the spring of 1962. Hugh Martin served as chairman of the Editorial Committee, E. P. Sharpe as chairman of the Music Advisory Committee. Maintaining the high quality of other contemporary English hymnals, this publication offers to the English Baptist churches an excellent collection of hymns for congregational singing. The influence of Sankey is evident in the number of gospel songs found in this hymnal. Perhaps this also can be attributed to the evangelistic crusades conducted in England by Billy Graham. Of unusual interest is the first hymnal inclusion of two hymn tunes by Geoffrey Beaumont, composer of the *Twentieth-Century Folk Mass,* written in 1957, and sometimes referred to as the "Jazz Mass." One of these tunes is GRACIAS (99), a rather startling contrast to NUN DANKET as a setting for "Now thank we all our God." The musical characteristics of this tune—melodically, rhythmically, and harmonically—are strongly reminiscent of American Tin Pan Alley tunes of the twenties and thirties, which were definitely considered "back numbers" in the forties.

The Anglican Hymn Book, edited by Arthur Pollard (literary editor) and Robin Sheldon (musical editor), was published in 1965 and was intended to be "a completely new hymn book . . . for use in the Church of England," as indicated in its preface. Among the tunes commissioned for this hymnal is David Willcocks' CONQUERING LOVE (100), given as an alternate setting for the Ascension hymn, "Let all the multitudes of light" by Frederick B. Macnutt.

The *New Catholic Hymnal* published in 1971 contains both a representative collection of texts and tunes covering a broad historical development and a good selection of tunes and texts published for the first time. Edited by Anthony Petti and Geoffrey Laycock, the hymnal provides interesting new materials, both textually and musically. The greatest number of new texts (fourteen) was contributed by Brian Foley. Among the composers whose tunes are included are Lennox Berkeley, Edmund Rubbra, Jean Langlais, and Benjamin Britten, who provided realizations of two melodies from Schemelli's *Gesangbuch,* 1736. One of the more attractive new tunes is Laycock's VERBUM DEI (103), written to be used with Fred Kaan's "God who spoke in the beginning." Another successful combination is Hamish Swanston's "In Babylon Town," which was given a hauntingly beautiful melodic setting in Ian Copley's tune of the same name (104), which was commissioned for this hymnal and which illustrates the continuing influence of the English carol tradition.

English Hymnal Companions The "historical edition" of *Hymns Ancient and Modern* (1909) was so designated because of its inclusion of an extended essay by W. H. Frere treating the historical development of hymnody. *The Historical Companion to Hymns Ancient and Modern* (1962), edited by Maurice Frost, retained much of Frere's historical introduction and added detailed notes on the texts and tunes of the 1950 edition, with brief notes on material contained in other editions.

As a source of reference to be used with his *Songs of Praise*, Percy Dearmer produced *Songs of Praise Discussed* (1933). *Companion to Congregational Praise*, published in 1953, was edited by K. L. Parry, with notes on the music by Erik Routley. *The Baptist Hymn Book Companion* appeared in the same year as its hymnal namesake, 1962.

Contemporary English Hymn Writers   In England in the 1960's and 1970's there has occurred what Erik Routley has labeled an "English Renaissance in hymn writing."[7] During these years, several hymnists have produced texts that speak in fresh, contemporary vocabulary and phraseology. These texts have appeared with increasing frequency in hymnals and hymnal supplements published since 1970.

The writer whose texts have been used most widely is Fred Kaan[8] (103). Over two hundred of his hymns exist, most of which were written for Pilgrim Congregational Church in Plymouth, England, which he served as minister. A large number of these texts were first published in *Pilgrim Praise*, the earliest edition of which appeared in 1968, and contained fifty of Kaan's hymn texts.

Other important contemporary contributors to the mainstream of British hymnody are Frederick Pratt Green (101), who first turned to hymn writing in 1967 when he was appointed to the committee to compile a supplement to the British *Methodist Hymn Book*, Brian Wren, and Albert Bayly.

Sidney Carter, in his *Songs of Sydney Carter in the Present Tense*, has produced unique texts that have proven popular and, at times, controversial. One of the most widely used of his texts is "Lord of the Dance."

Hymnal Supplements   As an indication of the continuing search for fresh materials, from both historical sources and contemporary writers, for use in the churches of England, several supplements to major hymnals were published in the late 1960's and early 1970's. In the summer of 1969, British Methodists issued *Hymns and Songs* as a supplement to *The Methodist Hymn Book* (1933). This collection included hymns and tunes of the "traditional" type and a sizable number of songs reflecting the folk influence on contemporary hymnody. In the same year, the proprietors of *Hymns Ancient and Modern* published *100 Hymns for Today*. Both of these 1969 supplements included materials from both English and American sources.

Praise for Today, a supplement to *The Baptist Hymn Book* of 1962, not only reflects the influence of contemporary developments in England and the United States, but includes hymns from a variety of other national origins.

---

[7] Erik Routley, "Hymn Writers of the New English Renaissance," *The Hymn*, Vol. 28, No. 1 (January, 1977), pp. 6–10.

[8] For an interesting autobiographical insight into the purposes and methods of Mr. Kaan's hymn writing, see Fred Kaan, "Saturday Night and Sunday Morning," *The Hymn*, Vol. 27, No. 4 (October, 1976), pp. 100–108.

70   Published in 1974, it is one of several hymnals from this decade to carry a number of hymns by Fred Kaan (eleven in this compilation).

Two important supplements appeared in 1975. The title of *English Praise: a Supplement to the English Hymnal* is self-explanatory. Though this collection contains fewer "new" texts than the others, it is significant because of its emphasis upon tunes that bear the characteristics of the carol and folk song. Serving a dual function, *New Church Praise* is intended as a supplement for both *The Church Hymnary* (third edition, 1973) and *Congregational Praise* (1951). A substantial percentage of the texts were produced by four contemporary writers: Frederick Pratt Green, Fred Kaan, T. C. Micklem, and Brian Wren. Principal contributors of new tunes were Micklem, Peter Cutts, and Erik Routley.

6

American Hymnody, I

If therefore the verses are not always so smooth and elegant as some may desire or expect; let them consider that Gods Altar needs not our pollishings.

FROM THE PREFACE TO THE BAY PSALM BOOK

Huguenot immigrants to the coast of South Carolina and Florida in 1562–1565 were the first to bring French metrical psalms and psalm tunes to American soil. It is said that native Indians, friendly to these settlers, picked up the French tunes and sang them long after the French settlements were wiped out by the Spaniards. Baird mentions that later visitors to this area would be greeted "with some snatch of a French Psalm uncouthly rendered by Indian voices, in strains caught from the Calvinists."[1]

English psalm tunes first reached America through the visit of Sir Francis Drake to the coast of northern California in June 1579. During the five weeks he and his men camped ashore while ship repairs were being made, friendly Indians visited their camp. Drake's chaplain, Francis Fletcher, tells of the impression that psalm singing made on the Indians during their frequent visits.

> In the time of which prayers, singing of Psalmes, and reading of certaine Chapters in the Bible, they sate very attentively: and observing the end at every pause, with one voice still cried, Oh, as greatly rejoycing in our exercises. Yea they tooke such pleasure in our singing of Psalmes, that whensoever they resorted to us, their first request was commonly this, *Gnaah,* by which they intreated that we would sing.[2]

[1] Charles W. Baird, *History of the Huguenot Emigration to America* (New York: Dodd, Mead & Company, Inc., 1885), I, 68.

[2] Francis Fletcher, "The World Encompassed by Sir Francis Drake," in H. S. Burrage, ed., *Early English and French Voyages* (New York: Charles Scribner's Sons, 1906), p. 163.

72   PSALMODY IN COLONIAL AMERICA

The Jamestown settlers who arrived in 1607 brought with them from England the Old Version sung to the tunes in Este's *Psalter,* 1592.

The Pilgrims   The Pilgrims who settled at Plymouth, Massachusetts, in 1620, were part of an English Separatist group, led by Robert Browne, who moved to Amsterdam, and later to Leyden, before they ventured to the New World. Because of the beginning of the Thirty Years' War in Germany and the hostility of Cardinal Richelieu in France, the Pilgrim fathers turned to the New World for freedom to exercise their religious and spiritual ideals.

By the time the Pilgrims arrived in Holland, the *Dutch Psalter,* Peter Datheen's 1566 translation of the *Genevan Psalter,* was known and used widely. This was the point of immediate contact through which the French psalm tunes from Geneva came to be known by the Pilgrims, who in turn brought them to America. Henry Ainsworth, a Hebrew scholar and teacher and one of the "Brownists," prepared for this group a new psalter which they felt adhered more closely to the meaning of the original than had the Sternhold and Hopkins psalm versions. The *Ainsworth Psalter,* published in Amsterdam in 1612, contained a new prose translation of each psalm placed adjacent to its metrical versification. Thirty-nine different tunes, borrowed from the traditions of both the Sternhold and Hopkins and Genevan psalters, were provided with Ainsworth's publication. Longfellow refers to this psalter in *The Courtship of Miles Standish,* as he describes Priscilla sitting at home singing.

> Open wide in her lap lay the well-worn psalmbook of Ainsworth
> Printed in Amsterdam, the words and music together,
> Rough-hewn, angular notes, like stones in the wall of a churchyard,
> Darkened and overhung by the running vine of the verses.

Although Ainsworth's *Psalter* was used at Plymouth until the end of the seventeenth century, it did not exert great influence in the further development of psalmody in America.

When the French and the Dutch settled New Amsterdam in 1628, they sang the metrical versions in their respective languages, using the *Genevan Psalter* and the *Dutch Psalter,* but they sang the same tunes. The melodies that Bourgeois had prepared for Calvin's psalters in Geneva were well known to the Dutch.

The Bay Psalm Book   A decade after the landing of the Pilgrims at Plymouth, a larger and more aristocratic group of settlers from England arrived north of Boston. Within ten years of the arrival of these Puritans, they produced their own psalter and printed it on their own press at Cambridge. This book, *The Whole Booke of Psalmes Faithfully Translated into English Metre,* 1640, commonly known as the *Bay Psalm Book,* was the first book of any kind published in the American Colonies. New translations were made by prominent New England divines who considered Sternhold and Hopkins crude, unscholarly, and much too free. Concerning the origin of this book, Cotton Mather related:

> Resolving then upon a New Translation, the chief Divines in the Country, took each of them a Portion to be Translated: Among whom were Mr. Welde and Mr. Eliot of Roxbury, and Mr. Mather of Dorchester. These, like the rest, were of so different a Genius for their Poetry, that Mr. Shephard of Cambridge, on the Occasion addressed them to this Purpose.

> You Roxb'ry Poets, keep clear of the Crime,
> Of missing to give us very good Rhime.
> And you of Dorchester, your Verses lengthen,
> But with the Texts own Words, you will them strengthen.[3]

The ministers who provided the psalm versions for the *Bay Psalm Book*[4] employed only six metrical forms. No tunes were included in this first edition, but the compilers recommended the tunes contained in the *Ravenscroft Psalter* and, for a few psalms, tunes from "our English psalme books," presumably musical editions of Sternhold and Hopkins. The final paragraph of John Cotton's preface to the new psalter sets forth the sincere conviction of those men who contributed to America's first book for Christian song.

> If therefore the verses are not always so smooth and elegant as some may desire or expect; let them consider that Gods Altar needs not our pollishings: Ex. 20. for wee have respected rather a plaine translation, than to smooth our verses with the sweetnes of any paraphrase, and soe have attended Conscience rather than Elegance, fidelity rather than poetry, in translating the hebrew words into english language, and Davids poetry into english meetre; that soe we may sing in Sion the Lords songs of prayse according to his owne will; until hee take us from hence, and wipe away all our teares, and bid us enter into our masters ioye to sing eternall Halleluiahs.

In the decade following the publication of the *Bay Psalm Book* there apparently developed dissatisfaction with many of the versifications which, because of various imperfections in poetic structure, were unsuitable for congregational singing. As Cotton Mather later wrote:

> It was thought that a little more of Art was to be employ'd upon them: And for that Cause, they were commited to Mr. Dunster, who Revised and Refined this Translation; and (with some Assistance from one Mr. Richard Lyon. . .) he brought it into the Condition wherein our Churches have ever since used it.[5]

[3] Quoted in Zoltan Haraszti, *The Enigma of the Bay Psalm Book* (Chicago: University of Chicago Press, 1956), p. 12. This most definitive work was published with a facsimile publication of the *Bay Psalm Book*.

[4] The supposition that Thomas Welde, John Eliot, and Richard Mather were the sole authors of the psalm versions appearing in the *Bay Psalm Book*—an idea conveyed for many years in writings concerning early New England psalmody—has been convincingly refuted in Haraszti, pp. 12–18, 31–60.

[5] Quoted in Irving Lowens, *Music and Musicians in Early America* (New York: W. W. Norton & Company, Inc., 1964), p. 31.

74 The collaboration of Henry Dunster, president of Harvard, and Lyon resulted in the publication in 1651 of the third edition of the *Bay Psalm Book* under a new title, *The Psalms Hymns and Spiritual Songs of the Old and New Testament, faithfully translated into English metre.* It was in this revised form, which became known as the *New England Psalm Book,* that the psalter continued in use for more than a century.

The ninth edition of the *Bay Psalm Book,* 1698, was the first to include music. The thirteen tunes, which appeared in the back of the book, were mostly in common meter and were printed in two parts—soprano and bass—with the sol-fa names printed under the notation on the staff.[6] As a source for these tunes, the editors had used Playford's *Introduction to the Skill of Musick,* the eleventh edition of which had appeared in London in 1687. In addition to these thirteen tunes, the editors reprinted Playford's "instructions for singing the psalms." This seems to be the earliest publication in America using the old English method of solmization, sometimes referred to as "Lancashire Sol-fa." The syllable names for the notes of the scale, fa, sol, la, fa, sol, la, mi, fa, are identical to those associated with "fasola" singing of the *Southern Harmony* and *Sacred Harp,* oblong tune books found in the southern region of the United States in the nineteenth and twentieth centuries.

The *Bay Psalm Book* enjoyed widespread popularity, which extended throughout New England and as far south as Pennsylvania. It replaced Ainsworth's *Psalter* in the Salem church in 1667, and in the Plymouth church in 1692. Twenty-seven editions were published in New England by 1762, and seven years after the first edition appeared, it was reprinted in England, where at least twenty editions followed, the latest being that of 1754. In January 1947, the *Bay Psalm Book* became a matter of public interest when one of the eleven extant first edition copies was sold at public auction in New York for $151,000, the highest price ever paid for a book in the English language.

Psalterium Americanum Cotton Mather, whose writings have provided several helpful bits of information concerning early American psalmody, himself produced a unique, though unsuccessful psalter. His *Psalterium Americanum,* published in 1718, provided psalm versions in blank verse (so that the meaning of the original Hebrew would not be distorted "for the sake of preserving the Clink of the Rhime," as he said in his preface). The psalm versions were written in common meter, but several were adapted to the use of long meter tunes by the addition of two extra syllables, placed in brackets, with each six-syllable line. Thus, the first two lines of Mather's version of Psalm 23 reads:

My Shepherd is th'Eternal God.
I shall not be in [any] want;

[6] Twelve pages from the *Bay Psalm Book,* ninth edition, 1698, containing the instructions for singing and the thirteen tunes, are reproduced in Hamilton C. MacDougall, *Early New England Psalmody* (Brattleboro, Vt.: Stephen Daye Press, 1960), pp. 13–41.

Psalm Translations for the Indians   John Eliot, "Apostle to the Indians," published at Cambridge in 1661 a versification of the psalms in the language of the Algonquin Indians entitled *Wame Ketoohomae Uketoohomaongash David.* These metrical psalms, bound with the translation of the Bible that Eliot had made earlier, represented some of the first efforts at presenting the gospel to the Indians.

ATTEMPTS TO IMPROVE PSALM SINGING

During the latter part of the seventeenth century, the repertoire of psalm tunes used by the colonists gradually dwindled, and their manner of singing the tunes that were retained became freer, more improvisatory, rather than precisely according to the notes and rhythms in which the tunes had been originally written.[7] Thomas Symmes, in his pamphlet, *The Reasonableness of Regular Singing, or Singing by Note,* explains this trend by saying:

> The declining from, and getting beside the rule, was gradual and insensible. Singing Schools and Singing books being laid aside, there was no way to learn; but only by hearing of tunes sung, or by taking the run of the tune, as it is phrased. The rules of singing not being taught or learnt, every one sang as best pleased himself, and every leading singer, would take the liberty of raising any note of the tune, or lowering of it, as best pleased his ear; and add such turns and flourishes as were grateful to him; . . .

The lack of tune books necessitated the singing of the few tunes familiar to everyone in any given gathering of people. Had there been sufficient tune books, the inability of most people to read by note would have still required the use of only those tunes that were familiar.

The traditional practice of "lining out" the psalm became symptomatic of the conditions of the time. Because of the absence of psalters from which the congregation could sing, a deacon was appointed to "line out" the psalm. He would read aloud a line or two, and then the congregation would join in singing the text that had just been read. In many churches a precentor would lead the singing through the strength of his own voice.[8] As indicated by Symmes's comment cited above, the congregational singing of the psalm tune was characterized by a general lack of uniformity in both melody and rhythm.

---

[7] In Gilbert Chase, *America's Music* (New York: McGraw-Hill Book Company, Inc., 1955), pp. 22–40, this development is treated as the emergence of a folk tradition in American church music.

[8] The experiences of one New England precentor, Samuel Sewell, are recounted in Robert Stevenson, *Protestant Church Music in America* (New York: W. W. Norton & Company, Inc., 1966), pp. 16–18, and Henry Wilder Foote, *Three Centuries of American Hymnody* (Cambridge: Harvard University Press, 1940), pp. 94–95.

76   Tunes were distorted until they became almost unrecognizable, and the breakdown of rhythmic structure reduced the tempo to the slowest possible movement.

The Reformers   In an effort to restore the former practice of psalm singing and to improve the manner in which the people sang, a group of young ministers initiated needed reforms. They desired to teach the people to read music from notes, enabling them to sing from the printed page rather than from memory only. This movement became known as the "new way," "regular singing," and "singing by note," as opposed to the "old way" of singing, sometimes called the "common way" or "singing by rote." The leaders of the "regular singing" movement were John Tufts, Thomas Symmes, and Thomas Walter.

Tufts published a small collection, *An Introduction to the Singing of Psalm-Tunes,* c. 1721. No copies of the first four editions of this first American reprint exclusively devoted to music are known to exist today.[9] An examination of a facsimile reprint of the fifth edition, 1726, reveals thirty-seven tunes arranged for three-part singing.[10] Initial letters, F, S, L, M, of the syllable names, fa, sol, la, mi, were used instead of notes on the staff, and the rhythm was indicated by a system of dot punctuation. For example, "F" was a quarter note; "F." was a half note; and "F:" was a whole note.

> These letters will serve also to measure the *Length* of the Notes, or to show how long each Note is to be sounded. For instance in Common Time, A Letter with two Points on the right side of it thus (F:) is to be sounded as long as you would be distinctly telling, *One, Two, Three, Four.* A Letter with but One Point thus, (F.) is to be sounded while you are telling *One, Two.* A Letter without any Point thus (F) only half so long.[11]

The tunes for the 1726 edition were drawn primarily from John Playford's *Whole Book of Psalms* and Thomas Walter's *Grounds and Rules of Music Explained* (1721 and 1723). Tufts's instructions for singing indicated his familiarity with similar writings by Ravenscroft, Playford (in his *Introduction to the Skill of Musick*) and Christopher Simpson *(Compendium of Practical Music).* Tufts's *Introduction* evidently filled a genuine need, for it went through eleven editions and was frequently bound with copies of the *Bay Psalm Book.*

Thomas Symmes made two important literary contributions to the "regular singing" cause. *The Reasonableness of Regular Singing, or Singing by Note,* printed anonymously in 1720, proposed that the "new way" of singing by note was actually not new, but was the oldest way of psalm singing and needed to be

---

[9] The early history of Tufts's *Introduction* is treated in Lowens, pp. 39–57.

[10] John Tufts, *An Introduction to the Singing of Psalm-Tunes,* a facsimile reprint of the fifth edition, with foreword by Irving Lowens (Philadelphia: Printed for *Musical Americana* by Albert Saifer, Publisher, 1954).

[11] Tufts, pp. 5–6.

revived. In *Utile Dulci or a Joco-Serious Dialogue, concerning Regular Singing,* a pamphlet published in 1723, Symmes presented a humorous refutation of the principal arguments against the "new way."

Thomas Walter's *The Grounds and Rules of Musick Explained,* 1721, was the other primary literary vehicle for the propagation of the ideas of the reformers.

EARLY AMERICAN SINGING SCHOOLS

The persuasiveness of the advocates of "regular singing" generated a renewed interest in expanding the repertoire of congregational singing and in developing music-reading abilities, especially in urban areas. From this interest emerged the singing school, which became institutionalized in colonial America after the midpoint of the eighteenth century as a means of providing instruction in music reading and in singing psalm tunes and anthems.[12] New and larger tune books were needed as these singing schools increased in popularity.

Urania The first of the larger tune books was published in 1761 by James Lyon. *Urania,* as Lyon's compilation was entitled, contained psalm tunes, hymn tunes, and anthems from both British and American sources. Among other distinctives, *Urania* was the first American publication to contain a considerable number of settings for four voices, rather than two or three, and it was the first to include fuguing tunes, a type of hymn tune that was to become extremely popular in the late eighteenth century.

The American fuguing tune, like its British counterpart, featured contrasts between homophonic and polyphonic textures. The opening section was customarily homophonic and ended with a cadence, usually on the tonic. There follows a section in which the various voice parts enter imitatively, after which the homophonic texture returns for the final cadence.

Urania was followed by other collections, including Josiah Flagg's *Collection of the Best Psalm Tunes* (1764), Daniel Bayley's *American Harmony* (1769), and Simeon Jocelyn's *Chorister's Companion* (1782). The latter publication included Lewis Edson's LENOX (106), which became one of the most popular fuguing tunes of the period.

William Billings and His Contemporaries The best-known among the singing-school teachers of the Revolutionary War period was William Billings

[12] For an interesting description of a "typical" singing school, see George Pullen Jackson, *White Spirituals in the Southern Uplands* (New York: Dover Publications, Inc., 1965; reprint of the book first published by University of North Carolina Press, Chapel Hill, 1933), pp. 8–9.

78   (1746–1800), who was only twenty-four when he published his first tune book, *The New England Psalm Singer,* in 1770. Billings used this and subsequent collections as he organized and conducted singing schools throughout the area surrounding Boston. These collections, *The Singing Master's Assistant* (1778), *Music in Miniature* (1779), *The Psalm Singer's Amusement* (1781), *Suffolk Harmony* (1786), and *Continental Harmony* (1794), enjoyed widespread usage. While Billings did not originate the fuguing tune,[13] he was successful in composing and popularizing the form. None of Billings' tunes, however, have been retained in present-day hymnals. The texts for which Billings wrote his tunes were drawn from a wide variety of sources, the favorite being the psalm versions and hymns of Isaac Watts.

Billings was not alone in his significance as compiler or composer during the Revolutionary War era. The more significant among his contemporaries were Daniel Read (106), Samuel Holyoke, and Oliver Holden, whose hymn tune CORONATION is the earliest American tune still in common usage. It was first published in Holden's *Union Harmony,* 1793.

IMMIGRANTS AND INFLUENCES

Immigration in the late seventeenth and early eighteenth centuries resulted in the establishment of numerous settlements of Europeans, largely in Pennsylvania. The first of these, a small group of Mennonites, settled at Germantown in 1683. The Dunkards, or German Baptists, arrived at Germantown in 1719, and the Moravians, Schwenkfelders, and others established their own settlements, exercising great diligence in maintaining their distinctive characteristics, as well as their native language, in colonial America. Along with their customs, manners, and religious beliefs, they brought their hymns and tunes.

The hymnal the Mennonites brought to America was *Ausbund, Das ist: Etliche schöne Christliche Lieder.* The first American edition was published in Germantown in 1742 and was followed by more than a dozen reprints. It is still used in the present day by the Old Order Amish in Pennsylvania and has the distinction of being the oldest hymn book officially in use by any church in America.[14] *Die Kleine Geistliche Harfe der Kinder Zions,* Germantown, 1803, was the first American Mennonite hymnal.

In 1735 a small group of Moravians landed at Savannah, Georgia. These were followed a few months later by a larger group whose fellow passengers on the voyage were the Wesleys and Governor James Oglethorpe. The mis-

---

[13] An enlightening essay concerning the origins of the American fuguing tune appears in Lowens, pp. 237–48.

[14] Lester Hostetler, *Handbook to the Mennonite Hymnary* (Newton, Kans.: General Conference of the Mennonite Church of North American Board of Publications, 1949), p. xxx.

sionary work in Georgia was abandoned in 1740, after which these Moravians settled in Philadelphia. The following year a settlement was established at Bethlehem, Pennsylvania. Some of the group moved to North Carolina a few years later, where the chief settlement was established at the site of today's Winston-Salem. In their hymn singing, the Moravians used their Herrnhut hymnal, *Das Gesangbuch der Gemeine in Herrnhut*, 1735, and after their settlement in Pennsylvania, their first American hymnal, *Hirten Lieder von Bethlehem*, was printed at Germantown in 1742. The reluctance of this group to abandon their native tongue for the language of their adopted country is evidenced by the fact that their first hymnal in English, a reprint of the *British Province Hymnal* of 1801, did not appear until 1813.[15]

American Printings of Watts and Wesley The transition from psalms to hymns in the American colonies, as in England, was a very gradual process which hinged on the psalm versions of Isaac Watts. The poor manner of singing and the controversy of "regular singing" as opposed to "common singing" did not provide fertile soil for the immediate transplanting of Watts's psalms and hymns. A decade after its first appearance in England, Watts's *Psalms* was reprinted in Philadelphia in 1729 by Benjamin Franklin. Apparently Franklin's publication of this work was motivated by his admiration for Watts rather than public demand for the work, for he complained two years later that the copies remained unsold in his shop. The first American edition of Watts's *Hymns and Spiritual Songs* was published in 1739.

John Wesley's *Charlestown Collection*, 1737, published on his visit to Georgia, had no influence on hymnic development in the American colonies at that time. The translations of German hymns which Wesley made on this visit cannot be acknowledged as belonging to American hymnody, yet it is true that they are the earliest English hymns written in America.

> It is interesting to reflect that both the beginning of Wesleyan hymnody and the opening to the English-speaking world of the treasury of German worship-song took place in Georgia in the fourth decade of the eighteenth century, when that colony was still only an outpost in the wilderness.[16]

HYMN SINGING OF THE GREAT AWAKENING

A revival of religion, known as the Great Awakening, occurred in the American colonies and was accompanied by fervent singing. Launched by Jonathan Edwards, pastor of the Congregational church in Northampton, Massachusetts, this movement endeavored to rescue deteriorating Con-

[15] *Hymnal and Liturgies of the Moravian Church* (Unitas Fratrum), p. 4.

[16] Henry Wilder Foote, *Three Centuries of American Hymnody* (Cambridge: Harvard University Press, 1940), p. 145.

80   gregationalism, the established denomination in Massachusetts. Edwards' efforts were greatly aided by the English preacher, George Whitefield, who visited the colonies in 1739–1740. Whitefield preached to great throngs on his tour through the middle and southern colonies and news of his successes reached New England before his arrival there in 1740. Emphasizing individual conversion, the preaching of Edwards, Whitefield, and others of the Great Awakening aroused evangelical enthusiasm and opened the way for the Calvinistic hymns of Isaac Watts. Whitefield's admiration for Watts and his high regard for the singing in his services were major factors in the transition from psalmody to hymnody. The spread of Watts's hymns by this movement created a demand for their publication, and the first reprintings were made in Boston, 1739; in Philadelphia, 1742 (by Benjamin Franklin); and in New York, 1752. These opened the way for a flood of publications of Watts's *Psalms and Hymns,* and from Benjamin Franklin's 1729 edition until 1778, almost fifty editions appeared. Many of these contained, in addition to the psalms and hymns of Watts, hymns added by the compilers in an effort to provide a collection acceptable to a particular denominational group. This resulted in the publication of collections known as *Barlow's Watts, Dwight's Watts, Winchell's Watts, Worcester's Watts,* and *Worcester's Watts and Select.*

DENOMINATIONAL ACTIVITY

With the growth of denominational groups following the Revolutionary War, the hymns they sang and the collections they used became more significant. Opposition to the introduction of new psalm versions among the Presbyterians brought about the "Great Psalmody Controversy." Presbyterian churches split into the "Old Side" and the "New Side" in 1741, and the controversy continued for almost a century. The "Old Side," representing largely the Scottish and Irish influence, clung tenaciously to the psalters of Rous or Barton, while the "New Side" adopted the New Version of Tate and Brady, or Watts's *Psalms.* The Synod of 1787 gave cautious approval to *Barlow's Watts* and left the decision on whether it should replace Rous to the local parishes. In 1802, the General Assembly gave formal authorization to *Dwight's Watts,* and the first official Presbyterian hymnal appeared in 1831.

The Church of England congregations among the colonies used the metrical psalms of the Old Version or the New Version which were bound in at the end of the Book of Common Prayer. The forming of these congregations into the Protestant Episcopal Church began in Philadelphia in 1784, and an American edition of the Prayer Book was published and officially adopted in 1790, which predated by thirty years the official acceptance of hymn singing by the Church of England. Twenty-seven hymns were added to the metrical psalms and the inclusion of these hymns marked the first official acceptance of hymnody into Episcopal usage. While it was not achieved without opposition, this transition did not result in the bitter controversy and harmful division experienced by other groups.

Because of the controversies over congregational singing, the practice among Baptist churches developed slowly. No doubt, among the earliest Baptist churches in New England, any singing used in the services was similar to the psalm singing in other churches, and the *Bay Psalm Book* was used. The settlement of a group of Welsh Baptists in Delaware in the early eighteenth century introduced congregational singing to the middle and southern colonies. While singing had been introduced in the First Baptist Church of Boston by 1728, it was not accepted in the First Baptist Church of Providence, Rhode Island, until 1771, and even then it was accomplished "by allowing the women to vote for it, and caused a division."[17]

Those Baptist churches that felt the impact of the Great Awakening became receptive to Watts, and several collections intended to be supplementary to Watts appeared containing additional hymns emphasizing the believer's baptism. None of these collections proved to be of lasting quality. *Winchell's Watts,* 1818–1819, and *Rippon's Watts,* Philadelphia, 1820, became significant collections for Baptists during the early nineteenth century. This latter collection was an American reprint of John Rippon's *Selection,* first published in London in 1787.

CAMP-MEETING SONGS

Following the Revolutionary War, pioneer settlements sprang up west of the Alleghenies. Wilderness life in these primitive societies was culturally and spiritually destitute. Moral standards were lax in the dull, isolated existence of the frontier.

> Hard-working Methodist circuit riders, poverty-stricken Baptist farmer-preachers, and self-sacrificing Presbyterian teacher-preachers fought the continuing battle for the Christian faith in that remote border region.[18]

The sudden outbreak of the Great Revival of 1800 occurred in Logan County, Kentucky, under the leadership of James McGready, a Presbyterian preacher. The outdoor revival, or camp meeting, became immensely popular as Presbyterians, Methodists, and Baptists joined forces in meetings that attracted thousands. From Kentucky, the camp-meeting movement spread

---

[17] Louis F. Benson, *The English Hymn* (New York: George H. Doran Company, 1915), p. 196.

[18] Charles A. Johnson, *The Frontier Camp Meeting* (Dallas: Southern Methodist University Press, 1955), p. 18.

82 through Tennessee and the Carolinas into Ohio, Georgia, Virginia, Maryland, Delaware, Pennsylvania, New York, Massachusetts, Connecticut, Vermont, and New Hampshire.[19]

This evangelistic movement on the American frontier produced the camp-meeting hymn. The words were in ballad style, couched in the simplest language, mainly concerned with the salvation of the sinner. The tunes were simple and folklike in character. The refrain, which was most important, was sometimes appended to an existing hymn and tune. Collections of these camp-meeting hymns were not plentiful in the early camp meetings, and those available usually contained words without any tunes. The teaching of these hymns by rote demanded that the tunes be easy, singable, and instantly contagious. Under these circumstances, a popular "catchy," repetitious refrain was of invaluable assistance.

Among the collections prepared for these camp meetings were: David Mintz's *Spiritual Song Book,* North Carolina, 1805; Solomon Wiatt's *Impartial Selection of Hymns and Spiritual Songs,* Philadelphia, 1809; John C. Totten's *A Collection of the Most Admired Hymns and Spiritual Songs, with the choruses affixed as usually sung at camp-meetings,* New York, 1809; Thomas S. Hinde's *The Pilgrim Songster,* Cincinnati, 1810; Peggy Dow's *A Collection of Camp-Meeting Hymns,* Philadelphia, 1816; John J. Harrod's *Social and Camp Meeting Songs for the Pious,* Baltimore, 1817; and J. Clarke's *The Camp Meeting Chorister,* Philadelphia, 1827.

After 1805, Presbyterian activity in camp meetings rapidly declined, and by 1825, the outdoor camp meeting was almost exclusively a Methodist institution. Baptists had moved in the direction of the "protracted meeting" held in their churches. Methodist camp-meeting activity continued, particularly among the Pentecostal Holiness branch of Methodism, into the beginning of the twentieth century.

FOLK HYMNODY

American folk hymnody encompasses that body of literature in which hymn texts are sung to folk or folklike melodies. In some instances, the text also stems from folk tradition, but frequently it can be identified with a specific hymn writer and traced to an earlier hymnal. Among the earliest collections to include folk materials were Joshua Smith's *Divine Hymns, or Spiritual Songs* (1794), Samuel Holyoke's *The Christian Harmonist* (1804), and Jeremiah Ingalls' *Christian Harmony* (1805), which contained I LOVE THEE (108). Texts from Watts, Wesley, Newton, and other familiar hymn poets were used, along with folk texts for which no author can be identified. The

[19] Johnson, pp. 67–68.

major emphases in subject matter were the repentance of the sinner, the anticipation of death, and the certainty of final judgment. Many of the new texts were written in the form of religious ballads. A large number of the tunes in these early collections show the influence of the fuguing tunes of the late eighteenth century singing school masters.

Though these earliest collections of folk hymns originated in New England, the major developments in the history of American folk hymnody occur in the South.

> The transit of folk-hymnody from the North to the South seems to have taken place during the second decade of the 19th century, roughly coinciding with the retreat of the quasi-folk composed American music of the singing-schools from urban to rural surroundings. During the crucial decade, these two related types of music joined hands, so to speak, and ever since then the Yankee fuguing tune and psalm-tune are found side by side with the folk-hymn. In this form they become a prominent feature of Southern musico-religious life throughout the 19th century.[20]

From this point forward, the history of folk hymnody is closely linked with the development and use of shaped notation.

SHAPED NOTATION

The "fasola" solmization, introduced in America by the English colonists in the seventeenth century and continued by Tufts and Walter, remained in use throughout the eighteenth century. Each subsequent compiler of singing school tune books included prefatory instructions designed to simplify the "rudiments" in order to make music reading easier. Most of these tune books, following European style, used diamond-headed half notes and square whole notes.

The beginning of the nineteenth century saw the introduction of shaped-note heads—a different shaped-note head representing each of the four syllables, *fa, sol, la, mi.* These first appeared in William Smith's and William Little's *The Easy Instructor* (1802) and Andrew Law's *Musical Primer,* fourth edition (1803). Smith and Little used a right-angle triangle for *fa;* a circle, or round head, for *sol;* a square for *la;* and a diamond head for *mi*—all on the five-line music staff. Law used the same four shapes with slightly different arrangement. His *fa* was square, his *la* was the right-angle triangle, and he eliminated the use of the staff. It was the Smith and Little pattern that was used extensively in the Southern folk hymn publications.

The first important collection to contain folk hymns in shaped notation was

[20] Lowens, pp. 139–40.

84   John Wyeth's *Respository of Sacred Music, Part Second,* published in Harrisburg, Pennsylvania, in 1813. Wyeth's compilation is significant both for the large number of folk tunes that were put into print for the first time (forty-four) and for its influence on the content of the first important Southern collection, the *Kentucky Harmony* of Ananias Davisson.[21]

Southern Shaped-Note Collections   The use of the shaped notes in four–shape notation spread rapidly to the South and West. As evidence of the increasing popularity of these collections, George Pullen Jackson lists thirty-eight tune books published in the first half of the nineteenth century, twenty-one of which were produced by compilers living in the Southern states.[22]

The first significant Southern collection, Davisson's *Kentucky Harmony,* was copyrighted in 1817, but may have been in use as long as two years before then. The book's 144 tunes were set in four-part harmony—in contrast to the three-voice pattern that was to become characteristic of many of the later Southern compilations—with the melody in the tenor. In this volume, as well as other folk hymn publications, it is difficult to determine the extent of the original contributions of the compiler, who often attached his name to tunes he had harmonized or arranged as well as to those he had composed.

William Caldwell's *Union Harmony* (1837) bears a close relationship to *Kentucky Harmony.* However, its significance lies in the large number of tunes to which Caldwell's name is attached, but with the admission that many are not original, having been collected and harmonized. Thus, Caldwell made an important contribution through his transcription of a number of melodies from oral tradition which then became a part of American folk hymn literature.

The most widely used of the Southern collections were *Southern Harmony* (1835) by William Walker and *Sacred Harp* (1844) by Benjamin F. White and E. J. King, which, in both sales volume and geographical coverage, were the most significant and enduring of the oblong tune books in four-shape notation.

Around the middle of the nineteenth century, a seven-shape notation pattern began to replace the four-shape notation in some circles. Jesse Aikin's *The Christian Minstrel* (1846) established the seven-shape system. When William Walker published his *Christian Harmony* in 1866, he abandoned the four-shape notation in favor of a seven-shape pattern (not identical to the one used by Aikin) and included an article defending the change. However, the editors of the 1869 edition of *Sacred Harp* decided to retain four-shape notation, after considering the seven shapes. (For illustrations of four- and seven-shaped notation, see page 102.)

[21] A detailed study of the relationship between Wyeth's *Repository of Sacred Music, Part Second,* and Davisson's *Kentucky Harmony* is made in Lowens, pp. 138–55, and in Lowens' new introduction to Ananias Davisson, *Kentucky Harmony* (Harrisonburg, Va.: The Author, 1816; facsimile reprint, Minneapolis: Augsburg Press, 1976).

[22] Jackson, p. 25.

Among the tunes from Southern shaped-note collections found in present-day hymnals are: AMAZING GRACE (117); FOUNDATION (118); MORNING SONG (119); LAND OF REST (120); HOLY MANNA (121); PISGAH (122); and KEDRON (124).

The tunes of Southern folk hymnody shared several common traits. They were frequently constructed as pentatonic or other "gapped scale" melodies, with a large proportion appearing in the natural minor or in other modes. Harmonizations often use open fourths and fifths rather than triads. Patterns of melodic repetition occur in many of the tunes.

OTHER EARLY NINETEENTH-CENTURY DEVELOPMENTS

The desire for a more definitely evangelical hymnody among the progressive Presbyterians and the Congregationalists resulted in Asahel Nettleton's *Village Hymns,* 1824. This collection included no tunes, but above each hymn was printed the name of one or more suitable tunes. Nettleton published shortly thereafter *Zion's Harp,* a collection of tunes for his *Village Hymns.* Nettleton's work became immensely popular, and *Village Hymns* ran through several editions in the first three years. Those churches that used Dwight and Worcester for their services found *Village Hymns* most effective for revival meetings, and the popular acceptance of this collection opened the way for similar collections to follow.

Even more evangelical in style and popular in appeal was *The Christian Lyre,* New York, 1831, by Joshua Leavitt, an associate of Charles G. Finney, the noted evangelist. This collection, primarily intended for use in Finney's meetings, was patterned after the work of Nettleton. Yet, Leavitt went considerably beyond his predecessor, since he "aimed to supply the revival need with somewhat lighter and more songlike hymns with rippling rhythms and sometimes 'chorusses.' "[23] In addition to the "revival hymns," Leavitt's collection contained several translations of German and Latin hymns, among which was J. W. Alexander's "O Sacred Head! now wounded" (9). The inclusion of these translations marked the first awareness in America of the richness of this heritage for hymnic use. The popularity of *The Christian Lyre* among the evangelicals is evidenced by the fact that it had passed through twenty-six editions by 1846. One of the tunes from this collection is PLEADING SAVIOUR (109).

Benjamin Carr   In the closing part of the eighteenth century and in the early nineteenth century a number of European musicians who came to America contributed significantly to the development of music in such growing cities as Charleston, Philadelphia, New York, and Boston. Among these

[23] Benson, p. 377.

86   professional immigrants was Benjamin Carr, who opened Philadelphia's first music store in 1793, and, as a music publisher, exerted great influence in music activities in that city. ADESTE FIDELIS (111), SPANISH HYMN (110), and PLEYEL'S HYMN (112) were introduced into American usage through his efforts.

Lowell Mason   Lowell Mason was the outstanding musician of his day. Having settled in Boston in 1827, Mason became associated with the Bowdoin Street Church, where his church choir earned national recognition for the quality of its singing. In an effort to improve music in both choir and congregation, Mason began music classes for the children of his church and published *The Juvenile Psalmist, or The Child's Introduction to Sacred Music,* 1829. His concern for the improvement of music in the churches was a basic objective of the Boston Academy of Music, which he founded in 1832. By 1838, he had gained approval for the teaching of vocal music in the public schools of Boston in "preparation for making the praise of God glorious in families and churches." In the years that followed, musical conventions became increasingly popular, resulting in 1853 in the formation of the first musical normal institutes. In this later activity Mason was assisted by George F. Root, Thomas Hastings, and William B. Bradbury.

> Lowell Mason carried on his pioneer work in the training of music teachers for nearly twenty-five years, and through teachers' classes, musical conventions, lectures on the pedagogy of music, teachers' institutes, and musical normal institutes, he provided the United States for more than a generation with most of its training of public school music teachers, as well as a large proportion of its trained church musicians and other professional musicians.[24]

Mason was prolific in his publication of collections of music in church and school. Rich lists at least eighty collections of music with which Mason was associated either as sole compiler or in collaboration with others.[25] These publications show his recognition of the need for better music, his contributions of original tunes, and his adaptation of tunes from other sources, especially European.[26] OLIVET and MISSIONARY HYMN (113) are his best-known original tunes, and ANTIOCH (114), AZMON (130), and HAMBURG (114) are the most widely used of his adaptations or arrangements.

    Greatly alarmed by the popularity of Leavitt's *Christian Lyre,* with what he considered "inferior music," Mason feared that this collection of lighter songs would undo his efforts to improve church music. With the assistance of Thomas Hastings, Mason published *Spiritual Songs for Social Worship,* 1832, to

---

[24] Arthur Lowndes Rich, *Lowell Mason* (Chapel Hill: The University of North Carolina Press, 1946), pp. 58–59.

[25] Rich, pp. 140–172.

[26] For a listing of these tunes, see Henry L. Mason, *Hymn Tunes of Lowell Mason* (Cambridge: The University Press, 1944).

stem the tide of Leavitt's influence. This venture was extremely successful, and this hymnal, designed not for church worship but for religious gatherings and revival meetings, was widely accepted. Hastings' TOPLADY (116) first appeared in this collection.

7

American Hymnody, II

The widespread influence of early nineteenth-century revivals resulted in increased denominational activity in America. The spiritual energy tapped by these revivals found expression in many areas of religious life. A reawakening of great concern for the spreading of the gospel brought about the establishment of various denominational boards to supervise missionary activity both at home and abroad. By 1812 pioneering missionaries had gone forth to such faraway places as India, Ceylon, Africa, and, later, to China and Japan. Opportunities for home missions expanded rapidly as the United States acquired more territory through the Louisiana Purchase, the regions of California, Oregon, and, finally, Texas. Before mid-century the boundaries of the United States reached from the Atlantic to the Pacific and from Mexico to Canada.

The idea of Sunday schools, introduced first by the Methodists following the Revolutionary War, was adopted by other groups. But, because of the lack of adequate public schools, these Sunday schools also were used to teach reading and writing. The American Sunday School Union founded in 1824 promoted the spread of Sunday schools and published needed materials for them.

The increase of denominational strength is further seen in the publication of denominational hymnals.

Episcopalians　With the approval of the 1826 General Convention, *Hymns of the Protestant Episcopal Church of the United States of America,* compiled by William A. Mühlenberg and Henry U. Onderdonck, was published in 1827. Bound with the *Book of Common Prayer,* it became known as the Prayer Book

Collection. Watts, Doddridge, Steele, Wesley, and other English hymn writers of the eighteenth century made the major contribution to the 212 hymns in this collection. Also included were hymns by Newton, Cowper, Montgomery, and Heber. In addition to these imports from England and hymns by the compilers, Mühlenberg and Onderdonck, there were hymns by Francis Scott Key, James W. Eastburn, and George Washington Doane.

Methodists   Wesleyan hymns made up the major portion of hymnic material used by the Methodists. Upon the authorization of the Methodist General Conference, *A Collection of Hymns for the use of the Methodist Episcopal Church, principally from the Collection of the Rev. John Wesley* was published in New York in 1821, slightly revised in 1832. This was the fifth Wesleyan collection produced in America. A sixth edition was published in 1836. These reprints of English Wesleyan collections were largely made up of the hymns of Charles Wesley and did not contain any hymns of American origin, nor any of the camp-meeting hymns so popular among the Methodists of the time.

Unitarians   The most important of several Unitarian collections of the nineteenth century were two compilations by the "two Sams," Samuel Johnson and Samuel Longfellow (102). *A Book of Hymns,* published in 1846 while both men were fellow students at the Harvard Divinity School, was an effort to produce a collection more in keeping with contemporary theological thought. *Hymns of the Spirit,* 1864, was a collection of theistic hymns, expressive of the compilers' philosophy of universal religion. Included in these collections were works of American Unitarian writers, John Greenleaf Whittier, James Russell Lowell, Jones Very, Theodore Parker, and Harriett Beecher Stowe, as well as hymns by Johnson and Longfellow.

Baptists   Numerous collections were used by Baptist churches in the first half of the nineteenth century. *Winchell's Watts* was generally used throughout the New England states, while *Watts and Rippon* was found in the middle states. Miller's *New Selection,* Cincinnati, 1835, and Buck's *The Baptist Hymnal,* Louisville, 1847, were popular in the South and the West. The finest collection for Baptists was *The Psalmist,* Boston, 1843, compiled by Baron Stow and Samuel F. Smith. Immensely successful in the North, *The Psalmist* met with strong opposition in the South because of the omission of many hymns popular in that area. Richard Fuller and J. B. Jeter published a *Supplement* in 1850, in an attempt to overcome this opposition by the addition of many of the omitted hymns.

Congregationalists   At mid-century two important hymnals were published for Congregational churches: Henry Ward Beecher's *Plymouth Collection,* 1855, and *The Sabbath Hymn Book,* 1858, compiled by two Andover Theological Seminary professors, Edwards A. Park and Austin Phelps.

90 Beecher's collection, primarily designed for his Plymouth Congregational Church in Brooklyn, New York, was definitely evangelical in character, while the Andover collection was more scholarly in content. Both hymnals were large in size. *The Plymouth Collection* contained 1,374 hymns, and *The Sabbath Hymn Book*, 1,290. These two hymnals mark the transition in the development of hymnody in America from the "psalms and hymns" era to the increasing acceptance of a free and catholic hymnody drawn from all available sources. Here were the forerunners of the modern church hymnal.

John Zundel, organist at Plymouth Church (125), and Charles Beecher served as music editors for the *Plymouth Collection*. This was the first church hymnal to print the tune above the words on the same page. No doubt the success and popularity of *The Christian Lyre* and *Spiritual Songs for Social Worship* led Henry Ward Beecher to adopt this format for his hymnal. With both words and tunes in the hands of the worshippers, congregational participation in hymn singing took on increased interest and significance in the service.

Mennonites   Throughout most of the nineteenth century, many Mennonite congregations retained their German language hymnals. The *Ausbund* continued in use and the *Gesangbuch* (1856), brought to this country by Swiss and South German Mennonites, enjoyed widespread usage, becoming the first official hymnbook of the General Conference Mennonite Church. The first American Mennonite hymnal in English was published in Harrisonburg, Virginia, in 1847. Joseph Funk, significant in developments related to shape-note tunebooks in the Shenandoah valley, was a member of the hymnal committee.[1]

Moravians   The first original hymnal for the Moravian church in America was published in 1851, revised in 1876. In this initial effort, the Moravians relied heavily on Moravian hymnals published in England, adding little of significance from their own congregations. These compilers boldly maintained the hymnody of Moravian tradition, yet there is increasing evidence of the infiltration of hymns and tunes from non-Moravian English and American sources.

Lutherans   Before the late 1800's, most Lutheran hymnals in America were published as two separate books: the hymnal, which contained only the texts, and the chorale book, which included the tunes and was intended to be used by the organist.

"In the course of its youthful years, Lutheran churches in America seemingly did very little to influence the use of Lutheran hymns and chorales in other

---

[1] Harry Lee Eskew, "Shape-Note Hymnody in the Shenandoah Valley, 1816–1860" (unpublished Ph.D. dissertation, Tulane University, 1966), p. 98.

denominations. Furthermore, instead of creating their own unique hymnody, English-speaking congregations relied on the use of their American neighbors."[2]

One of the earliest English hymnals for American Lutherans was the 1795 *A Hymn and Prayer Book,* prepared by John Christopher Kunze. The first American Lutheran Hymnal of widespread significance was the *Church Book,* published in 1868 for the use of Evangelical Lutheran Congregations.

New Sects In addition to the expansion and growth of denominational groups, a further outgrowth of the early nineteenth-century revivals was the appearance of new sects. The most important of these were the Shakers, the Adventists, and the Mormons—all of which had their beginnings in New York or New England. In the activities of these groups and the propagating of their beliefs, hymn singing was a constant aid. Aggressive, intense sectarianism characterized the hymnody of each group.

The hymns of the Shakers expressed belief in the mystical union of the believer with God's Holy Spirit, and in God as a dual person, both male and female. Expressions of praise and exaltation of Mother Ann Lee, the founder of the Shakers, are frequently seen in these hymns. The early Adventist hymns reflect the strong faith of this group in the imminent second coming of Christ. The followers of William Miller, leader of the Adventist movement, were prolific in their hymn writing, and numerous collections appeared.

The beginning of Mormonism occurred in Manchester, New York, in 1827, and Joseph Smith's *Book of Mormon* was published in 1830. The Preface to the *Hymns* of the Church of Jesus Christ of the Latter Day Saints, Salt Lake City, Utah, 1948, states:

> Within a few months of the organization of His restored Church, the Lord directed that Emma Smith, wife of the Prophet Joseph Smith, should make a selection of sacred hymns for use by the Saints in their worshipping assemblies.

Here is an instance of origin unique in hymnic history, with the responsibility for the development of the hymnody of a religious sect given to the wife of the leader of the group. The result of Emma Smith's efforts is seen in *A Collection of Sacred Hymns,* published first in New York, 1836, and again in Nauvoo, Illinois, 1841. This collection and others that followed were filled with hymnic writing expressing the strong sectarianism of the Mormons. Many of these hymns tell of the glories of Mormon history—the revelation to Joseph Smith, the trials and tribulations of the westward journey, and the joyful anticipation of reaching the "promised land" of Utah.

By far the best-known Mormon hymn is William Clayton's "Come, come ye saints," written to fit a tune which seems to have originated in Georgia at least

---

[2] Dale Eugene Warland, "The Music of Twentieth-Century Lutheran Hymnody in America" (unpublished D.M.A. dissertation, University of Southern California, 1965), p. 7.

two years previously. Clayton was a member of the first group of Mormon pioneers to make the westward trek. His wife had remained at Nauvoo, Illinois, and, later along the journey, word reached Clayton that she had given birth to a son. The brief letter from his wife closed with the reassuring phrase, "All is well." No doubt these words recalled to his mind this hymn, and he framed new stanzas of comfort and strength retaining the significant lines, "All is well." His diary entry for April 15, 1846, states, "This morning I composed a new song, 'All Is Well.' "[3]

This tune, ALL IS WELL, appeared in the *Sacred Harp*, 1844, one of ten tunes in this collection credited to J. T. White, a nephew of the compiler, B. F. White. In the *Original Sacred Harp*, Atlanta, Georgia, 1911 (an enlarged and annotated edition of the 1844 *Sacred Harp*), the editor, Joe S. James, states that this tune had been published before it appeared in the 1844 collection. It is altogether possible that this could have been one of the many tunes that appeared in *The Organ*, the county newspaper published at Hamilton, Harris County, Georgia, which B. F. White edited for three or four years prior to the publication of the *Sacred Harp*. Many of these tunes, which first appeared in the county weekly newspaper, were used later in the *Sacred Harp*. The first two stanzas of the original text are:

What's this that steals, that steals upon my frame!
  Is it death? is it death?
That soon will quench, will quench this mortal flame.
  Is it death? is it death?
If this be death, I soon shall be
From ev'ry pain and sorrow free,
I shall the King of glory see.
  All is well! All is well!
Weep not, my friends, my friends weep not for me,
  All is well! All is well!
My sins forgiv'n, forgiv'n, and I am free,
  All is well! All is well!
There's not a cloud that doth arise,
To hide my Jesus from my eyes,
I soon shall mount the upper skies.
  All is well! All is well!

In some unknown manner this tune migrated north to Illinois, came to Clayton's attention, and became the vehicle for his new text. J. Spencer Cornwall, former director of the famed Mormon Tabernacle Choir, states:

Over the years the choir has received more fan mail concerning the singing of this hymn than any other number it has performed. When the choir sang it in

[3] The sectarian views expressed in Clayton's original text limit this hymn to Mormon usage. While retaining the vigor and strength of expression, Joseph F. Green's altered version (123), makes this hymn appropriate for much wider usage in the broad stream of hymnody.

Europe, on the 1955 tour, it had to be repeated in every concert. It was sung in English, but its message, "All is Well," went over to everyone in every country regardless of language.[4]

THE EMERGENCE OF THE GOSPEL SONG

The issue of slavery became the first major political issue to confront the rapidly expanding nation in the nineteenth century. The revivals early in the century had produced strong opposition to slavery at the grass-roots level. The churches of America were caught in the maelstrom of this upheaval, and major splits resulted in the three most influential groups—Methodists, Baptists, and Presbyterians—prior to the outbreak of war between the states. Of increasing significance was the growth and popularity of the Sunday school movement and the expanding influence of the Young Men's Christian Association (founded in England in 1844, with an organized branch in Boston in 1851). However, by mid-century, the enthusiasm for missions had waned, and in the business prosperity of the decade, 1845–1855, interest in churches declined in the towns and cities. In 1857 the third great panic in American history caused thousands of businessmen to close their doors, as banks failed and railroads went into bankruptcy. A new wave of revivalism followed, known as the Second Great Awakening. This reappearance of evangelical fervor found its greatest expression in the interdenominational noonday prayer meetings held daily in churches and theaters. For use in these noonday meetings, the Sunday School Union published *Union Prayer Meeting Hymns,* 1858, largely a collection of familiar hymns. The revivalism that immediately preceded the Civil War did much to prepare the way for Moody, Whittle, Pentecost, and other evangelists who appeared later.

Expansion of the Frontier The population expansion westward continued the movement of the American frontier. The religious activity along this frontier was fervently evangelical in nature and largely led by Methodists, Baptists, and small splinter sects. There were no metropolitan areas of culture, no influential educational centers. In the struggling frontier settlements, the music used in the religious services consisted of folk and camp-meeting hymns. Itinerant evangelists imported the gospel songs to these areas as they became popular in the East and Midwest.

---

[4] J. Spencer Cornwall, *A Century of Singing* (Salt Lake City: Deseret Book Company, 1958), pp. 303–304.

94   **Music Copyrights**   Music copyrights played no small role in the development of American hymnody, as legal developments provided protection for music compositions.[5] The Copyright Act of 1831 was the first to include music. This became increasingly significant after the Civil War, when the Registry of Copyrights office was opened about 1870 at Washington in the Library of Congress. Prior to this, the registry of music was handled in the various districts of the states. Refusal to grant permission or the demand for exorbitant fees reduced the number of copyrighted tunes in many denominational hymnals. As a result, the compilers imported an increasing number of public-domain tunes from England. Quite frequently that which was musically superior was at the same time less expensive to use.

The Gospel Song   Perhaps most phenomenal of the developments of Christian song in the second half of the nineteenth century was the appearance and widespread popularity of the gospel song. Neither the name nor the type of these songs was new, but this label was attached to the songs popularized in the Moody-Sankey revivals. In 1874, P. P. Bliss compiled a small collection, *Gospel Songs,* which was published by the John Church Company, Cincinnati. That title became the generic label by which all subsequent songs of this type became known.

Antecedents   The gospel song had its roots in American folk hymnody, which emerged at the turn of the century in Jeremiah Ingalls' *Christian Harmony,* 1805, and the evangelical collections of Asahel Nettleton and Joshua Leavitt. Of equal importance were the camp-meeting collections, the singing-school tune books, and the songs designed for use in the Sunday school movement. All these forces met, merged, and contributed to the development of the gospel song.

The use of the gospel song in the evangelistic movement from about 1870 on had its immediate roots in at least four lines of development: (1) the "praise services" of Eben Tourjee; (2) the hearty singing of large groups attending the annual national conventions of the YMCA and the Sunday School Union; (3) Philip Phillips' "services of song" given at Sunday school conventions and evangelistic campaigns both in America and around the world;[6] and (4) the influence of Philip P. Bliss in connection with Moody's early work in Chicago. Tourjee, who founded the New England Conservatory of Music in 1867, began holding "praise services," or "sings," in his home in Warren, Rhode Island, as early as 1851. The popularity of these meetings increased, and Tourjee's reputation as a musical leader became widely known.

---

[5] See the discussion of music copyright law in Burton, "Copyright and the Creative Arts," in Paul H. Lang, *One Hundred Years of Music in America* (New York: G. Schirmer, Inc., 1961), pp. 282–301.

[6] For a detailed description see Philip Phillips, *Song Pilgrimage Around the World* (Chicago: Fairbanks, Palmer & Co., 1880).

When the great revival meetings commenced at the Tabernacle in Boston, Dr. Tourjee came forward with a choir of about two thousand voices . . . In no city have the revivalists been sustained by better music than in Boston; and it is certainly most gratifying to see the accomplished director of the largest musical conservatory in the world thus lending his own personal influence to swell the tide of song that rises from the mighty concourse to the praise of the Redeemer.[7]

Sunday School Songs   The enormous output of Sunday school collections beginning in the twenties and continuing into the seventies had much to do with cultivating a taste for a lighter type of religious song among young people. Leaders in publication of these were William B. Bradbury, George F. Root, Silas J. Vail, Asa Hull, William H. Doane, and Robert Lowry. Many of the familiar gospel songs found in denominational hymnals today, such as "What a friend we have in Jesus" (126), "He leadeth me, O blessed thought" (127), "All the way my Saviour leads me" (128), and "To God be the glory" (129) first appeared in these collections.

The Revivalist   One of the numerous evangelical collections that immediately preceded Bliss and Sankey was *The Revivalist*, 1868, compiled by Joseph Hillman, with Lewis Hartsough as music editor. This collection ran through eleven editions within a few years following its appearance and was most popular among the Methodists in New York. John W. Dadmun, William Hunter, William MacDonald, and William G. Fischer were among the more significant contributors to this collection and its subsequent editions.

Philip P. Bliss   Bliss was one of the most widely known and best loved musicians of his day. His activities in music-school teaching and in musical conventions took him from New York to Wisconsin and from Michigan to Alabama. For several years he was associated with Root and Cady, a well-known music-publishing firm in Chicago for whom he wrote many songs and also represented in his travels in music-convention work. Later, he was associated with the John Church Company of Cincinnati, which published four of his books: *The Charm*, 1871; *The Song Tree*, 1872; *Sunshine*, 1873; and *Gospel Songs*, 1874. Bliss first met Dwight L. Moody in Chicago during the summer of 1869. When he was at home in Chicago between engagements, he frequently sang in Moody's services. The effectiveness of Bliss's singing in these services first brought to Moody an awareness of the real value of music in his work. At Moody's insistence, Bliss abandoned his teaching in 1874 and became song leader for Major D. W. Whittle, a prominent evangelist. Bliss was a prolific songwriter, usually providing both words and music. One of his best-known gospel songs is "Sing them over again to me" (131).

[7] Elias Nason and J. Frank Beale, Jr., *Lives and Labors of Eminent Divines* (Philadelphia. John E. Potter & Co., 1895), p. 298.

Sankey's "Sacred Songs and Solos" After several years as a YMCA worker, Ira D. Sankey began his work as song leader and soloist with Dwight L. Moody in 1870, following their first meeting at a YMCA convention in Indianapolis. In 1872, Moody and Sankey visited England, where Sankey used Philip Phillips' *Hallowed Songs,* with some additional songs in manuscript he had picked up in Chicago before his departure. The demand in England for these manuscript songs prompted him to request the publishers of *Hallowed Songs* to bring out a new edition to which his songs might be appended. When this request was refused, an English publisher, Morgan and Scott, published a twenty-four page pamphlet of Sankey's songs in 1873, entitled, *Sacred Songs and Solos.* Additional songs were put into subsequent editions, until the 1903 edition contained 1,200 songs. The sales of this collection reflect its extraordinary popularity in England, for in the first fifty years after its publication more than eighty million copies had been sold.[8]

The "Gospel Hymns" Series Upon his return to America, Sankey discovered *Gospel Songs,* 1874, by Bliss and suggested that they merge their materials and publish a joint collection. *Gospel Hymns and Sacred Songs* appeared in 1875 and was followed by *Gospel Hymns No. 2* in 1876; *No. 3* in 1878; *No. 4* in 1883; *No. 5* in 1887; and *No. 6* in 1891. These six editions were jointly published by Biglow and Main, New York and Chicago, and the John Church Company, New York and Cincinnati. The strange coincidence of copublication no doubt added greatly to the circulation and popularity of these books.

The combination of the two compilers, Bliss and Sankey, and the two publishers, Biglow and Main and the John Church Company, explains to a large degree the dominant role played by this series of gospel song books. Biglow and Main (Sankey's publisher) was founded in 1868 primarily to publish the collections of William B. Bradbury. This firm was familiar to churches as a publisher of Sunday school song books prior to the Bliss and Sankey series. The John Church Company (Bliss's publisher), organized in 1859, was well-established in general music publishing, specializing in vocal and piano music as well as Sunday school collections. They had developed a successful merchandising operation through local retail music dealers, as well as a nationwide mail-order business. No better plan for merchandising and promoting this book could have been available for Bliss and Sankey. After the death of Bliss in 1876, Sankey was assisted in the later editions of *Gospel Hymns* by James McGranahan and George C. Stebbins.

The mainstream of gospel hymnody followed *Gospel Hymns,* and this series remained unchallenged to the end of the century. Gospel songs, which first appeared in other collections, later became immensely popular through their inclusion in one of these six editions. This series culminated in *Gospel Hymns Nos. 1–6 Complete,* 1894, containing 739 hymns.[9]

---

[8] *The Ira D. Sankey Centenary* (New Castle, Pa., 1941), p. 15.

[9] The six collections of *Gospel Hymns* have recently been reprinted in Ira D. Sankey et al., *Gospel Hymns Nos. 1 to 6,* new introduction by H. Wiley Hitchcock (New York: Da Capo Press, 1972).

Moody Bible Institute For the training of evangelists and song leaders, Dwight L. Moody founded Moody Bible Institute in Chicago in 1890. This institution has played a major role in gospel hymnody in America. Daniel B. Towner, noted gospel song composer, served as head of the music department from 1893 until his death in 1919. In this strategic position, he exerted a wide influence throughout the nation as he trained evangelical church music leaders.

Fanny J. Crosby The author of "All the way my Saviour leads me" (128) and "To God be the glory" (129) was by far the most prolific writer of gospel song texts. Beginning in the early 1830's, her hymn writing continued at a phenomenal rate until shortly before her death in 1915 at the age of ninety-five. An estimate of the number of hymns she wrote has been placed at 8,000. Though blind from infancy, Fanny Crosby lived a radiant life and, to a greater extent than any other person, captured the spirit of literary expression of the gospel song era. Most of her life was spent in New York City, where she was a member of St. John's Methodist Episcopal Church. While most of her writing was for the Biglow & Main Company, she supplied texts for such composers as Bradbury, Root, Doane, Lowry, Sankey, Sweney, Kirkpatrick, and others.

Distinguishing Characteristics Simple expressions of Christian experience and salvation characterize these gospel songs.

> The American Gospel Hymn is nothing if it is not emotional. It takes a simple phrase and repeats it over and over again. There is no reasoning, nor are the lines made heavy with introspection. "Tell me the story simply, as to a little child." The feelings are touched; the stiffest of us become children again.[10]

These songs, which appealed to the masses of people, were used most effectively in services of evangelistic emphasis. The tunes were simple, popular melodies, which usually included a refrain. They were quickly learned and easily remembered by the common people. The melodic line was supported by simple harmonic structure with infrequent changes of chord.

> The old hymn-tune, with fundamental harmony at each beat, moves with the stride and strength of a giant, while the attenuated effect of these American tunes is largely due to their changing the harmony but once in a bar.[11]

Nonetheless, in spite of texts that are light and lacking in lyrical beauty or doctrinal strength and tunes that are melodically trite and harmonically dull, the gospel songs continue after a century of usage, strongly favored by evangelical Christians around the world.

---

[10] John Spencer Curwen, *Studies in Worship Music,* 2d series (London: J. Curwen & Sons, 1885), p. 40.
[11] Curwen, p. 39.

Gospel hymnody has the distinction of being America's most typical contribution to Christian song. Gospel hymnody has been a plough digging up the hardened surfaces of pavemented minds. Its very obviousness has been its strength. Where delicacy or dignity can make no impress, gospel hymnody stands up triumphing. In an age when religion must win mass approval in order to survive, in an age when religion must at least win a majority vote from the electorate, gospel hymnody is inevitable. Sankey's songs are true folk music of the people. Dan Emmett and Stephen Foster only did in secular music what Ira D. Sankey and P. P. Bliss did as validly and effectively in sacred music.[12]

Translation into Other Languages   American missionaries, carrying the gospel of Christ to other nations, have translated gospel songs into the language of the people and have used them as effective tools of missionary enterprise. An examination of evangelical hymnals from many countries today, in both the eastern and western hemispheres, reveals a surprisingly large number of the songs of Sankey and his followers.

LATE NINETEENTH-CENTURY HYMNALS

Gospel hymnody had the least influence in those denominational groups that had an authorized hymnal compiled and sanctioned by ecclesiastical authority. This was especially true of the Episcopalians.

Episcopalians   An American edition of *Hymns Ancient and Modern* was issued in 1862 and was licensed for use in some dioceses. In spite of the fact that this hymnal was not widely used, it left an indelible imprint upon subsequent Episcopal hymnals. *The Hymnal,* 1871–1874, contained no tunes, but five musical editions were published: Goodrich and Gilbert, 1875; Hall and Whiteley; Hutchins, 1872; Pearce, 1872 (?); and Tucker and Rousseau, 1875.

The next revision of *The Hymnal,* 1892, likewise contained no tunes. Six musical editions were published: Messiter, 1893; Tucker and Rousseau, 1894; Hutchins, 1894; Darlington, 1897; Parker, 1903; and Helfenstein, 1909. Of these six musical editions, the one prepared by Hutchins was the most popular and the most widely used.

The Hymnal, 1916, was followed by an authorized music edition entitled *The New Hymnal,* 1918, the first Episcopal hymnal since 1785 to contain tunes and the first effort of the Episcopal Church to standardize the tunes used to the hymns of the official hymnal.

[12] Robert M. Stevenson, *Patterns of Protestant Church Music* (Durham, N.C.: Duke University Press, 1953), p. 162.

Methodists A number of Methodist hymnals appeared during the nineteenth century published by the three branches of American Methodism. The Methodist Episcopal Church issued hymnals in 1849 and again in 1878. The Methodist Protestant Church issued hymnals in 1838 and 1859. *Tribute of Praise and Methodist Protestant Hymnal*, 1882, was a combination of Eben Tourjee's *Tribute of Praise*, 1874, with revisions of previous Methodist hymnals, and was the first hymnal by the Methodist Protestants to contain tunes. The last official hymnal of this group was published in 1901.

The Methodist Episcopal Church, South, published its first hymnal in 1847. This collection was amplified in 1851 by *Songs of Zion*. The first tune book for this group, *Wesleyan Hymn and Tune Book*, 1859, contained the hymns of the 1847 collection, with suitable tunes selected by L. C. Everett. In response to the demand for a smaller and less expensive collection, the *New Hymn Book* was issued in 1881. The last official hymnal of this group appeared in 1889.

The first merging of hymnic endeavors among Methodists occurred with the joint publication of the *Methodist Hymnal*, 1905, by the Methodist Episcopal Church and the Methodist Episcopal Church, South. The commission that compiled this hymnal had the musical assistance of Peter C. Lutkin, who served as music editor.

Presbyterians Presbyterian hymnals in the last half of the nineteenth century reflected strong influences of *Hymns Ancient and Modern*. The Presbyterian *Hymnal*, 1870, drew heavily on the new translations of Latin hymns, and even to a greater extent on the tunes of Monk and his fellow composers. This collection was replaced by the *Hymnal*, 1895, prepared with great care and effort by the Board of Publication, Philadelphia.

> The whole field of Hymnody was freshly studied with the resources of the new Hymnology; the hymns were chosen in the interests of devotion as distinguished from homiletics, and their text was determined with scrupulousness that had been more common in literature than in Hymnody.[13]

In addition to the tunes of the English composers, the committee selected tunes by American composers which had appeared in the musical editions of the Episcopal *Hymnal* of 1892. Because of its increased popularity, this Presbyterian hymnal established a measure of uniformity in the hymn singing of Presbyterian churches. A revision was made in 1911.

While denominational hymnals were gaining in importance, independent collections were still widely used. A well-known Presbyterian minister, Charles S. Robinson, published no less than fifteen collections, of which the most significant were: *Songs of the Church*, 1862; *Songs for the Sanctuary*, 1865; *Psalms and Hymns and Spiritual Songs*, 1875; *Laudes Domini*, 1885; and *In Excelsis*, 1897. While Robinson included contemporary material in his collection, his hymnals

[13] Louis F. Benson, *The English Hymn* (New York: George H. Doran Company, 1915), p. 555.

100   were not as advanced as the denominational collections. Much of the popularity of these books can be attributed to the use of popular tunes by Mason, Hastings, Bradbury, Root, and Greatorex, as well as the work of Joseph P. Holbrook, music editor for most of Robinson's collections.

The southern branch of American Presbyterianism was more conservative and, at the same time, more evangelical than the northern branch and less influenced by Anglican hymnody. Robinson's *Psalms and Hymns and Spiritual Songs*, 1875, was officially adopted by this group. In 1901, *New Psalms and Hymns* was authorized and published in Richmond.

Congregationalists   While many Congregational churches used hymnals compiled by Robinson, there were efforts within the denomination to produce hymnals for these churches. The two most important of this type published in the last half of the nineteenth century were *Hymns of the Faith with Psalms*, Boston, 1887; and Lyman Abbott's *Plymouth Hymnal*, 1893. While both of these collections reveal strong influences of Anglican hymnody, the latter was the more advanced in this respect.

Baptists   The only new Baptist collection to appear during the Civil War was William B. Bradbury's *Devotional Hymn and Tune Book*, published by the American Baptist Publication Society, Philadelphia, 1864. Among the new material in this collection was Bradbury's SOLID ROCK (132).

Of the major denominational groups, the Baptists were least affected by the influences of the Oxford Movement and the liturgical hymn. In this period, the most widely used collections, particularly in the North, were: *The Service of Song for Baptist Churches*, 1871, compiled by S. L. Caldwell and A. J. Gordon; *The Calvary Selection of Spiritual Songs*, 1878, a Baptist edition of Robinson's *Psalms and Hymns and Spiritual Songs*, 1875, edited by R. S. MacArthur, pastor of the Calvary Baptist Church, New York; and *The Baptist Hymnal*, 1883. William H. Doane's work as one of the music editors of this hymnal is evidence of the growing popularity of his gospel songs among Baptists and of an effort on the part of the denomination to meet the competition of commercially published collections. Hymns by Anglican writers were included, along with seventeen hymns by Fanny J. Crosby. Tunes by Barnby and Dykes were outnumbered by those of Mason and Doane.

The finest Baptist collection of this period was *Sursum Corda*, 1898, edited by E. H. Johnson and published by the American Baptist Publication Society. This hymnal reveals Johnson's disinterest in the gospel song and his greater enthusiasm for Anglican hymns. In an effort to promote Anglican hymn tunes, Johnson included 1,346 tunes for the 856 hymns in this collection. Apparently *Sursum Corda* was too advanced for its day, for it did not approach the popular acceptance of the *Baptist Hymnal*. Regarding Johnson's efforts to raise the standards of hymnody among Baptists, Benson comments:

It is indeed easier to plan, within the walls of a Seminary, the elevation of the literary and musical standards of a Church's devotion, than to change the habits and tastes of a great body of people who do not share the Seminary's advantages.[14]

Baptist churches in the South used a varied assortment of hymnals during this period. The collections mentioned above, together with more evangelical collections independently published, were used in some churches. Collections then issued in the South, and most popular in the areas where they were produced, were: *The Southern Psalmist,* Nashville, 1858, edited by J. R. Graves and J. M. Pendleton; J. M. D. Cates's *The Sacred Harp,* Nashville, 1867; J. R. Graves's *The New Baptist Psalmist,* Memphis, 1873; and A. B. Cates's *Baptist Songs, with Music,* Louisville, 1879.

Hymns and Hymn Writers New hymns by American authors are found in the collections that appeared in the last half of the nineteenth century. Among the more important of these hymns are John White Chadwick's "Eternal Ruler of the ceaseless round," 1864 (50); Phillips Brooks's "O little town of Bethlehem," 1868; Mary Ann Thomson's "O Zion haste, thy mission high fulfilling," 1868 (135); Daniel C. Roberts's "God of our fathers, whose almighty hand," 1876; Washington Gladden's "O Master, let me walk with thee," 1879 (80); Ernest W. Shurtleff's "Lead on, O King Eternal," 1887; and Katherine Lee Bates's "O beautiful for spacious skies," 1893.

EXPANSION OF SOUTHERN SHAPED-NOTE SINGING

One of the most interesting and seldom-mentioned developments of sacred song in America is the expansion of the shaped-note tradition following the Civil War and continuing to the present day. The "four shape fasola singing" of the *Sacred Harp* tradition still exists with little change having transpired either in the material used or in the manner of singing (see Figure 2).

Of unique significance and influence, particularly in the rural areas of the South, were the "singing conventions" using the paperback "seven shape" collections of such publishers as the Vaughan Music Company, the Stamps-Baxter Music Company, and the Stamps Quartet Music Company. This line of development may be traced back to Joseph Funk, the Mennonite publisher of Virginia, whose shaped-note collection, *Choral Music,* 1816, was produced for the German-speaking population of Pennsylvania. His English collection,

---

[14] Benson, p. 559.

SEVEN-SHAPE NOTATION

Harmonia Sacra, 1851, jokingly called the "Hominy Soaker," was most popular in Virginia and North Carolina, and was also used in other southern states.

Following the Civil War, Joseph Funk's grandson, Aldine S. Kieffer, established the Ruebush-Kieffer Music Company in Dayton, Virginia, later called Singer's Glen. B. C. Unseld of New York, a student of Eben Tourjee and Theodore F. Seward, was invited to teach the first normal music school in Virginia in 1874, and he continued in this capacity for eight years. To promote the normal schools and advertize new publications, Kieffer began in 1870 a monthly periodical, *Musical Million,* which continued until 1915.

Among the more prominent music teachers produced in Unseld's normal schools in Virginia were Samuel W. Beasley, D. M. Click, A. B. Funk, E. P. Hauser, J. H. Hall, E. T. Hildebrand, George B. Holsinger, A. J. Showalter, and W. M. Weakley. In the years that followed, normal music schools were conducted in Virginia, West Virginia, North and South Carolina, Georgia, Alabama, Kentucky, Tennessee, Louisiana, Arkansas, Missouri, Texas, and Oklahoma (then Indian Territory).

Growth of the "Singing Convention" Tradition   As the popularity of these schools spread, the demand for new songs and new collections greatly increased, and the activity related to this expansion can be traced as it moved westward across the South. A. J. Showalter, a descendant of the Funks of

Pennsylvania and an associate of Kieffer, established a music publishing company in Dalton, Georgia, in 1885. James D. Vaughan and R. E. Winsett became active music publishers in Tennessee. Vaughan's first shaped-note songbook appeared in 1900,[15] and Winsett's initial book appeared in 1903. E. M. Bartlett began the Hartford Music Company in Hartford, Arkansas, about 1922. In Texas, the Stamps-Baxter Music and Printing Company (beginning in 1925) and the Stamps Quartet Company (beginning in 1945) became the most influential publishers in the Southwest.[16]

The expansion and development of twentieth-century shaped-note singing in America, while closely related to evangelical church groups, has been non-denominational in character. Largely a rural activity, singing conventions have been most popular among Baptist, Methodist, Nazarene, Church of God, Pentecostal, and Holiness groups. In addition to the annual publication of one or two "convention" books, most music publishers produced a shaped-note hymnal for churches, making use of the well-known standard hymns and gospel songs (of the Sankey, Crosby, Doane, Stebbins tradition), to which were added those "convention" songs that had become favorites. One of the best known of these is "Farther Along" (133).

The peak of popularity of convention singing seemed to occur in the 1940's. Following World War II, there was a gradual decline and a period of transition. The urbanization of the South, the closing of rural community schools in favor of consolidated district schools, the mechanization of farm operation, the advances in transportation and communication, and the general trend of the times all contributed to this change. The migration of families from southern states into Ohio, Illinois, Indiana, and Michigan during these years accounts for the emerging popularity of convention shaped-note singing in these areas, where the practice was referred to as "Southern" gospel music.

The publishing of new gospel songs in sheet music format emerged in the late 1940's, and the demand for paperback shaped-note gospel songbooks diminished. This development marked the beginning awareness of the value of copyright ownership of gospel songs and all the rights inherent in the Copyright Law—performance rights, publishing rights, mechanical reproduction rights, and film synchronization rights. The number of publishers greatly expanded as individual song writers joined as owners in forming new companies. Some individuals, by becoming publisher (as well as writer, recording artist, and performer), thereby controlled all rights for the music. *The*

---

[15] Jo Lee Fleming, "James D. Vaughan, Music Publisher, Lawrenceburg, Tennessee, 1912–1964" (unpublished D.S.M. dissertation, Union Theological Seminary, 1972), p. 51.

[16] In 1977 the James D. Vaughan interests and copyrights were owned by the Tennessee Music Company, Cleveland, Tennessee. The Stamps Quartet Company interests and copyrights were owned by the Blackwood Brothers and J. D. Sumner, Memphis, Tennessee. The Hartford Music Company interests and copyrights were owned by Albert Brumley, Powell, Missouri. The Stamps-Baxter Music and Printing Company interests and copyrights were owned by the Zondervan Corporation, Grand Rapids, Michigan.

104   *Gospel Music 1977 Directory and Yearbook*[17] lists 135 gospel music publishers as
active in the industry.

From "Singing Convention" to "Gospel Sing"   Many factors contributed
to the transition of the 1950's and 1960's from the singing convention, where
everybody sang from the latest paperback songbooks, to the gospel sing,
where those in attendance were entertained by singing quartets and groups
and were motivated to buy the latest record albums.[18] This transition occurred in the churches where "fifth Sunday singings" were as regular as
"preaching," and this remains in many areas.[19] However, the increased popularity of the quartets and groups and the growing crowds demanded larger
quarters, and larger auditoriums—school field houses, gymnasiums, city auditoriums, theaters—were rented for this purpose. As costs went up, admission fees were charged. Promoters appeared on the scene to handle the details
of facilities, schedules, equipment, and so on, and to free the musicians to be
artists and performers. Fancy attire, custom buses, elaborate sound equipment, instrumental rhythm groups for accompaniment, and high professional
promotional techniques are the rule. In 1976, there were twenty-three talent
agencies engaged in the booking of gospel music groups on the national and
international scene.[20]

Recordings have become an essential part of the gospel music business.
Albums are sold at each personal appearance and distributed to radio disc
jockeys for air play. While live broadcasts of gospel music began in the early
1920's, the playing of gospel music records by radio stations came along in
later decades and has increased at a phenomenal rate. In 1976, there were 830
radio stations programming gospel music as a total format or a significant part
of their broadcast time.

The Gospel Music Association, with headquarters in Nashville, Tennessee,
has become a focal point of promotion and communication about this expression of gospel music in a highly successful manner. Ironically, since the vast
public following of this music has little need for seeing the printed songs sung
by gospel music groups, the identification of shaped-notation with this music
has greatly diminished. The printed page is not important to the listener, and
he cares not whether the song is printed in round or shaped notation. He is
interested only in what he hears. The sound of the music sung in the 1970's by
the Speer Family, the Imperials, the Oak Ridge Boys, the Happy Goodmans,
and other groups has roots in that tradition associated with Stamps, Bartlett,

[17] *Gospel Music 1977 Directory and Yearbook* (Nashville: Gospel Music Association, 1976), pp.
120–122.

[18] This phenomenon has been carefully researched in Stanley H. Brobston, "Daddy Sang Bass"
(unpublished doctoral dissertation, New York University, 1977).

[19] These are frequently referred to as "new book singings," to distinguish them from the "old
book singings"—Sacred Harp singings.

[20] *Gospel Music 1977 Directory and Yearbook*, p. 108.

Vaughan, Showalter, Kieffer, Funk, and others mentioned earlier. But the distinctive technique for teaching music reading so long identified with this musical tradition in America has all but disappeared.

TWENTIETH-CENTURY HYMNALS

Remarkable progress has characterized American hymnody in the twentieth century. Strict denominational lines have given way to a merging of many traditions, as hymnal committees have drawn on the resources of a common heritage for congregational singing. A common core of hymnody has emerged as each new publication has borrowed freely from previous hymnals of other faiths. Editorial standards have steadily risen, resulting in hymnals far superior to those of the previous century. Of particular significance have been the joint efforts of denominational groups in compiling and publishing hymnals. Three major branches of Methodism joined in compiling the *Methodist Hymnal*, 1935. Four Presbyterian groups cooperated in the compilation of *The Hymnbook*, 1955, and the *Service Book and Hymnal*, 1958, was the cooperative effort of eight different Lutheran groups in America.

During recent decades, more well-edited hymnals have been published than in any other period of American hymnody. To make a critical comparative study of these hymnals would be unrealistic and inappropriate. A denominational hymnal is prepared, not for competition or comparison with hymnals of other denominational groups, but solely as a collection of hymns for congregational use in churches of that denomination. While a common core of hymnody is increasingly evident, there remain major distinctive characteristics of the denominational groups themselves. These characteristics, having to do with differences in forms of worship, hymnological heritage, and cultural and economic backgrounds of the people, are inevitable factors in hymnal compilation. Those denominations whose constituency encompasses the full scope of economic, cultural, and geographical distribution encounter the greatest difficulty in providing an acceptable hymnal. In those evangelical groups where local congregations are autonomous, or subject to little ecclesiastical control, acceptability of a hymnal by local congregations becomes of major concern. Acceptability by the people becomes of less concern to groups who by historical tradition have used without question the hymnals prepared by ecclesiastical leadership. This acceptance and leadership usually has produced hymnals of high literary and musical quality.

Presbyterians *The Hymnal*, 1933, was published by the Presbyterian Church, U.S.A. Clarence Dickinson served as editor, and his experienced judgment as a church musician is reflected in the high quality of the hymns and tunes included. While this has been referred to as a "musician's hymnal"

106 and has been widely used, it has not been a popular collection with the more evangelical congregations in Presbyterianism. This reaction was revealed at the time of the compilation of the 1955 *Hymnbook*, when regional groups requested a more functional hymnal, less high church in character.

The Hymnbook, 1955, was jointly prepared by the Presbyterian Church in the United States, the Presbyterian Church in the United States of America, the United Presbyterian Church of North America, and the Reformed Church in America. This collection is the successor to the individual hymnals of these various groups. The need to satisfy the particular demands of these groups accounts for the inclusion of a body of metrical psalms for the Reformed Church and the evangelistic hymns for the Southern Presbyterians. A good selection of contemporary English and American hymn tunes was included. *The Hymnbook* was ably edited by David Hugh Jones.

The Worshipbook, 1972, was produced for the Cumberland Presbyterian Church, the Presbyterian Church in the United States, and the United Presbyterian Church in the U.S.A. The organization of content is interesting, in that the hymns are arranged alphabetically by first line. As many as 122 of the hymns have either text or tune from the twentieth century.

Methodists *The Methodist Hymnal*, 1935, edited by Robert G. McCutchan, was jointly prepared by three major Methodist groups. Genuine effort was made to prepare a collection suitable for congregations both large and small, both urban and rural. Primarily for the benefit of rural churches in the South, a shaped-note edition was provided for several years.

The Methodist Hymnal, 1966, succeeded the 1935 publication of the same title as the principal hymnal for American Methodists. In preparation for the compilation of this hymnal, a six-page questionnaire, covering every facet of the hymnal, was mailed to 22,000 Methodist ministers to solicit their responses on the basis of their experience with the 1935 hymnal. The single item that drew the greatest number of responses from the 11,000 questionnaires returned was that dealing with gospel hymns; sixty-two percent requested more gospel hymns than appeared in the 1935 hymnal.[21] Carlton Young served as editor of the 1966 *Methodist Hymnal*, which maintained an excellent balance between broad historical and ecumenical representation, representative hymns from the Methodist tradition (there are 77 by Charles Wesley), and contributions of the twentieth century. Among the more appealing new tunes included in this hymnal are Lloyd Pfautsch's WALDA (156) and Katherine K. Davis' MASSACHUSETTS (155).

Episcopalians *The Hymnal 1940*, authorized in that year and published in 1943, has been considered an important landmark in the development of American hymnals. The scholarly influence of Winfred Douglas made this Episcopal hymnal significant not only for the literary quality of its hymns, but

---

[21] *The Christian Advocate*, Vol. V, No. 25 (December 7, 1961), pp. 10–12.

also for the character of its tunes. Distinctive musical features involved the use of numerous plainsong melodies and a large number of tunes of American origin, in addition to the established repertoire of psalm and hymn tunes. The absence of meter signatures on all the hymn tunes reflects the influence of rhythmically free plainsong. The resources of contemporary English hymn tunes—those of Vaughan Williams, Holst, and Geoffrey and Martin Shaw—were used extensively, a practice that soon became a trend in future hymnal compilations.

Lutherans *The Lutheran Hymnal,* 1941, was published by the Evangelical Lutheran Synodical Conference of North America. This collection strongly reflects the Lutheran musical heritage of the chorale. Over one-half of the texts are set to tunes of German origin, most of them written prior to 1850.[22]

Service Book and Hymnal, 1958, was prepared jointly by eight synodical Lutheran groups—a cooperative effort that produced the most catholic hymnal ever used by Lutheran congregations. Quite significant is the wide variety of tunes. This is explained in the "Introduction to the Common Hymnal":

> The music, like the texts, is ecumenical. The characteristic Lutheran form, the chorale, is well-represented in rhythmic, isometric and Bach arrangements. An increased number of plainsong melodies on one hand, and some Gospel hymns on the other, will provide for a wide variety of taste among our people. About two hundred fifty hymns have tunes of English origin, including both the standard tunes of the nineteenth century and some by contemporary composers. Psalm tunes from English, Scottish, Swiss, and French sources appear, as well as eight Welsh tunes and a number of French tunes based on plainsong. Carols and more than thirty folksongs, largely from North European sources, add much new and interesting music. American composers are well represented, some by tunes which appear here for the first time.[23]

Luther D. Reed was the chairman of the joint commission that prepared this hymnal.

Congregationalists *The Pilgrim Hymnal,* 1958, which bears the same title as the Congregational hymnal that appeared in 1904, revised in 1931, was a new hymnal rather than another revision.

> Although making wise use of that hymnal, the present volume draws more heavily on the best hymnody of the Church Universal, while at the same time making fuller use of our particular heritage: the *Genevan Psalters,* the Bay Psalm Book, Isaac Watts—all the richness of the Reformed and Free Church traditions. Elements have also been incorporated from older musical and liturgical sources which have been long neglected and surrendered by default. Finally, looking to

---

[22] Warland, pp. 73–74.

[23] *Service Book and Hymnal of the Lutheran Church in America* (Minneapolis: Augsburg Publishing House, 1958), p. 286.

the future, the hymnal has benefited from the broadening and enriching impetus of the ecumenical movement.[24]

The successful achievement of those objectives stated in the Preface is reflected in the contents of this excellent hymnal, making this collection a notable contribution to mid-century American hymnody. Dr. and Mrs. Hugh Porter served as musical editors.

The Hymnal, 1974, produced by the United Church of Christ (which includes the Congregationalists) will be used to supplant the *Pilgrim Hymnal*.

Baptists *Christian Worship*, 1941, was jointly compiled by the Disciples of Christ and the Northern Baptist Convention, now the American Baptist Convention. The *Hymnbook for Christian Worship*, 1970, provides another compilation by these same groups, with a substantial amount of new material, including twenty new texts drawn from the publications of the Hymn Society of America.

Baptist Hymnal, 1956, edited by W. Hines Sims and published by the Southern Baptist Convention, was the first collection to bear that title since the *Baptist Hymnal*, 1883. The 1956 publication gradually replaced the *Broadman Hymnal*, 1940, compiled by B. B. McKinney, which had been the first hymnal to be used by a substantial majority of Southern Baptist congregations and was widely used by other denominations. The 1956 *Baptist Hymnal* was strongly evangelical in character, revealing the extensive influence of the gospel song tradition among Southern Baptist congregations.

The *Baptist Hymnal*, 1975 edition, under the general editorship of William J. Reynolds, is by far the most eclectic hymnal ever produced for Southern Baptists. New materials range from harmonized plainsong to recent expressions of the folk and "pop gospel" styles. There is strong emphasis upon the inclusion of contemporary materials, both texts and tunes. The largest number of original tunes by a contemporary composer is Reynolds' ten, representing a span of nearly two decades of contributions. Among the numerous excellent texts from contemporary writers is Elton Trueblood's "Thou, whose purpose is to kindle" (157).

Other Denominational Hymnals *The Hymnal*, 1941, was published by the General Synod of the Evangelical and Reformed Church, a merger of the Evangelical Synod of North America and the Reformed Church in the United States.

The 1969 *Hymnal and Liturgies of the Moravian Church*, published by authority of the provincial synods of The Moravian Church in America, replaced the 1923 publication bearing the same title. The most recent hymnal, like its predecessor, draws heavily upon its European chorale heritage. However, the 1969 hymnal includes some of the chorale melodies in their early

---

[24] *The Pilgrim Hymnal* (Boston: The Pilgrim Press, 1958), p. v.

rhythmic versions (instead of the isometric adaptations of later centuries) for the first time in an American Moravian hymnal. Of the 623 hymns contained, 191 are from Moravian sources.

The *Mennonite Hymnal,* 1969, edited by Lester Hostetler and Walter E. Yoder, offers a diverse selection of tunes, but without extensive use of contemporary materials. This collection succeeds *The Mennonite Hymnary,* published in 1940, and the *Mennonite Church Hymnal,* 1927.

Roman Catholic Hymnals   Before the mid-twentieth century, the content of Roman Catholic hymnals was predominantly Latin hymns and liturgical settings, with the remaining portion devoted to vernacular hymns by Catholic authors and a few translations from Latin by non-Catholics. Two of the principal hymnals used in this period were the *St. Basil's Hymnal,* revised in 1935, and the *St. Gregory Hymnal,* 1941. A similar division of content was present in the *Pius X Hymnal,* 1953. However, in the *Mediator Dei Hymnal,* edited by Cyr de Brant (a pen name used by the distinguished Catholic hymnologist J. Vincent Higginson), there appeared a substantial number of translations of Latin hymns—most of them from the Breviary—set to tunes from German, French, and English sources.

Of considerable significance to the contemporary situation in Roman Catholic hymnody was the publication in 1955 of the *People's Hymnal.* This small paperbound collection contained a substantial number of both texts and tunes selected from contemporary Protestant hymnals and introduced for the first time into Catholic worship. Many of these were subsequently included in later Catholic hymnal compilations.

The effect of the Second Vatican Council (beginning in October, 1962) upon Catholic hymnody has been predictably revolutionary. There has been a continuing search for appropriate vernacular hymnic expressions for use both within and outside of the structures of the liturgy. One of the most widely-used collections has been the *People's Mass Book,* 1964, compiled by Omer Westendorf and published by the World Library of Sacred Music, which he founded. This book, according to its editor, "was compiled and published specifically to implement the celebration of the new English mass."[25] F. E. L. Church Publications has produced several collections oriented toward the "youth music" movement, including *Hymnal for Young Christians,* which was the first hymnal to include the now popular "They'll know we are Christians by our love" by Peter Scholtes.

Hymnal Supplements   Some denominations have produced supplements to their hymnals to provide new materials for their congregations. *Contemporary Worship I—Hymns,* published in 1969 by the Inter-Lutheran Commission on Worship, was the first of a series of publications leading toward a new

[25] Omer Westendorf, "Review Article: Handbook for American Catholic Hymnals," *Journal of Church Music,* Vol. 19, No. 2 (February, 1977), p. 9.

110   *Service Book and Hymnal,* which is projected for publication in 1978.[26] The collection includes twenty-one hymns and provides guitar chords in addition to harmonization in the traditional manner.

More Hymns and Spiritual Songs, 1971, prepared by the Joint Commission on Church Music of the Episcopal Church, contains seventy hymns and tunes. Drawing upon both British and American sources for new materials, the collection is intended to supplement *The Hymnal 1940.*

Worship Supplement, published in 1972 to be used alongside *The Lutheran Hymnal,* 1941, offers ninety-three hymns reflecting historically-based content. Approximately thirty of the hymns were produced by twentieth-century writers. Early in 1977 work was begun on a supplement to the *Methodist Hymnal,* 1966. The projected publication date for this collection is 1980.

Institutional and Other Hymnals   In recent decades, a few colleges and universities have made significant contributions to the growing body of hymnals in print. The *Hymnal for Colleges and Schools,* edited by E. Harold Geer and published by Yale University Press in 1956, provides a compilation broadly representative of the historical development of hymnody with an overall content selected for its appeal and appropriateness for an academic community. Of particular interest is the section containing brief notes on the hymns.

The Harvard University Hymn Book, 1964, was compiled by Samuel H. Miller and John Ferris. This hymnal is similar in many respects to the *Hymnal for Colleges and Schools.* It includes a more detailed treatment in the section "Notes on the Hymns," but contains fewer hymns.

Westminster Praise, edited by Erik Routley and published in 1976 by Hinshaw Music, Inc., is intended to be a hymn supplement compiled for use at the chapel services of Westminster Choir College. One of the attractive new tunes appearing in this collection is Alice Parker's WEST END (102). Austin Lovelace, Erik Routley, Alec Wyton, and Carlton Young collaborated in the compilation of *Ecumenical Praise,* which is scheduled for publication by Agape (a division of Hope Publishing Company) in 1977. Either of the latter collections could be used as a supplement to almost any American hymnal, since there is little duplication of materials previously used in hymnals of this country.

AMERICAN HYMNAL COMPANIONS

Of invaluable worth has been the willingness of various denominations to provide handbooks or companion books for their hymnals. Accurate information of genuine interest relative to both hymn and tune, together

---

[26] Eugene L. Brand, "New Lutheran Hymnal and Service Book: Progress Report I," *Church Music* (75–2), pp. 19–20.

with biographical sketches of authors and composers, all help broaden under-standing. A page-by-page study of a hymnal and its handbook is a most rewarding adventure in Christian song.

The first significant American handbook of our century was Robert G. McCutchan's *Our Hymnody*, 1937, prepared as a manual for the 1935 *Methodist Hymnal*. McCutchan's painstaking research, his love and concern for congregational song, and his familiarity with hymnic literature are revealed in the pages of his handbook. Leonard Ellinwood's *The Hymnal 1940 Companion*, 1949, and Armin Haeussler's *The Story of Our Hymns*, 1952 (Evangelical and Reformed Church *Hymnal*, 1941), were scholarly works in the finest tradition, bringing to light the most recent hymnological discoveries of the time. Other hymnal companions produced around the mid-century were W. G. Polack's *The Handbook to the Lutheran Hymnal*, 1942, and *Handbook to the Mennonite Hymnary*, 1949, by Lester Hostetler.

More recently, new volumes have been produced to serve as companions for hymnals dating from the late 1950s through the mid-1970s. *Guide to the Pilgrim Hymnal*, 1966, was written by Albert C. Ronander and Ethel K. Porter. The collaboration of Fred D. Gealy, Austin C. Lovelace, and Carlton R. Young, under the general editorship of Emory Stevens Bucke, resulted in *Companion to the Hymnal*, 1970, a handbook to the *Methodist Hymnal* of 1966.

In 1976 William J. Reynolds completed *Companion to Baptist Hymnal* (1975). Twelve years earlier he had written *Hymns of Our Faith* as a handbook for the 1956 *Baptist Hymnal*. Also in 1976 there appeared the long-awaited companion to the Lutheran *Service Book and Hymnal*, William R. Seaman's *Companion to the Hymnal*.

J. Vincent Higginson made a unique and valuable contribution to the continually expanding area of Catholic hymnody in his *Handbook of American Catholic Hymnals*, 1976. Rather than serving as a companion to a single hymnal, Higginson's book covers the larger body of Catholic hymnody, encompassing many hymnals, in dealing with texts and tunes from Catholic hymnals in common use through 1964.

TWENTIETH-CENTURY TEXTS AND TUNES

Obviously the test of time has not yet applied to a large portion of the hymnic writing that has appeared in this century. However, a number of hymns that seem to merit a place in the development of American hymnody have found their way into several contemporary collections.

Hymns from the early part of this century that appear in the section of illustrative hymns are: Julia Cady Cory's "We praise thee, O God, our Redeemer, Creator," 1902 (137); Frank Mason North's "Where cross the

112   crowded ways of life," 1903 (61); Harry Webb Farrington's "I know not how that Bethlehem's babe," 1910 (79); Louis F. Benson's "The light of God is falling," 1910 (64); William Pierson Merrill's "Rise up, O men of God," 1911 (141); and Jay T. Stocking's "O Master Workman of the race," 1912 (93).

More recent hymns in the same section include: Harry Emerson Fosdick's "God of grace and God of glory," 1930 (87); Sarah E. Taylor's "O God of light, thy Word a lamp unfailing," 1952 (134); Georgia Harkness' "Hope of the World, thou Christ of great compassion," 1954 (35); D. Elton Trueblood's "Thou, whose purpose is to kindle," 1967 (157); and "My God is there, controlling" by William Watkins Reid (158), which was published by the Hymn Society of America in a collection of Reid's hymns under the same title.

American composers have made important contributions to hymn tune repertoire. Among those that have found their way into hymnal publications are: Annabeth McClelland Gay's SHEPHERDS' PIPES (147), Austin C. Lovelace's HINMAN (148), Robert G. McCutchan's ALL THE WORLD (139), Leland B. Sateren's MARLEE (153), Leo Sowerby's TAYLOR HALL (146), Ralph Alvin Strom's NAME OF JESUS (150), Arnold G. H. Bode's LARAMIE (145), Katherine K. Davis' MASSACHUSETTS (155), Lloyd Pfautsch's WALDA (156), and Daniel Moe's CITY OF GOD (149).

INFLUENCES IN TWENTIETH-CENTURY DEVELOPMENTS

The development of hymnody in America has been greatly enriched by the contribution of several scholars who have devoted a large share of their time and energies to this area of understanding. One of the most prominent among these contributors was Louis F. Benson—hymnologist, hymn writer, hymnal editor, author, and lecturer. He excelled in many areas, including the writing of hymn texts such as "The light of God is falling" (64). His persistent, careful scholarship has resulted in the writing of *The English Hymn* and *The Hymnody of the Christian Church,* which are important landmarks in American hymnological activity.

The numerous people cited earlier in this chapter for their role in the development of twentieth-century hymnals and hymnal companions have been a vital part of the movement bringing about the continuing enrichment of the American hymn tradition. To this list must be added the names of scholars whose research and writing has contributed valuable insight into specialized areas of hymnology. Included among these are Ruth Ellis Messenger, for her work in Latin hymnody, George Pullen Jackson, who was a pioneer in the since-productive field of research into American folk hymnody, and Henry Wilder Foote, for his writings concerning American hymnody.

The most prolific and provocative hymnologist of the present day is Erik Routley, the distinguished British scholar whose writings have spanned almost three decades and who recently moved to the United States to teach at Westminster Choir College. His numerous books and frequent articles have provided scholarly treatment of historical material and penetrating insight into contemporary developments and trends.

The Hymn Society of America One of the most vital forces currently engaged in the interest of hymnody in the United States is The Hymn Society of America. Founded in 1922, the membership of this organization has grown steadily. *The Hymn,* a quarterly publication issued by the Society, the *Papers* of the Hymn Society, a series of monographs on selected specialized topics, and the hymn "searches" conducted by the organization have provided a strong stimulus to hymnological and hymn-writing activity in this country.[27] Local chapters have been organized in a number of cities, and hymn festivals have been encouraged. The hymn-writing competitions on specific themes ("Ecumenical Hymns," "Hymns on the Bible," "Hymns on the City," "Hymns on the Mission of the Church," and so on) have produced a large number of texts of high quality, first published by the Society, many of which have subsequently appeared in hymnals in this country and abroad.

Denominational Influences Denominational groups and their affiliate publishing houses have occasionally given encouragement to the creation of new hymn texts and tunes other than those originally provided for new hymnals or hymnal supplements. Two Lutheran publishing firms have issued leaflets containing new hymns. In 1964 Augsburg Publishing House released "Four Contemporary Hymns," including Daniel Moe's CITY OF GOD (149) as a setting for Bradford Gray Webster's "O Jesus Christ, to Thee may hymns be rising." Two years later, Augsburg published a second set of four, all of them by Moe.

Concordia Publishing Company issued a pamphlet of thirteen hymns under the title "A New Song," but for most of these, both texts and tunes were drawn from historical sources. "Praise the Lord" (159) was one of "Five Hymns" by Heinz Werner Zimmermann published by Concordia in 1973.

From the mid-1960s through 1971, Southern Baptists sponsored a series of hymn-writing competitions and searches for new texts and tunes and published the best materials received in a series of pamphlets, including "Eight New Christian Service Hymns" (1966), "Seven Hymns of Concern and Ministry" (1969), and "New Hymns for This Day" (1971).

---

[27] Information concerning membership and publications of the Society may be obtained from The Hymn Society of America, National Headquarters, Wittenberg University, Springfield, Ohio 45501.

114 CONTEMPORARY TRENDS

Christian song is never static, never quite the same from one generation to another. When viewed from two or three decades the changes may appear rather small. However, a backward look of fifty years reveals more distinct differences, and these differences become more sharply defined over a passing century. The last hundred years have witnessed a marked change in the concept of worship as reflected in American hymnody. The increasing significance of corporate worship, the shifting of emphasis from the fear and awe of God and impending judgment to an expression of love and gratitude to God, and the meaning and comfort of worship to the individual, all are reflected in succeeding hymnal compilations. Hymnic expressions yearning for the "Promised Land" have given way to hymns revealing a desire for a more abundant life in this world. Hymns with missionary emphasis express concern and hope for the gospel message of peace on earth, rather than redemptive salvation for "pagans" or "the heathen." Texts of nineteenth-century English missionary hymns have been carefully pruned to remove expressions reflecting British colonialism. Hymns of vital Christian living emphasizing active service and the welfare of humanity are replacing those speaking only of passive, pious Christian living.

Watts and Wesley are both well-represented in our hymnals today, but not in the proportion of a century ago. Hymns of the eighteenth century have rapidly declined in number during the last century as many literary expressions of that era have become obsolete and meaningless in Christian experience. The hymnody of the Oxford Movement of nineteenth-century England has become more widely accepted in America among both liturgical and non-liturgical groups.

While contemporary denominational hymnals reveal certain denominational characteristics, these have become less sharply defined. Hymnic material from the Reformation and pre-Reformation traditions, as well as Wesleyan, Anglican, and Evangelical influences make up a common body of hymnody which can be found in the hymnals of all major denominations.

This merging of influence is also seen in hymn tunes. Plainsong melodies, once the sole property of the Roman Catholic Church, may now be found in Protestant hymnals, along with Lutheran chorale melodies and French and English psalm tunes. On the other hand, the gospel song, a product of American revivalism, appears in hymnals of liturgical tradition, which in years past have paid scant attention to this area.

Hymn Tune Developments Among the specific trends in our time, the decline of many tunes popular fifty to a hundred years ago is readily apparent. Only the most hearty of the Victorian tunes are surviving in the critical atmosphere of the mid-twentieth century. A renewed interest in plainsong explains the presence of such tunes as DIVINUM MYSTERIUM (4) and VENI

CREATOR (6) in several Protestant hymnals. EIN' FESTE BURG, NUN DANKET, NEUMARK (19), and PASSION CHORALE (9) are among the numerous Lutheran chorale melodies that commonly appear in hymnals outside the Lutheran tradition. Lutheran, Congregational, and Presbyterian hymnals now include a number of gospel songs, recognizing the popularity of these songs among these denominational groups.

Unison singing has become increasingly popular, and strong unison tunes, such as LASST UNS ERFREUEN (23), SINE NOMINE (91), and SLANE (88) are regular items found in most collections. American composers have contributed to the growing repertoire of unison melodies with vigorous tunes such as WALDA (156) and MASSACHUSETTS (155). Several splendid tunes from European sources have been added to our musical repertoire as hymnal editors have diligently searched for worthy material. One such example is the Norwegian tune KIRKEN DEN ES ET (154), which remained for almost a century exclusively in Lutheran usage. Other Scandinavian tunes have greatly enriched our musical treasures of Christian song.

While English and European folk material have long been standard fare, American hymnal compilers have now discovered the rich heritage of our own native folk song. Most of these are of Southern origin and include such tunes as MORNING SONG (119), KEDRON (124), FOUNDATION (118), and AMAZING GRACE (117). Negro spirituals have become increasingly popular for hymnal usage during the last three decades. "Were you there" (140) and "Lord, I want to be a Christian" (144) are among the spirituals most frequently found in current hymnals.

One of the most interesting developments in the hymnody of our time is the appearance in American hymnals of hymns and tunes of Far East origin. During the last century and a half missionaries journeyed to India, China, and many other remote places. Now Christian hymns return from these mission fields, reflecting the literary and musical culture of these distant places. From Chinese sources have come such hymns as "Father, long before creation," "The bread of life" (151), and "Rise to greet the sun" (152). CHINESE MELODY (142), SHENG EN (151), and LE P'ING (152) illustrate tunes from Oriental sources. Bliss Wiant has been most helpful in arranging and harmonizing many of these tunes for American collections without losing the distinctive Oriental characteristics of the music. Recent hymnals have also included tunes from Thailand, Nigeria, Korea, and Indonesia. The international interchange of hymnic ideas, both texts and tunes, has been significantly aided by the four editions (1924, 1930, 1951, and 1974) of *Cantate Domino*, the hymnal published by the World Student Christian Federation.

Folk and "Pop" Music Influences   In the mid-1960s, there emerged a growing body of song literature for group singing that was written to appeal to the musical tastes of young people. Utilizing melodic and harmonic materials associated with folk music and the various styles of "pop" music, the sounds of "youth music" began to appear with increasing frequency in the church. Youth musicals—semidramatic productions designed both for presentation within the church and as a vehicle for taking the message of faith outside of the church into secular society—by such composers as Ralph Carmichael, Kurt Kaiser, Bill Cates, Otis Skillings, Buryl Red, and Philip Landgrave, to name but a few, often included at least one song that was readily adapted to group singing.[28]

Paperback collections that combined the new songs with selected spirituals and familiar hymns appeared with increasing frequency in the late 1960's and early 1970's, as publishers attempted to provide materials in response to the trend toward the use of folk and "pop" styles. A typical collection would include a few traditional hymns, a group of spirituals, some of the new songs that had been widely used, and several selections either by the compiler(s) of the collection or by composers closely affiliated with the publisher. *Jesus Style Songs* (Augsburg Publishing House), *Sing 'N' Celebrate* (Word, Incorporated, 1971), *Jesus Songs* (Broadman Press, 1971), and *Hymnal for Contemporary Christians* (Singspiration Music, 1971) are but a few representative titles under which the collections were published. Either guitar chords or keyboard accompaniment, or both, may be provided, varying with each collection. *Songbook for Saints and Sinners* (Agape, 1971), compiled by Carlton R. Young, drew from an unusually wide variety of sources for its contents.

Two of the most widely used songs were Ray Repp's "Allelu!" and Peter Scholtes' "They'll know we are Christians by our love," both originally published by F. E. L. Publications in 1966. Other composers whose songs appeared in several of the youth collections include Ralph Carmichael, Kurt Kaiser, Buryl Red, and Don Wyrtzen. *Sing 'N' Celebrate II,* published in 1975 by Word, Incorporated, contained thirteen selections by the talented blind composer-lyricist Ken Medema.

Other Developments The influence of the gospel song of the late nineteenth century has continued through three-quarters of the twentieth century, not only by the continued use of the texts and tunes written in that era, but also through its effect upon a subsequent style of writing that might be called the contemporary gospel song. More sophisticated musically than its nineteenth century predecessor, the contemporary gospel song seeks to communicate its message through directness and simplicity of language and the instant appeal of its music. One of the most prolific composers of contemporary gospel songs during the past two decades has been John W. Peterson. More recently, the music of William J. Gaither has gained widespread acceptance and popularity.

Sharply contrasted with the style of the contemporary gospel song have

---

[28] The 1975 *Baptist Hymnal* included five hymn tunes (CATES, PASS IT ON, SKILLINGS, TABERNACLE, and WOODLAND) that had their origin in a youth musical. For four of these, the text was written for the same musical.

been the hymns, or songs, written with the intent of communicating textually in a manner that is unique, unexpected, and nontraditional. The foremost exponents of this approach have been Richard Avery and Donald Marsh, who have collaborated to produce a series of publications, beginning with *Hymns Hot and Carols Cool*, 1967, designed to create a sense of both freshness and drama in the worship experience.

The stream of our hymnody continues to widen as each succeeding generation expresses its judgment on its hymnic inheritance and makes its own contribution of new material. The hymnody of today encompasses a far wider range of material—both texts and tunes—than ever before in Christian history. The richness of our heritage and the creative activity of the present should enable contemporary congregations to become involved in meaningful hymn singing to a degree unparalleled in the history of the church's song.

Suggestions for Supplementary Study

1. Early Church Song

Apel, Willi. *Gregorian Chant*. Bloomington: Indiana University Press, 1958.

Bailey, Albert Edward. *The Gospel in Hymns*. New York: Charles Scribner's Sons, 1950. Pp. 211–307.

Benson, Louis F. *The Hymnody of the Christian Church*. Richmond: John Knox Press, 1956 (reprinted from the 1927 edition by George H. Doran Co., New York). Pp. 15–75.

Britt, Dom Matthew (ed.). *The Hymns of the Breviary and Missal*. New York: Benziger Brothers, 1948.

Douglas, Winfred. *Church Music in History and Practice*. Revised with additional material by Leonard Ellinwood. New York: Charles Scribner's Sons, 1962. Pp. 124–154.

Duffield, Samuel Willoughby. *The Latin Hymn-Writers and Their Hymns*. Ed. R. E. Thompson. New York: Funk and Wagnalls, 1889.

Julian, John. *A Dictionary of Hymnology*. 2 vols. New York: Dover Publications, 1957 (reprint of the Second Revised Edition, 1907). Articles on "Greek Hymnody," "Latin Hymnody," "Sequence," and individual hymns listed under their Latin and Greek titles.

Messenger, Ruth Ellis. "Christian Hymns of the First Three Centuries," *Papers of the Hymn Society of America*, No. IX, 1942.

———. "Latin Hymns of the Middle Ages," *Papers of the Hymn Society of America*, No. XIV, 1948.

———. *The Medieval Latin Hymn*. Washington: Capital Press, 1953.

———. "The Praise of the Virgin in Early Latin Hymns," *Papers of the Hymn Society of America*, No. III, 1932.

120   Patrick, Millar. *The Story of the Church's Song.* Rev. ed. by James Rawlings Sydnor. Richmond: John Knox Press, 1962. Pp. 11–69.

Pierik, Marie. *The Song of the Church.* New York: Longmans, Green and Co., 1947.

Reese, Gustave. *Music in the Middle Ages.* New York: W. W. Norton & Co., 1940. Pp. 57–197.

Routley, Erik. *Hymns and Human Life.* London: John Murray, 1952. Pp. 13–32.

Ryden, E. E. *The Story of Christian Hymnody.* Rock Island, Ill.: Augustana Press, 1959. Pp. 3–54.

Wellesz, Egon. *A History of Byzantine Music and Hymnography.* Second edition. Oxford: Clarendon Press, 1962.

Werner, Eric. *The Sacred Bridge.* New York: Columbia University Press, 1959. Pp. 1–49, 207–272.

2. The Lutheran Chorale

Bailey, *The Gospel in Hymns,* pp. 308–346.

Blume, Friedrich, ed. *Protestant Church Music.* New York: W. W. Norton & Co., 1974. Pp. 3–105, 127–161, 236–245, 251–262, 593–607.

Duerksen, Rosella Reimer. "Anabaptist Hymnody of the Sixteenth Century." Unpublished D.S.M. dissertation. Union Theological Seminary, 1956.

Jenny, Markus. "The Hymns of Zwingli and Luther: a Comparison." In *Cantors at the Crossroads.* Ed. Johannes Riedel. St. Louis: Concordia Publishing House, 1967. Pp. 45–63.

Julian, *A Dictionary of Hymnology,* articles on "German Hymnody" and individual hymn writers.

Leupold, Ulrich S., ed. *Liturgy and Hymns.* Vol. 53 of *Luther's Works.* Philadelphia: Fortress Press, 1965.

Liemohn, Edwin. *The Chorale, Through 400 Years of Musical Development as a Congregational Hymn.* Philadelphia: Muhlenberg Press, 1953.

Reed, Luther D. "Luther and Congregational Song," *Papers of the Hymn Society of America,* No. XII, 1947.

Riedel, Johannes. *The Lutheran Chorale: Its Basic Traditions.* Minneapolis: Augsburg Publishing House, 1967.

Routley, Erik. *The Music of Christian Hymnody.* London: Independent Press, 1957. Pp. 8–24, 69–84, 102–107.

Ryden, *The Story of Christian Hymnody,* pp. 57–246.

3. Psalmody

Bailey, *The Gospel in Hymns,* pp. 2–17.

Blankenburg, Walter. "Church Music in Reformed Europe," in *Protestant Church Music.* Ed. Friedrich Blume. New York: W. W. Norton & Co., 1974. Pp. 509–590.

Douen, E. O. *Clement Marot et le Psautier Huguenot.* Paris: L'Imprimerie Nationale, 1878–1879.

Frost, Maurice. *English and Scottish Psalm and Hymn Tunes.* London: S.P.C.K. and Oxford University Press, 1953.

Julian, articles on "Psalters, English," "Psalters, French," and "Old Version."

Patrick, *The Story of the Church's Song*, pp. 86–113.

———. *Four Centuries of Scottish Psalmody.* London: Oxford University Press, 1950.

Pidoux, Pierre. *Le Psautier Huguenot du XVIe Siecle.* 2 vols. Basel: Edition Barenreiter, 1962.

Pratt, Waldo Selden. *The Music of the French Psalter of 1562.* New York: AMS Press, 1966 (reprint of edition by Columbia University Press, New York, 1939).

———. "The Significance of the Old French Psalter," *Papers of the Hymn Society of America*, No. IV, 1933.

Prothero, Rowland E. *The Psalms in Human Life.* London: Thomas Nelson & Sons, 1903. Pp. 168–267.

Reese, Gustave. *Music in the Renaissance.* Rev. ed. New York: W. W. Norton & Co., 1959. Pp. 355–362, 501–506.

Routley, *The Music of Christian Hymnody*, pp. 25–68, 85–90.

Stroud, William Paul. "The Ravenscroft Psalter (1621): The Tunes, with a Background on Thomas Ravenscroft and Psalm Singing in His Time." Unpublished D.M.A. dissertation. University of Southern California, 1959.

4. English Hymnody, I

Bailey, *The Gospel in Hymns*, pp. 18–140.

Benson, Louis F. *The English Hymn.* Richmond: John Knox Press, 1962 (reprinted from the 1915 edition published by the George H. Doran Company, New York). Pp. 19–357.

———. *The Hymnody of the Christian Church*, pp. 86–95, 105–138.

Benson, Louis F. "The Hymns of John Bunyan," *Papers of the Hymn Society of America*, No. I, 1930.

Bishop, Selma L., ed. *Isaac Watts: Hymns and Spiritual Songs, 1707–1748.* London: The Faith Press, 1962.

Escott, Harry. *Isaac Watts, Hymnographer.* London: Independent Press, 1962.

Haas, Alfred Burton. "Charles Wesley," *Papers of the Hymn Society of America*, No. XXII, 1957.

Hope, Norman Victor. "Isaac Watts and His Contribution to English Hymnody," *Papers of the Hymn Society of America*, No. XIII, 1947.

Johansen, John Henry. "The Olney Hymns," *Papers of the Hymn Society of America*, No. XX, 1956.

Martin, Hugh. *They Wrote Our Hymns.* Naperville, Ill.: Alec R. Allenson, 1961. Pp. 1–56.

Parks, Edna. *The Hymns and Hymn Tunes Found in the English Metrical Psalters.* New York: Coleman-Ross Company, 1966.

Patrick, *The Story of the Church's Song*, pp. 114–141.

Routley, *Hymns and Human Life*, pp. 63–125.

———. *The Music of Christian Hymnody*, pp. 91–101.

———. *The Musical Wesleys.* London: Herbert Jenkins, 1968. Pp. 1–42.

Ryden, *The Story of Christian Hymnody*, pp. 255–319.

122   Stevenson, Robert M. *Patterns of Protestant Church Music*. Durham, N.C.: Duke University Press, 1953. Pp. 93–138.
      Young, Robert H. "The History of Baptist Hymnody in England from 1612 to 1800." Unpublished D.M.A. dissertation. University of Southern California, 1959.

5. English Hymnody, II

Bailey, *The Gospel in Hymns*, pp. 141–210, 347–476.
Benson, *The English Hymn*, pp. 435–460, 493–543.
Dearmer, Percy. *Songs of Praise Discussed*. London: Oxford University Press, 1933.
Higginson, J. Vincent. "John Mason Neale and 19th-Century Hymnody: His Work and Influence," *The Hymn*, Vol. 16, No. 4 (October, 1965), pp. 101–117.
Julian, *A Dictionary of Hymnology*, articles on "England Hymnody, Church of," and individual hymns and hymn writers.
Kaan, Fred. "Saturday Night and Sunday Morning," *The Hymn*, Vol. 27, No. 4 (October, 1976), pp. 100–108.
Martin, *They Wrote Our Hymns*, pp. 57–140.
Parry, K. L., and Erik Routley. *Companion to Congregational Praise*. London: Independent Press, 1953.
Patrick, *The Story of the Church's Song*, pp. 142–165.
Routley, Erik. *Hymns and Human Life*, pp. 129–223.
———. "Hymn Writers of the New English Renaissance," *The Hymn*, Vol. 28, No. 1 (January, 1977), pp. 6–10.
———. *The Music of Christian Hymnody*, pp. 108–150.
Ryden, *The Story of Christian Hymnody*, pp. 321–464.
Westermeyer, Paul. "The Hymnal Noted: Theological and Musical Intersections," *Church Music*, 73–2, pp. 1–9.

6. American Hymnody, I

Barbour, J. Murray. *The Church Music of William Billings*. East Lansing: Michigan State University Press, 1960.
Benson, *The English Hymn*, pp. 161–204, 280–314, 358–434.
Britton, Allen P. "Theoretical Introductions in American Tune-Books to 1800." Unpublished Ph.D. dissertation. University of Michigan, 1949.
Chase, Gilbert. *America's Music; From the Pilgrims to the Present*. New York: McGraw-Hill Book Company, 1955. Pp. 3–64, 123–163, 183–258.
Davisson, Ananias. *Kentucky Harmony*. New introduction by Irving Lowens. Minneapolis: Augsburg Press, 1976 (facsimile reprint of the 1816 edition published in Harrisonburg, Va.).
Downey, James Cecil. "The Music of American Revivalism." Unpublished Ph.D. dissertation. Tulane University, 1968.
Ellinwood, Leonard. *The History of American Church Music*. New York: Morehouse-Gorham Company, 1953. Pp. 3–52, 67–71, 101–109.

Eskew, Harry Lee. "Shape-Note Hymnody in the Shenandoah Valley, 1816–1860." Unpublished Ph.D. dissertation. Tulane University, 1966.

Foote, Henry Wilder. *Three Centuries of American Hymnody.* Cambridge, Mass.: Harvard University Press, 1940. Pp. 3–202, 373–386.

Haraszti, Zoltan. *The Enigma of the Bay Psalm Book.* Chicago: University of Chicago Press, 1956.

Jackson, George Pullen. *Spiritual Folk-Songs of Early America.* New York: Dover Publications, 1964 (republication of the work published by J. J. Augustin, New York, 1937).

——. *White Spirituals in the Southern Uplands.* New York: Dover Publications, 1965 (republication of the work published by the University of North Carolina Press, Chapel Hill, 1933).

Lowens, Irving. *Music and Musicians in Early America.* New York: W. W. Norton & Co., 1964.

Lyon, James. *Urania; A Choice Collection of Psalm-Tunes, Anthems, and Hymns.* New preface by Richard Crawford. New York: Da Capo Press, 1974 (unabridged republication of the first edition published in Philadelphia, 1761).

MacDougall, Hamilton C. *Early New England Psalmody: An Historical Appreciation, 1620–1820.* Brattleboro: Stephen Daye Press, 1940.

McCurry, John G. *The Social Harp.* Ed. Daniel W. Patterson and John F. Garst. Athens: University of Georgia Press, 1973.

McKay, David P., and Richard Crawford. *William Billings of Boston.* Princeton: Princeton University Press, 1975.

Mason, Henry Lowell. "Lowell Mason: An Appreciation of His Life and Work," *Papers of the Hymn Society of America,* No. VIII, 1941.

Sims, John N. "The Hymnody of the Camp-Meeting Tradition." Unpublished D.S.M. dissertation. Union Theological Seminary, 1960.

Stevenson, Robert. *Protestant Church Music in America.* New York: W. W. Norton & Co., 1966. Pp. 3–105.

White, B. F., and E. J. King. *The Sacred Harp.* Nashville: Broadman Press, 1968 (facsimile edition of the third edition, 1859).

7. American Hymnody, II

Bailey, *The Gospel in Hymns,* pp. 482–577.

Benson, *The English Hymn,* pp. 460–492, 513–590.

——. *The Hymnody of the Christian Church,* pp. 262–277.

Douglas, *Church Music in History and Practice,* pp. 220–241.

Foote, Henry Wilder. "Recent American Hymnody," *Papers of the Hymn Society of America,* No. XVII, 1952.

——. *Three Centuries of American Hymnody,* pp. 202–369.

Haeussler, Armin. *The Story of Our Hymns: The Handbook to the Hymnal of the Evangelical and Reformed Church.* Saint Louis: Eden Publishing House, 1952. Pp. 17–45.

Hymnal 1940 Companion, The. Third edition, revised. New York: The Church Pension Fund, 1956. Pp. xix–xxvii.

Jost, Walter James. "The Hymn Tune Tradition of the General Conference Mennonite Church." Unpublished D.M.A. dissertation. University of Southern California, 1966.

124   Noyes, Morgan P. "Louis F. Benson, Hymnologist," *Papers of the Hymn Society of America,* No. XIX, 1955.

Patrick, *The Story of the Church's Song,* pp. 166–192.

Reed, Luther D. *Worship: A Study of Corporate Devotion.* Philadelphia: Muhlenberg Press, 1959. Pp. 150–157, 230–239.

Ryden, *The Story of Christian Hymnody,* pp. 487–638.

Sankey, Ira D. *Sankey's Story of the Gospel Hymns.* Philadelphia: The Sunday School Times Co., 1906.

Stevenson, *Protestant Church Music in America,* pp. 106–132.

Warland, Dale Eugene. "The Music of Twentieth-Century Lutheran Hymnody in America." Unpublished D.M.A. dissertation. University of Southern California, 1965.

Weight, Newell Bryan. "An Historical Study of the Origin and Character of Indigenous Hymn Tunes of the Latter-Day Saints." Unpublished D.M.A. dissertation. University of Southern California, 1961.

Wohlgemuth, Paul W. "Mennonite Hymnals Published in the English Language." Unpublished D.M.A. dissertation. University of Southern California, 1958.

Illustrative Hymns

In the historical development of Christian hymnody presented in the preceding chapters, many hymns and tunes have been mentioned. The pages to follow present a selection of illustrative hymns and tunes which have come from the cathedral and the camp meeting, from liberal and conservative thought, from the well known and also the unknown, as mankind has sought to express his praise to God.

Let all the world in every corner sing,
 My God and King!
The heavens are not too high,
His praise may thither fly;
The earth is not too low,
His praises there may grow.
Let all the world in every corner sing,
 My God and King!

Let all the world in every corner sing,
 My God and King!
The Church with psalms must shout,
No door can keep them out;
But above all, the heart
Must bear the longest part,
Let all the world in every corner sing,
 My God and King!

GEORGE HERBERT, 1593–1632

O Splendor of God's Glory Bright

Latin: *Splendor paternae gloriae*
St. Ambrose, 340-397
Tr. Robert S. Bridges, 1844-1930

SPLENDOR PATERNAE L.M.
Sarum Plainsong, Mode I

1 O Splen-dor of God's glo-ry bright, O thou that bring-est
2 O thou true Sun, on us thy glance Let fall in roy-al
3 The Fa-ther, too, our prayers im-plore, Fa-ther of glo-ry
4 To guide what-e'er we no-bly do, With love all en-vy

light from light, O Light of light, light's liv-ing spring,
ra-di-ance; The Spir-it's sanc-ti-fy-ing beam
ev-er-more, The Fa-ther of all grace and might,
to sub-due; To make ill-for-tune turn to fair,

O Day, all days il-lu-min-ing,
Up-on our earth-ly sen-ses stream.
To ban-ish sin from our de-light:
And give us grace our wrongs to bear. A-men.

SOURCE OF TEXT: One of the fourth-century Ambrosian hymns. SOURCE OF TRANSLATION: Bridges's *Yattendon Hymnal*, London, 1899. SOURCE OF TUNE: The Sarum form of the traditional plainsong melody.

Christians, to the Paschal Victim

Ascribed to Wipo, d.c.1050
Tr. Anonymous

VICTIMAE PASCHALI, *Irregular*
Ascribed to Wipo, d.c.1050

1 Chris-tians, to the Pas-chal vic-tim Of-fer your thank-ful prais-es!

2 A lamb the sheep re-deem-eth: Christ, who on-ly is sin-less, Re-con-cil-eth

Sin-ners to the Father. 3 Death and life have contended In that combat stu-

SOURCE OF TEXT: First found in an Einsiedeln manuscript, dating from the end of the eleventh century. SOURCE OF TRANSLATION: *Antiphoner and Grail*, London, 1880. The selection of stanzas used here first appeared in *The English Hymnal*, London, 1906. SOURCE OF TUNE: This plainsong sequence dates from the eleventh century.

pen-dous: The Prince of life, who died, reigns im-mor-tal. 4 Speak, Ma-ry, de-clar -

ing   What thou sawest, way-faring. 5 "The tomb of Christ, who is liv - ing,

The glo-ry of Je-sus' re-sur-rec - tion; 6 Bright an-gels at-test - ing,

The shroud and nap-kin rest-ing. 7 Yea, Christ my hope is a - ris - en:

To Gal - i - lee he goes be - fore you." 8 Christ in-deed from death is ris-en,

rit.

Our new life ob-tain-ing Have mercy, victor King, ev - er reigning! A-men.

3   Day of Wrath! O Day of Mourning!

Probably by Thomas of Celano, 13th century
Tr. William J. Irons, 1812-1883, St. 1-18
Tr. Isaac Williams, 1802-1865, St. 19

DIES IRAE 8.8.8.
Plainsong sequence,
13th century

In unison, with insistent rhythm, not slow

1 Day of wrath! O day of mourn-ing! See ful - filled the
2 O what fear man's bo - som rend-eth When from heav'n the
7 What shall I, frail man, be plead-ing? Who for me be
8 King of ma - jes - ty tre - men-dous, Who dost free sal -
13 Thou the sin - ful wo-man sav - edst; Thou the dy - ing
14 Worth-less are my prayers and sigh - ing, Yet, good Lord, in

pro-phets' warn-ing, Heav'n and earth in ash - es burn - ing!
Judge de - scend-eth, On whose sen - tence all de - pend-eth!
in - ter - ced - ing, When the just are mer - cy need - ing?
va - tion send us, Fount of pi - ty, then be - friend us!
thief for - gav - est; And to me a hope vouch-saf - est.
grace com - ply - ing, Res - cue me from fires un - dy - ing!

SOURCE OF TEXT: The Latin text is found in two manuscripts compiled *c.* 1255. SOURCE OF TRANSLA-
TION: First appeared in the privately printed *Introits and Hymns for Advent*, London, *n.d.* SOURCE
OF TUNE: A plainsong sequence of thirteenth-century origin.

3 Won-drous sound the trum - pet fling-eth; Thru earth's sep-ul-chers
4 Death is struck, and na ture quak-ing, All cre - a - tion is
9 Think, good Je-sus, my sal - va - tion Cost thy won-drous in -
10 Faint and wea-ry, thou hast sought me, On the cross of suf-
15 With thy fa - vored sheep O place me, Nor a-mong the goats
16 While the wick-ed are con-found-ed, Doomed to flames of woe

it ring-eth; All be - fore the throne it bring-eth.
a - wak-ing, To its Judge an an-swer mak - ing.
car - na - tion; Leave me not to rep - ro - ba - tion!
f'ring bought me. Shall such grace be vain-ly brought me?
a - base me, But to thy right hand up-raise me.
un-bound-ed, Call me with thy saints sur-round-ed.

5 Lo! the book, ex - act - ly word - ed, Where - in all hath
6 When the Judge his seat at - tain - eth And each hid - den
11 Right - eous Judge! for sin's pol - lu - tion Grant thy gift of
12 Guil - ty, now I pour my moan - ing, All my shame with
17 Low I kneel, with heart sub - mis - sion: See, like ash - es,

been re - cord - ed: Thence shall judg - ment be a - ward - ed.
deed ar - raign - eth, Noth - ing un - a - venged re - main - eth.
ab - so - lu - tion, Ere the day of ret - ri - bu - tion.
an - guish own - ing; Spare, O God, thy sup - pliant groan - ing!
my con - tri - tion; Help me in my last con - di - tion.

PART II

18 Ah! that day of tears and mourn - ing! From the dust of

earth re-turn-ing, Man for judg-ment must pre-

pare him; Spare, O God, in mer cy spare him!

Somewhat slower

19 Lord, all pitying, Je-sus blest, Grant them thine e-ter-nal rest. A - men.

4   Of the Father's Love Begotten

Latin: Prudentius, 348-c.410
Tr. John M. Neale, 1818-1866, St. 1, alt.
Tr. Henry W. Baker, 1821-1877, Sts. 2,3

DIVINUM MYSTERIUM 8.7.8.7.8.7.7.
13th-century Plainsong, Mode V

1 Of the Fa-ther's love be-got-ten, Ere the worlds be-gan to be,
2 O ye heights of heaven a-dore him; An-gel hosts, his prais-es sing;
3 Christ, to thee with God the Fa-ther, And, O Ho-ly Ghost, to thee,

He is Al-pha and O-me-ga, He the source, the end-ing he;
Powers, do-min-ions, bow be-fore him, And ex-tol our God and King;
Hymn and chant and high thanks-giv-ing, And un-wea-ried prais-es be:

Of the things that are, that have been, And that
Let no tongue on earth be si - lent, Ev-ery
Hon-or, glo-ry, and do-min - ion, And e-

SOURCE OF TEXT: From the "Hymnus omis horae" in Prudentius' *Cathemerinon*. SOURCE OF TRANSLA-TION: Neale's *Hymnal Noted*, London, 1851. SOURCE OF TUNE: Thirteenth-century plainsong (Sanctus trope). *Piae Cantiones*, Nyland, 1582. Thomas Helmore set this tune to Neale's translation in the musical edition of *The Hymnal Noted*, London, 1854. Harmonization by C. Winfred Douglas (1887-1944).

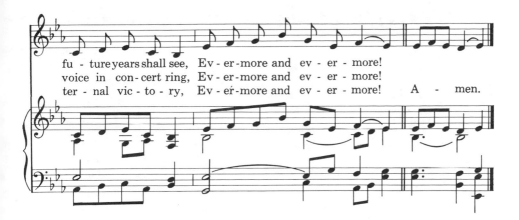

fu - ture years shall see, Ev - er-more and ev - er - more!
voice in con - cert ring, Ev - er-more and ev - er - more!
ter - nal vic - to - ry, Ev - er-more and ev - er - more! A - men.

To Thee Before the Close of Day   5

Latin: c.7th century
Tr. John M. Neale, 1818-1866, alt.

JAM LUCIS L.M
Plainsong, Mode VI

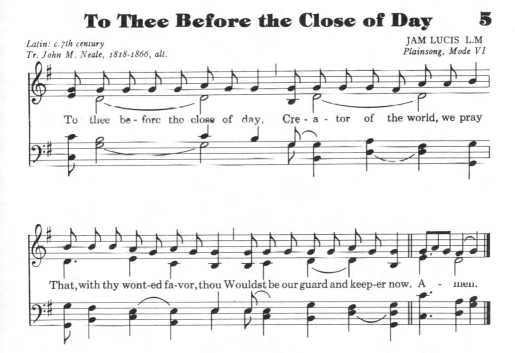

To thee be - fore the close of day, Cre - a - tor of the world, we pray

That, with thy wont-ed fa-vor, thou Wouldst be our guard and keep-er now. A - men.

SOURCE OF TEXT: While this hymn is found in the earliest Ambrosian manuscripts of the seventh century, it is not of Ambrosian authorship. It is an Office Hymn sung at Complin. Neale's translation appeared in the *Hymnal Noted*, 1851. SOURCE OF TUNE: Traditional plainsong melody.

6 Come, Holy Ghost, Our Souls Inspire

Latin: 9th century
Tr. John Cosin, 1594-1672

VENI CREATOR L.M.
Plainsong
"Vesperale Romanum" (Mechlin)

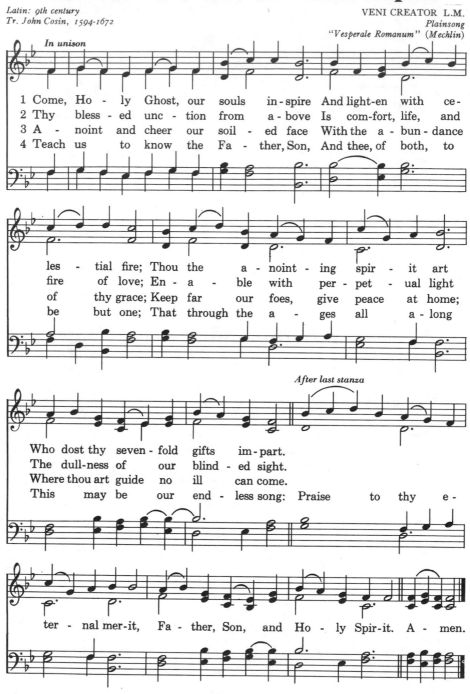

1 Come, Ho - ly Ghost, our souls in-spire And light-en with ce-
2 Thy bless - ed unc - tion from a - bove Is com-fort, life, and
3 A - noint and cheer our soil - ed face With the a - bun - dance
4 Teach us to know the Fa - ther, Son, And thee, of both, to

les - tial fire; Thou the a - noint - ing spir - it art
fire of love; En - a - ble with per - pet - ual light
of thy grace; Keep far our foes, give peace at home;
be but one; That through the a - ges all a - long

After last stanza

Who dost thy seven - fold gifts im-part.
The dull-ness of our blind - ed sight.
Where thou art guide no ill can come.
This may be our end - less song: Praise to thy e-

ter - nal mer-it, Fa - ther, Son, and Ho - ly Spir-it. A - men.

SOURCE OF TEXT: Anonymous Latin hymn of the ninth century. SOURCE OF TRANSLATION: Cosin's *Collection of Private Devotions in the Practice of the Ancient Church, Called the Hours of Prayer* . . ., 1627. It was included in the *Book of Common Prayer*, 1662. SOURCE OF TUNE: A medieval melody in the Mechlin *Vesperale Romanum*, 1848.

Out of the Depths I Cry to Thee

7

Martin Luther, 1483-1546
Tr. Catherine Winkworth, 1827-1878, alt.

AUS TIEFER NOTH (COBURG) 8.7.8.7.8.8.7.
German Hymn Melody, 16th century

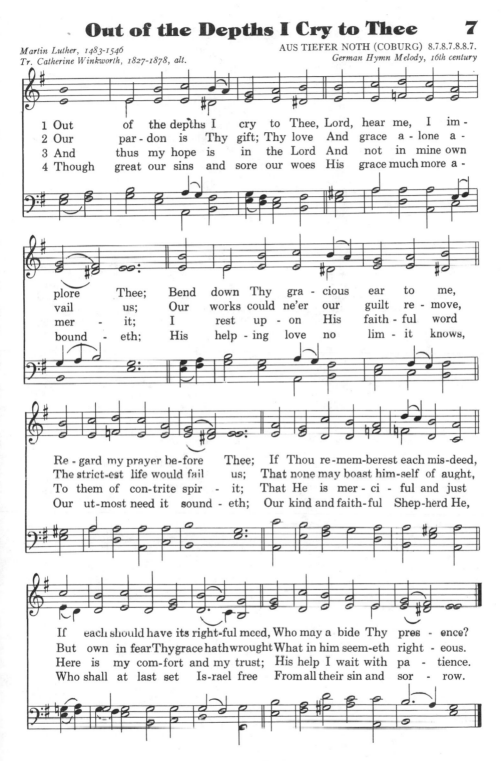

1 Out of the depths I cry to Thee, Lord, hear me, I im-
2 Our par-don is Thy gift; Thy love And grace a-lone a-
3 And thus my hope is in the Lord And not in mine own
4 Though great our sins and sore our woes His grace much more a-

plore Thee; Bend down Thy gra-cious ear to me,
vail us; Our works could ne'er our guilt re-move,
mer-it; I rest up-on His faith-ful word
bound-eth; His help-ing love no lim-it knows,

Re-gard my prayer be-fore Thee; If Thou re-mem-berest each mis-deed,
The strict-est life would fail us; That none may boast him-self of aught,
To them of con-trite spir-it; That He is mer-ci-ful and just
Our ut-most need it sound-eth; Our kind and faith-ful Shep-herd He,

If each should have its right-ful meed, Who may a-bide Thy pres-ence?
But own in fear Thy grace hath wrought What in him seem-eth right-eous.
Here is my com-fort and my trust; His help I wait with pa-tience.
Who shall at last set Is-rael free From all their sin and sor-row.

SOURCE OF TEXT: *Etlich Christlich Lieder*, Wittenberg, 1524. SOURCE OF TRANSLATION: Winkworth's *Chorale Book for England*, London, 1863. SOURCE OF TUNE: Walther's *Geistliche Gesangbüchlein*, Wittenberg, 1524. Probably composed by Walther or Luther.

8

All Glory Be to God on High

Attr. to Nicolaus Decius, d.1541
Tr. Catherine Winkworth, 1827-1878, alt.

ALLEIN GOTT IN DER HOH' 8.7.8.7.8.8.7.
"Geistliche Lieder," Leipzig, 1539

1 All glo-ry be to God on high, Who hath our race be-friend-ed!
2 We praise, we wor-ship thee, we trust And give thee thanks for-ev-er,
3 O Je-sus Christ, our God and Lord, Be-got-ten of the Fa-ther,
4 O Ho-ly Spir-it, pre-cious Gift, Thou Com-fort-er un-fail-ing,

To us no harm shall now come nigh, The strife at last is end-ed;
O Fa-ther, that thy rule is just And wise, and chang-es nev-er;
O thou who hast our peace re-stored, And the lost sheep dost gath-er,
Do thou our trou-bled souls up-lift, A-gainst the foe pre-vail-ing;

God show-eth his good-will to men, And peace shall reign on
Thy bound-less power o'er all things reigns, Thou dost what-e'er thy
Thou Lamb of God, en-throned on high, Be-hold our need and
A-vert our woes and calm our dread: For us the Sav-ior's

earth a-gain; O thank him for his good-ness!
will or-dains; 'Tis well thou art our rul-er!
hear our cry; Have mer-cy on us, Je-sus!
blood was shed; Do thou in faith sus-tain us! A-men.

SOURCE OF TEXT: A German paraphrase of the "Gloria in excelsis," first appeared in the Rostock *Gesangbuch*, 1525. SOURCE OF TRANSLATION: Winkworth's *Chorale Book for England*, London, 1863. SOURCE OF TUNE: Composed or arranged by Nicolaus Decius, in *Geistliche Lieder*, Leipzig, 1539.

O Sacred Head, Now Wounded 9

Latin: 12th century
German; Paul Gerhardt, 1607-1676
Tr. James W. Alexander, 1804-1859, alt.

PASSION CHORALE 7.6.7.6.D.
Melody by Hans Leo Hassler, 1564-1612
Harm. by J.S. Bach, 1685-1750

1 O sa - cred Head, now wound-ed, With grief and shame weighed down,
2 What thou, my Lord, hast suf - fered Was all for sin - ners' gain;
3 What lan-guage shall I bor - row To thank thee, dear - est friend;

Now scorn-ful - ly sur - round-ed With thorns, thy on - ly crown,
Mine, mine was the trans-gres - sion, But thine the dead-ly pain.
For this thy dy - ing sor - row, Thy pit - y with-out end?

How art thou pale with an - guish, With sore a - buse and scorn!
Lo, here I fall, my Sav - ior! 'Tis I de - serve thy place;
O make me thine for - ev - er; And, should I faint-ing be,

How does that vis - age lan - guish Which once was bright as morn!
Look on me with thy fa - vor, Vouch-safe to me thy grace.
Lord, let me nev - er, nev - er, Out - live my love to thee! A-men.

SOURCE OF TEXT: Latin, fourteenth century. SOURCE OF TRANSLATION: Gerhardt's German translation — Crüger's *Praxis Pietatis Melica* — Frankfurt, 1656. Alexander's English translation first appeared in Leavitt's *Christian Lyre*, New York, 1831. SOURCE OF TUNE: Hassler's *Lustgarten neuer Teutscher Gesäng*, Nürnberg, 1601.

10 O Morning Star, How Fair and Bright

Philipp Nicolai, 1556-1608
Tr. Catherine Winkworth, 1827-1878, alt..

WIE SCHÖN LEUCHTET 8.8.7.8.8.7.4.8.4.8.
Melody by Philipp Nicolai, 1556-1608
Harm. by J. S. Bach, 1685-1750

1 O Morn-ing Star, how fair and bright Thou beam-est forth in truth and light! O Sov-ereign meek and low-ly! Thou Root of Jes-se, Da-vid's Son, My Lord and Mas-ter, thou hast won My heart to serve thee sole-ly! Thou art ho-ly, Fair and glo-rious, all-vic-to-rious,

2 Thou heaven-ly Bright-ness! Light di-vine! O deep with-in my heart now shine, And make thee there an al-tar! Fill me with joy and strength to be Thy mem-ber, ev-er joined to thee In love that can-not fal-ter; Toward thee long-ing Doth pos-sess me; turn and bless me;

SOURCE OF TEXT AND TUNE: Appendix to Nicolai's *Frewden-Spiegel des ewigen Lebens*, Frankfurt, 1599. SOURCE OF TRANSLATION: Winkworth's *Chorale Book for England*, London, 1863. SOURCE OF HARMONIZATION: Bach's *Cantata No. 1*, composed in 1740.

Rich in bless - ing, Rule and might o'er all pos - sess - ing.
Here in sad - ness Eye and heart long for thy glad - ness! A-men.

While Shepherds Watched Their Flocks 11

Nahum Tate, 1652-1715

WINCHESTER OLD C.M.
Thomas Este's "Whole Book of Psalms," 1592

1 While shep-herds watched their flocks by night, All seat - ed on the ground,
2 "Fear not," said he, for might-y dread Had seized their trou-bled mind,
3 "To you, in Da - vid's town, this day Is born of Da - vid's line
4 "The heaven-ly babe you there shall find To hu - man view dis - played,

The an - gel of the Lord came down, And glo - ry shone a - round.
"Glad ti-dings of great joy I bring To you and all man kind.
The Sav - ior, who is Christ the Lord; And this shall be the sign:
All mean-ly wrapped in swath-ing bands, And in a man-ger laid." A-men.

5 Thus spake the seraph; and forthwith
   Appeared a shining throng
Of angels praising God, who thus
   Addressed their joyful song:

6 "All glory be to God on high,
   And to the earth be peace;
Good will henceforth from heaven to men
   Begin and never cease."

SOURCE OF TEXT: Supplement to Tate and Brady's *New Version*, London, 1700. SOURCE OF TUNE:
Thomas Este's *Psalter*, London, 1592, in which the harmonization is credited to George Kirbye, one
of ten composers who assisted Este in preparation of the tunes.

12 Wake, Awake, for Night Is Flying

Philipp Nicolai, 1556-1608
Tr. Catherine Winkworth, 1827-1878

WACHET AUF *Irregular*
Philipp Nicolai, 1556-1608

1 Wake, a-wake, for night is fly - ing, The watch-men on
Mid-night hears the wel-come voic - es And at the thrill-

the heights are cry - ing, A - wake, Je - ru - sa - lem, at last!
ing cry re - joic - es: Come forth, ye vir - gins, night is past!

The Bridegroom comes, awake, Your lamps with glad-ness take; Al-le-lu - ia!

And for his mar-riage feast pre-pare, For ye must go to meet him there. A-men.

2 Zion hears the watchmen singing,
And all her heart with joy is springing,
    She wakes, she rises from her gloom;
For her Lord comes down all-glorious,
The strong in grace, in truth victorious,
    Her Star is risen, her Light is come.

Ah come, thou blessèd One,
God's own belovèd Son,
    Alleluia!
We follow till the halls we see
Where thou hast bid us sup with thee.

SOURCE OF TEXT AND TUNE: Appendix to Nicolai's *Frewden-Spiegel des ewigen Lebens*, Frankfurt, 1599. SOURCE OF TRANSLATION: Winkworth's *Lyra Germanica*, London, second series, 1858.

Wake, Awake, for Night Is Flying 13

Philipp Nicolai, 1556-1608
Tr. Catherine Winkworth, 1827-1878

WACHET AUF Irregular
Philipp Nicolai, 1556-1608
Adapted and harmonized by J. S. Bach, 1685-1750

1 Wake, a-wake, for night is fly - ing, The watch-men on the heights are cry - ing, A - wake, Je - ru - sa - lem, at last! The Bride-groom comes, a-wake, Your lamps with glad-ness take; Al - le - lu - ia! And for his mar-riage feast pre-pare, For ye must go to meet him there. A-men.

Mid-night hears the wel-come voic - es And at the thrill-ing cry re - joic - es: Come forth, ye vir-gins, night is past!

Wake, a-wake, for

3 Now let all the heavens adore thee,
   And men and angels sing before thee,
     With harp and cymbal's clearest tone;
   Of one pearl each shining portal,
   Where we are with the choir immortal
     Of angels round thy dazzling throne;

Nor eye hath seen, nor ear
Hath yet attained to hear
     What there is ours;
But we rejoice, and sing to thee
Our hymn of joy eternally. Amen.

SOURCE OF TEXT AND TUNE: Appendix to Nicolai's *Frewden-Spiegel des ewigen Lebens*, Frankfurt, 1599. SOURCE OF TRANSLATION: Winkworth's *Lyra Germanica*, London, second series, 1858. SOURCE OF HARMONIZATION: This is the final chorus in Bach's Cantata No. 140, *Wachet Auf*, composed for the twenty-seventh Sunday after Trinity, November 25, 1731.

14   Gentle Mary Laid Her Child

Joseph Simpson Cook, 1859-1933

TEMPUS ADEST FLORIDUM 7.6.7.6.D.
Spring carol, c.14th century
Arr. by Ernest C. MacMillan, 1893-

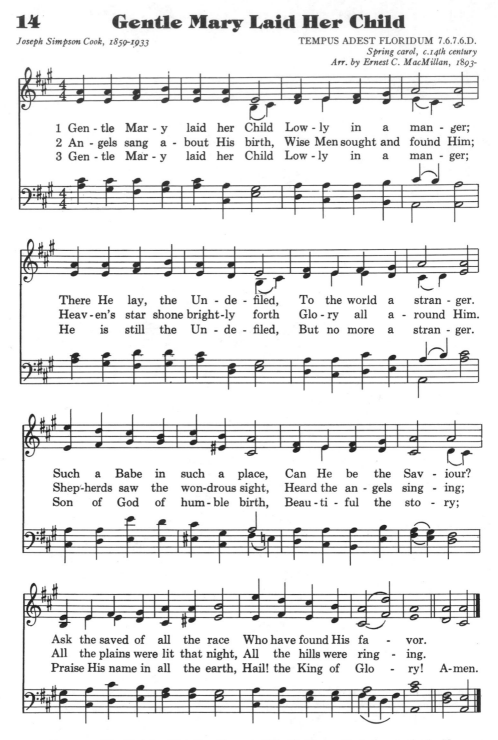

1 Gen-tle Mar-y laid her Child Low-ly in a man-ger;
2 An-gels sang a-bout His birth, Wise Men sought and found Him;
3 Gen-tle Mar-y laid her Child Low-ly in a man-ger;

There He lay, the Un-de-filed, To the world a stran-ger.
Heav-en's star shone bright-ly forth Glo-ry all a-round Him.
He is still the Un-de-filed, But no more a stran-ger.

Such a Babe in such a place, Can He be the Sav-iour?
Shep-herds saw the won-drous sight, Heard the an-gels sing-ing;
Son of God of hum-ble birth, Beau-ti-ful the sto-ry;

Ask the saved of all the race Who have found His fa-vor.
All the plains were lit that night, All the hills were ring-ing.
Praise His name in all the earth, Hail! the King of Glo-ry! A-men.

SOURCE OF TEXT: *The Christian Guardian*, Toronto, 1919. First hymnal inclusion was in the *Hymnary of the United Church of Canada*, Toronto, 1930. Used by permission of Alta Lind Cook, Toronto.
SOURCE OF TUNE: *Piae Cantiones*, Nyland, 1582. Harmonization from the *Hymmary of the United Church of Canada*, Toronto, 1930, used by permission of Sir Ernest MacMillan.

146

Unto Us a Boy Is Born 15

Latin carol, 15th century
Tr. Percy Dearmer, 1867-1936

PUER NOBIS 7.7.7.7.
"Piae Cantiones," 1582
Arr. by Geoffrey Shaw, 1879-1943

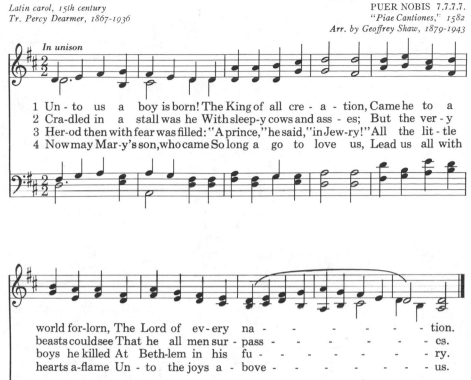

1 Un-to us a boy is born! The King of all cre-a-tion, Came he to a
world for-lorn, The Lord of ev-ery na - - - - - - - tion.

2 Cra-dled in a stall was he With sleep-y cows and ass-es; But the ver-y
beasts could see That he all men sur-pass - - - - - - - es.

3 Her-od then with fear was filled: "A prince," he said, "in Jew-ry!" All the lit-tle
boys he killed At Beth-lem in his fu - - - - - - - ry.

4 Now may Mar-y's son, who came So long a go to love us, Lead us all with
hearts a-flame Un-to the joys a-bove - - - - - - us.

5 Alpha and Omega he!
Let the organ thunder,
While the choir with peals of glee
Doth rend the air asunder.

SOURCE OF TEXT AND TUNE: A Latin carol, both words and music; first appeared in a fifteenth-century Trier manuscript. SOURCE OF TRANSLATION: *Oxford Book of Carols*, 1928. Words copyright. Reprinted by permission of the Oxford University Press, London. SOURCE OF TUNE ARRANGEMENT: *Oxford Book of Carols*. Reprinted by permission of A. R. Mowbray & Co., Limited, London.

16   All Glory, Laud, and Honor

Theodulph of Orleans, c.760-c.821
Tr. John M. Neale, 1818-1866, alt.

ST. THEODULPH 7.6.7.6.D.
Melody by Melchior Teschner, 1584-1635

1 All glo-ry, laud, and hon-or To thee, Re-deem-er, King,
2 Thou art the King of Is-rael, Thou Da-vid's roy-al son,
3 Thou didst ac-cept their prais-es; Ac-cept the prayers we bring,

To whom the lips of chil-dren Made sweet ho-san-nas ring!
Who in the Lord's name com-est, The King and bless-ed One;
Who in all good de-light-est, Thou good and gra-cious King.

The peo-ple of the He-brews With palms be-fore thee went;
To thee, be-fore thy pas-sion, They sang their hymns of praise;
All glo-ry, laud, and hon-or To thee, Re-deem-er, King,

Our praise and prayer and an-thems Be-fore thee we pre-sent.
To thee, now high ex-alt-ed, Our mel-o-dy we raise.
To whom the lips of chil-dren Made sweet ho-san-nas ring! A-men.

SOURCE OF TEXT: Unknown, written about 820. SOURCE OF TRANSLATION: Neale's *Medieval Hymns*, London, 1851. SOURCE OF TUNE: *Ein Andächtiges Gebet*, Leipzig, 1615.

Lo, How a Rose E'er Blooming 17

German: anon., 15th century
Tr. Theodore Baker, 1851-1934

ES IST EIN' ROS' 7.6.7.6.6.7.6.
German: Melody, 16th century
Arr. by Michael Praetorius, 1571-1621

1 Lo, how a Rose e'er bloom-ing From ten-der stem hath sprung!
2 I - sa - iah 'twas fore-told it, The Rose I have in mind,

Of Jes-se's lin-eage com-ing As men of old have sung.
With Mar-y we be-hold it, The Vir-gin Moth-er kind.

It came, a flower-et bright, A - mid the cold of
To show God's love a - right, She bore to men a

win - ter, When half spent was the night.
Sav - ior, When half spent was the night.

SOURCE OF TEXT: *Speirischen Gesangbuch*, Cologne, 1599. SOURCE OF TRANSLATION: Translated about 1897. Source unknown. SOURCE OF TUNE: A traditional melody harmonized by Praetorius for his *Musae Sionae*, Görlitz, 1609.

18   Jesus, Priceless Treasure

Johann Franck, 1618-1677
Tr. Catherine Winkworth, 1827-1878

JESU, MEINE FREUDE 6.6.5.6.6.5.7.8.6.
Traditional German Melody
Adapted by Johann Crüger, 1598-1662

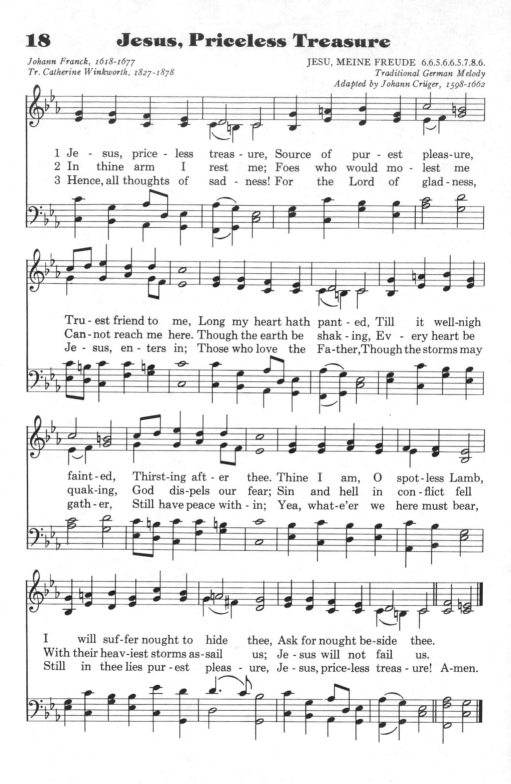

1 Je - sus, price - less treas - ure, Source of pur - est pleas-ure,
2 In thine arm I rest me; Foes who would mo - lest me
3 Hence, all thoughts of sad - ness! For the Lord of glad - ness,

Tru - est friend to me, Long my heart hath pant - ed, Till it well-nigh
Can - not reach me here. Though the earth be shak - ing, Ev - ery heart be
Je - sus, en - ters in; Those who love the Fa - ther, Though the storms may

faint - ed, Thirst - ing aft - er thee. Thine I am, O spot - less Lamb,
quak - ing, God dis - pels our fear; Sin and hell in con - flict fell
gath - er, Still have peace with - in; Yea, what - e'er we here must bear,

I will suf - fer nought to hide thee, Ask for nought be - side thee.
With their heav - iest storms as - sail us; Je - sus will not fail us.
Still in thee lies pur - est pleas - ure, Je - sus, price - less treas - ure! A - men.

SOURCE OF TEXT AND TUNE: Crüger's *Praxis Pietatis Melica*, fifth edition, Berlin, 1653. SOURCE OF TRANSLATION: Winkworth's *Chorale Book for England*, London, 1863.

If Thou But Suffer God to Guide Thee 19

Georg Neumark, *1621-1681*
Tr. Catherine Winkworth, *1827-1878*

NEUMARK 9.8.9.8.8.8.
Melody by Georg Neumark, 1621-1681

1 If thou but suf - fer God to guide thee, And hope in
2 On - ly be still, and wait his lei - sure In cheer - ful
3 Sing, pray, and keep his ways un - swerv - ing; So do thine

him through all thy ways, He'll give thee strength, what-e'er be - tide thee,
hope, with heart con - tent To take what-e'er thy Fa - ther's pleas-ure
own part faith - ful - ly, And trust his word, though un - de - serv-ing;

And bear thee through the e - vil days; Who trusts in God's un
And all de - serv - ing love have sent; Nor doubt our in - most
Thou yet shalt find it true for thee; God nev - er yet for-

chang - ing love Builds on the rock that nought can move.
wants are known To him who chose us for his own.
sook at need The soul that trust - ed him in - deed. A-men.

SOURCE OF TEXT AND TUNE: Neumark's *Fortgepflantzer Musikalisch-Poetischer Lustwald*, Jena, 1657.
SOURCE OF TRANSLATION: Winkworth's *Chorale Book for England*, London, 1863.

20   Ah, Holy Jesus

Johann Heermann, 1585-1647
Tr. Robert S. Bridges, 1844-1930

HERZLIEBSTER JESU 11.11.11.5.
Johann Crüger, 1598-1662

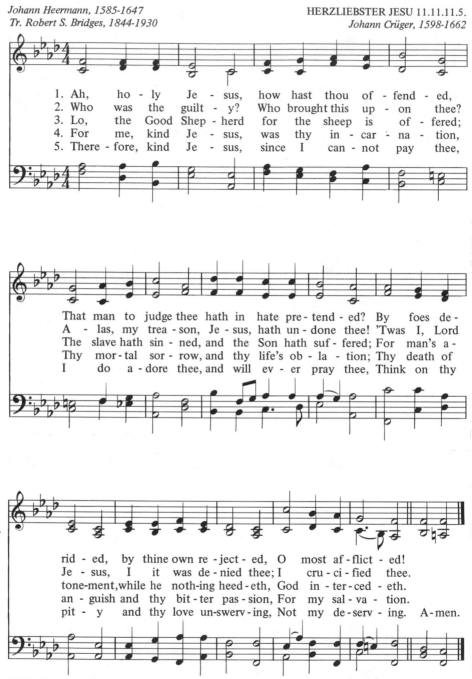

1. Ah, ho-ly Je-sus, how hast thou of-fend-ed,
2. Who was the guilt-y? Who brought this up-on thee?
3. Lo, the Good Shep-herd for the sheep is of-fered;
4. For me, kind Je-sus, was thy in-car-na-tion,
5. There-fore, kind Je-sus, since I can-not pay thee,

That man to judge thee hath in hate pre-tend-ed? By foes de-
A-las, my trea-son, Je-sus, hath un-done thee! 'Twas I, Lord
The slave hath sin-ned, and the Son hath suf-fered; For man's a-
Thy mor-tal sor-row, and thy life's ob-la-tion; Thy death of
I do a-dore thee, and will ev-er pray thee, Think on thy

rid-ed, by thine own re-ject-ed, O most af-flict-ed!
Je-sus, I it was de-nied thee; I cru-ci-fied thee.
tone-ment, while he noth-ing heed-eth, God in-ter-ced-eth.
an-guish and thy bit-ter pas-sion, For my sal-va-tion.
pit-y and thy love un-swerv-ing, Not my de-serv-ing. A-men.

SOURCE OF TEXT: Heermann's *Devoti Musica Cordis*, 1630. SOURCE OF TRANSLATION: Bridges' *Yattendon Hymnal, 1899.* SOURCE OF TUNE: Crüger's *Neues vollkommlenes Gesangbuch,* 1640, composed for Heermann's text. This harmonization first appeared in the *Chorale Book for England,* 1863.

152

Joachim Neander, 1650-1680
Tr. Catherine Winkworth, 1827-1878, alt.

LOBE DEN HERREN 14.14.4.7.8.
"Stralsund Gesangbuch," 1665

1 Praise to the Lord, the Al-might-y, the King of cre-a-tion!
2 Praise to the Lord, who o'er all things so won-drous-ly reign-eth,
3 Praise to the Lord, who doth pros-per thy work and de-fend thee;
4 Praise to the Lord! O let all that is in me a-dore him!

O my soul, praise him, for he is thy health and sal-va-tion!
Shel-ters thee un-der his wings, yea, so gen-tly sus-tain-eth!
Sure-ly his good-ness and mer-cy here dai-ly at-tend thee.
All that hath life and breath, come now with prais-es be-fore him.

All ye who hear, Now to his tem-ple draw near;
Hast thou not seen How thy de-sires e'er have been
Pon-der a-new What the Al-might-y can do,
Let the A-men Sound from his peo-ple a-gain:

Join me in glad ad-o-ra-tion!
Grant-ed in what he or-dain-eth?
If with his love he be-friend thee.
Glad-ly for aye we a-dore him. A-men.

SOURCE OF TEXT: Neander's *A und Ω Glaub- und Liebesübung*, Bremen, 1680. SOURCE OF TRANSLA-
TION: Winkworth's *Chorale Book for England*, London, 1863. SOURCE OF TUNE: *Ander Theil des
Erneuerten Gesangbuch*, Stralsund, 1665. Neander adapted this tune for this text in his 1680 collection.

22   Open Now Thy Gates of Beauty

Benjamin Schmolck, 1672-1737
Tr. Catherine Winkworth, 1827-1878

UNSER HERRSCHER 8.7.8.7.7.7.
Melody by Joachim Neander, 1650-1680

1 O - pen now thy gates of beau - ty, Zi - on, let me en - ter there,
2 Gra-cious God, I come be - fore thee, Come thou al - so un - to me;

Where my soul in joy - ful du - ty, Waits for him who an-swers prayer.
Where we find thee and a - dore thee, There a heaven on earth must be.

O how bless - ed is this place, Filled with sol - ace, light, and grace!
To my heart O en - ter thou, Let it be thy tem - ple now.

SOURCE OF TEXT: Schmolck's *Kirchen-Gefährte*, Schweidnitz, Silesia, 1732. SOURCE OF TRANSLATION: Winkworth's *Chorale Book for England*, London, 1863. SOURCE OF TUNE: Neander's *A und Ω Glaub und Liebesübung*, Bremen, 1680.

All Creatures of Our God and King   23

St. Francis of Assisi, 1182-1226
Tr. William H. Draper, 1855-1933

LASST UNS ERFREUEN 8.8.4.4.8.8. *with Alleluias*
Melody from "Geistliche Kirchengesäng," Cologne, 1623

In unison

1 All crea-tures of our God and King, Lift up your voice and with us sing
2 Thou rush-ing wind that art so strong, Ye clouds that sail in heaven a-long,
3 Thou flow-ing wa-ter, pure and clear, Make mu-sic for thy Lord to hear,
4 And all ye men of ten-der heart, For-giv-ing oth-ers, take your part,
5 Let all things their cre-a-tor bless, And wor-ship him in hum-ble-ness,

Al-le-lu-ia, Al-le-lu-ia! Thou burn-ing sun with gold-en
O praise him, Al-le-lu-ia! Thou ris-ing morn, in praise re-
Al-le-lu-ia, Al-le-lu-ia! Thou fire so mas-ter-ful and
O sing ye, Al-le-lu-ia! Ye who long pain and sor-row
O praise him, Al-le-lu-ia! Praise, praise the Fa-ther, praise the

beam, Thou sil-ver moon with soft-er gleam, O praise him, O
joice, Ye lights of eve-ning, find a voice, O praise him, O
bright, That giv-est man both warmth and light, O praise him, O
bear, Praise God and on him cast your care. O praise him, O
Son, And praise the Spir-it, three in One. O praise him, O

praise him, Al-le-lu-ia, Al-le-lu-ia, Al-le-lu-ia! A-men.

SOURCE OF TEXT: From "Sun Song," or "Song About Creatures," written about 1225. SOURCE OF
TRANSLATION: *School Worship*, London, 1926. Permission of J. Curwen & Sons, Ltd. SOURCE OF TUNE:
Melody from *Geistliche Kirchengesäng*, Cologne, 1623. Harmonization by Ralph Vaughan Williams.
From *The English Hymnal*, London, 1906, used by permission of Oxford University Press, London.

24 At the Cross, Her Station Keeping

Latin, 13th century
Tr. Edward Caswall, 1814-1878

STABAT MATER (MAINZ) 8.8.7.D.
Mainz "Gesangbuch," 1661

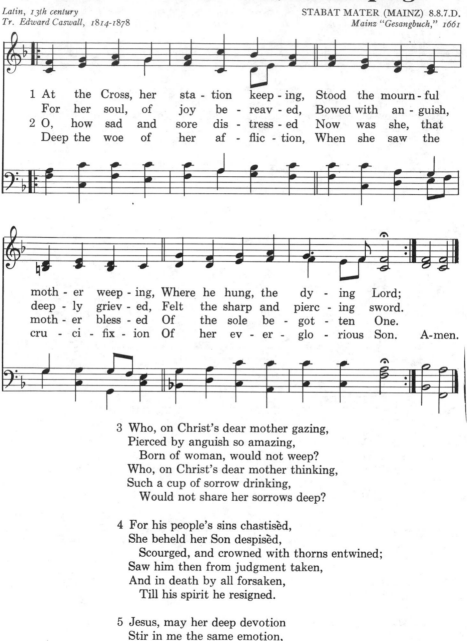

1 At the Cross, her sta-tion keep-ing, Stood the mourn-ful
  For her soul, of joy be-reav-ed, Bowed with an-guish,
2 O, how sad and sore dis-tress-ed Now was she, that
  Deep the woe of her af-flic-tion, When she saw the

moth-er weep-ing, Where he hung, the dy-ing Lord;
deep-ly griev-ed, Felt the sharp and pierc-ing sword.
moth-er bless-ed Of the sole be-got-ten One.
cru-ci-fix-ion Of her ev-er-glo-rious Son. A-men.

3 Who, on Christ's dear mother gazing,
  Pierced by anguish so amazing,
    Born of woman, would not weep?
  Who, on Christ's dear mother thinking,
  Such a cup of sorrow drinking,
    Would not share her sorrows deep?

4 For his people's sins chastisèd,
  She beheld her Son despisèd,
    Scourged, and crowned with thorns entwined;
  Saw him then from judgment taken,
  And in death by all forsaken,
    Till his spirit he resigned.

5 Jesus, may her deep devotion
  Stir in me the same emotion,
    Fount of love, Redeemer kind,
  That my heart, fresh ardor gaining
  And purer love attaining,
    May with thee acceptance find. Amen.

SOURCE OF TEXT: Anonymous Latin hymn of the thirteenth century. SOURCE OF TRANSLATION: Caswall's translation first appeared in his *Lyra Catholica*, London, 1849. The present form relies on other translations, and has been greatly edited and revised. SOURCE OF TUNE: The present tune is an adaptation of a melody which appeared in the Roman Catholic *Gesangbuch* of the Mainz diocese, 1661.

Spread, O Spread, Thou Mighty Word 25

Jonathan Friedrich Bohnmaier, 1774-1841
Tr. Catherine Winkworth, 1829-1878, alt.

GOTT SEI DANK 7.7.7.7.
Freylinghausen's "Gesangbuch," 1704

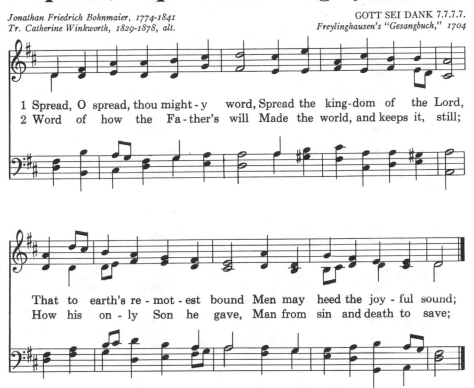

1 Spread, O spread, thou might-y word, Spread the king-dom of the Lord,
2 Word of how the Fa-ther's will Made the world, and keeps it, still;

That to earth's re-mot-est bound Men may heed the joy-ful sound;
How his on-ly Son he gave, Man from sin and death to save;

3 Word of how the Saviour's love
　Earth's sore burden doth remove;
　How for ever, in its need,
　Through his death the world is freed;

4 Mighty word God's Spirit gave,
　Man for heavenly life to save;
　Word through whose all-holy might
　Man can will and do the right;

5 Word of life, most pure and strong,
　Word for which the nations long,
　Spread abroad, until from night
　All the world awakes to light.

SOURCE OF TEXT: Privately printed in 1827, it was published the following year in the *Kern des deutschen Liederschatzes*, Nürnberg, 1828. SOURCE OF TRANSLATION: Winkworth's *Lyra Germanica*, second series, London, 1858. The altered version appearing here was made by Arthur Farlander and Winfred Douglas for *The Hymnal 1940*.

157

26 Sing Praise to God Who Reigns Above

Johann J Schütz, 1640-1690
Tr. Frances E. Cox, 1812-1897

MIT FREUDEN ZART 8.7.8.7.8.8.7.
Bohemian Brethren's "Kirchengesänge," 1566

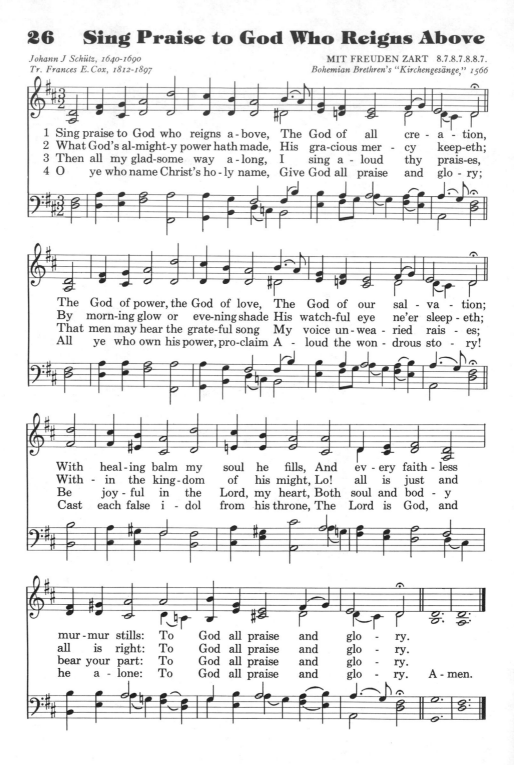

1 Sing praise to God who reigns a-bove, The God of all cre - a - tion,
2 What God's al-might-y power hath made, His gra-cious mer - cy keep-eth;
3 Then all my glad-some way a - long, I sing a - loud thy prais-es,
4 O ye who name Christ's ho-ly name, Give God all praise and glo - ry;

The God of power, the God of love, The God of our sal - va - tion;
By morn-ing glow or eve-ning shade His watch-ful eye ne'er sleep-eth;
That men may hear the grate-ful song My voice un-wea - ried rais - es;
All ye who own his power, pro-claim A - loud the won - drous sto - ry!

With heal-ing balm my soul he fills, And ev - ery faith - less
With - in the king-dom of his might, Lo! all is just and
Be joy - ful in the Lord, my heart, Both soul and bod - y
Cast each false i - dol from his throne, The Lord is God, and

mur - mur stills: To God all praise and glo - ry.
all is right: To God all praise and glo - ry.
bear your part: To God all praise and glo - ry.
he a - lone: To God all praise and glo - ry. A - men.

SOURCE OF TEXT: *Christliches Gedenckbuchlein*, Frankfurt, 1675. SOURCE OF TRANSLATION: *Lyra Eucharistica*, 1864, and in Cox's *Hymns from the German*, the same year. SOURCE OF TUNE: Bohemian Brethren's *Kirchengesänge*, Eibenschütz, Moravia, 1566.

Christian Hearts, in Love United 27

Nicolaus L. von Zinzendorf, 1700-1760
Tr. Frederick W. Foster, 1760-1835

CASSELL, 8.7.8.7.D.
German Melody

1 Chris-tian hearts, in love u-nit-ed, Seek a-lone in Je-sus rest;
2 Come then, come, O flock of Je-sus, Cov-e-nant with Him a-new;
3 Grant, Lord, that with Thy di-rec-tion, "Love each oth-er," we com-ply,
4 O that such may be our u-nion, As Thine with the Fa-ther is,

Has He not your love ex-cit-ed? Then let love in-spire each breast;
Un-to Him, Who con-quered for us, Pledge we love and ser-vice true;
Aim-ing with un-feigned af-fec-tion Thy love to ex-em-pli-fy;
And not one of our com-mun-ion E'er for-sake the path of bliss;

Mem-bers on our Head de-pend-ing Lights re-flect-ing Him, our Sun,
And should our love's u-nion ho-ly Firm-ly linked no more re-main,
Let our mu-tual love be glow-ing, Thus will all men plain-ly see,
May our light 'fore men with bright-ness, From Thy light re-flect-ed, shine;

Breth-ren His com-mands at-tend-ing, We in Him, our Lord, are one.
Wait ye at His foot-stool low-ly, Till He draw it close a-gain.
That we, as on one stem grow-ing, Liv-ing branch-es are in Thee.
Thus the world will bear us wit-ness, That we, Lord, are tru-ly Thine. A-men.

SOURCE OF TEXT: Zinzendorf's *Die letzten Reden unsers Herrn und Heylandes Jesu Christi vor seinem Creutzes-Tode*, Frankfurt and Leipzig, 1725. SOURCE OF TRANSLATION: Foster's translation appeared in the *Moravian Hymn Book*, London, 1789, and was altered to its present form in the 1886 edition. SOURCE OF TUNE: Unknown.

28 Gracious Lord, Our Shepherd and Salvation

Tobias Clausnitzer, 1619-1684
Tr. John Swertner, 1746-1813

COVENANT (MARTER CHRISTI) 10.7.10.7.10.10.7.7.
J. D. Grimm's "Choralbuch," 1755

1 Gra-cious Lord, our Shepherd and Sal - va-tion, In Thy pres-ence we ap - pear;
2 Lord, re-ceive the thanks and ad-o - ra-tion, Which to Thee we hum-bly pay,
3 Chos-en flock, thy faith-ful Shep-herd fol-low, Who laid down His life for thee;

Own us as Thy flock and con-gre-ga-tion, Let us feel that Thou art near:
For our call-ing and pre-des-ti-na-tion, Bless-ed Sav-iour, on this day;
All thy days un-to His ser-vice hal-low, Each His true dis-ci-ple be:

May we all en-joy Thy love and fav-or, And o-bey Thee as our Head and Sav-iour,
Give us grace to walk as Thine annointed, In the path Thou hast for us ap-point-ed;
Ev-er-more re-joice to do His pleasure, Be the full-ness of His grace thy trea-sure;

Who, by Thy most pre-cious blood, Mad'st us, sin-ners, heirs of God.
We de-vote most heart-i-ly Soul and bod-y un-to Thee.
Should suc-cess thy la-bor crown, Give the praise to Him a-lone. A-men.

SOURCE OF TEXT: *Altdorffisches Gesang-Büchlein,* 1663. SOURCE OF TRANSLATION: *Moravian Hymn Book,* London, 1789. SOURCE OF TUNE: It was known and sung at Herrnhut, *c.*1735, and appeared in the manuscript of J. D. Grimm's *Choralbuch,* 1755. The first Moravian collection to include this tune was the *Choralbuch der evangelischen Brüdergemeinen vom Jahr 1778 gehörige Melodien,* Leipzig, 1784.

Jesus Makes My Heart Rejoice 29

Henriette Luise von Hayn, 1724-1783
Tr. Frederick W. Foster, 1760-1835

HAYN 7.7.8.8.7.7.
"Herrnhuter Choralbuch," 1735

1 Je - sus makes my heart re - joice, I'm His sheep, and know his voice;
2 Trust - ing His mild staff al - ways, I go in and out in peace;
3 Should not I for glad - ness leap, Led by Je - sus as his sheep?

He's a Shep-herd, kind and gra-cious, And His past-ures are de - li - cious;
He will feed me with the treas-ure Of His grace in rich - est meas-ure;
For when these blest days are o - ver, To the arms of my dear Sav-iour

Con-stant love to me He shows, Yea, my ve - ry name He knows.
When a - thirst to Him I cry, Liv-ing wa - ter He'll sup - ply.
I shall be con-veyed to rest: A - men, yea, my lot is blest. A-men.

SOURCE OF TEXT: *Gesangbuch zum Gebrauch der evangelischen Brüdergemeinen*, Barby, 1778. SOURCE
OF TRANSLATION: *A Collection of Hymns for the use of the Protestant Church of the United Brethren*,
London, 1789. SOURCE OF TUNE: First appeared in the handwritten manuscript of the *Herrnhuter
Choralbuch*, Herrnhaag, 1735.

30   Jesus, Lead the Way

Nicolaus L. von Zinzendorf, 1700-1760
Tr. Arthur W. Farlander, 1898-1952

SEELENBRAUTIGAM, 5.5.8.8.5.5.
Adam Drese, 1620-1701

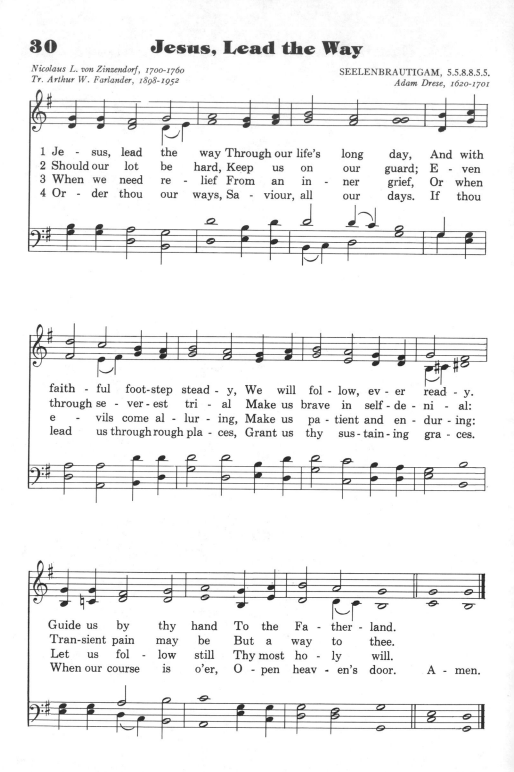

1 Je - sus, lead the way Through our life's long day, And with
2 Should our lot be hard, Keep us on our guard; E - ven
3 When we need re - lief From an in - ner grief, Or when
4 Or - der thou our ways, Sa - viour, all our days. If thou

faith - ful foot-step stead - y, We will fol - low, ev - er read - y.
through se - ver - est tri - al Make us brave in self - de - ni - al:
e - vils come al - lur - ing, Make us pa - tient and en - dur - ing:
lead us through rough pla - ces, Grant us thy sus - tain - ing gra - ces.

Guide us by thy hand To the Fa - ther - land.
Tran - sient pain may be But a way to thee.
Let us fol - low still Thy most ho - ly will.
When our course is o'er, O - pen heav - en's door. A - men.

SOURCE OF TEXT: This composite of two earlier hymns by Zinzendorf first appeared in *Sammlung geistlicher und lieblicher Lieder*, Leipzig, 1725. SOURCE OF TRANSLATION: *The Hymnal 1940*. SOURCE OF TUNE: *Geistreiches Gesangbuch*, Darmstadt, 1698

The Day Thou Gavest, Lord, Is Ended 31

John Ellerton, 1826-1893, alt.

LES COMMANDEMENS DE DIEU 9.8.9.8.
Attr. to Louis Bourgeois, c.1510-c.1561
"Genevan Psalter," 1543

1 The day thou gav - est, Lord, is end - ed,
2 We thank thee that thy Church, un - sleep - ing,
3 As o'er each con - ti - nent and is - land
4 The sun that bids us rest is wak - ing,
5 So be it, Lord; thy throne shall nev - er,

The dark - ness falls at thy be - hest;
While earth rolls on - ward in - to light,
The dawn leads on an - oth - er day,
Our breth - ren 'neath the west - ern sky,
Like earth's proud em - pires, pass a - way;

To thee our morn - ing hymns as - cend - ed,
Through all the world her watch is keep - ing,
The voice of prayer is nev - er si - lent,
And hour by hour fresh lips are mak - ing,
Thy king - dom stands, and grows for - ev - er,

Thy praise shall sanc - ti - fy our rest.
And rests not now by day or night.
Nor dies the strain of praise a - way.
Thy won - drous do - ings heard on high.
Till all thy crea - tures own thy sway. A - men.

SOURCE OF TEXT: *A Liturgy for Missionary Meetings*, 1870. SOURCE OF TUNE: *Genevan Psalter*, 1549. This is the tune used for the Decalogue and Psalm 140. It was included in Ainsworth's *Psalter*, 1612.

32 All People That on Earth Do Dwell

Based on Psalm 100
William Kethe, d. 1608?, alt.

OLD HUNDREDTH L.M.
Attr. to Louis Bourgeois, c.1510-c.1561
"Genevan Psalter," 1551

1 All peo-ple that on earth do dwell, Sing to the Lord with cheer-ful voice;
2 The Lord, ye know, is God in - deed; With - out our aid he did us make;
3 O en - ter then his gates with praise, Ap-proach with joy his courts un - to;
4 For why? the Lord our God is good, His mer - cy is for - ev - er sure;

Him serve with mirth, his praise forth tell, Come ye be-fore him and re-joice.
We are his folk, he doth us feed, And for his sheep he doth us take.
Praise, laud, and bless his name al - ways, For it is seem-ly so to do.
His truth at all times firm - ly stood, And shall from age to age en-dure. A-men.

SOURCE OF TEXT: Day's *Psalter*, London, 1560–1561. SOURCE OF TUNE: *Genevan Psalter*, 1551.

33 Stand Up, and Bless the Lord

James Montgomery, 1771-1854

OLD 134TH (ST. MICHAEL) S.M.
Adapted from "Genevan Psalter," 1551

1 Stand up, and bless the Lord, Ye peo - ple of His choice;
2 Though high a - bove all praise, A - bove all bless - ing high,
3 Oh, for the liv - ing flame From His own al - tar brought,
4 God is our strength and song, And His sal - va - tion ours;
5 Stand up, and bless the Lord; The Lord your God a - dore;

SOURCE OF TEXT: Written in 1824, and first published in Montgomery's *Christian Psalmist*, 1825.
SOURCE OF TUNE: *Genevan Psalter*, 1551.

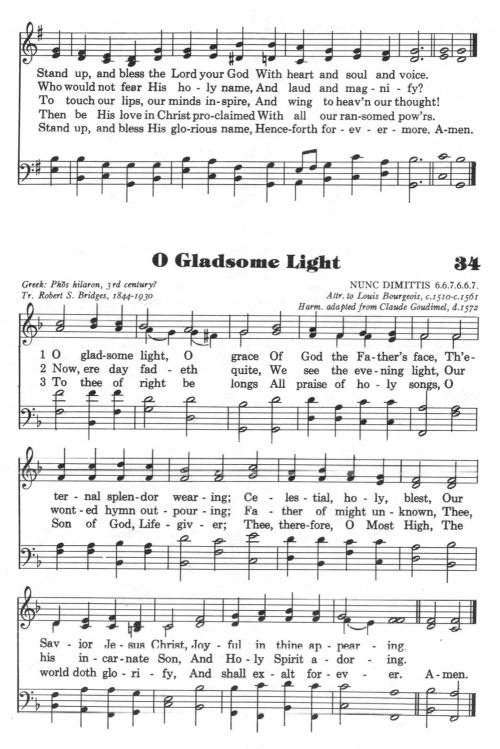

Stand up, and bless the Lord your God With heart and soul and voice.
Who would not fear His ho - ly name, And laud and mag - ni - fy?
To touch our lips, our minds in-spire, And wing to heav'n our thought!
Then be His love in Christ pro-claimed With all our ran-somed pow'rs.
Stand up, and bless His glo-rious name, Hence-forth for - ev - er - more. A-men.

O Gladsome Light 34

Greek: Phōs hilaron, 3rd century?
Tr. Robert S. Bridges, 1844-1930

NUNC DIMITTIS 6.6.7.6.6.7.
Attr. to Louis Bourgeois, c.1510-c.1561
Harm. adapted from Claude Goudimel, d.1572

1 O glad-some light, O grace Of God the Fa-ther's face, Th'e-
2 Now, ere day fad - eth quite, We see the eve-ning light, Our
3 To thee of right be longs All praise of ho - ly songs, O

ter - nal splen-dor wear-ing; Ce - les - tial, ho - ly, blest, Our
wont - ed hymn out - pour - ing; Fa - ther of might un - known, Thee,
Son of God, Life - giv - er; Thee, there-fore, O Most High, The

Sav - ior Je - sus Christ, Joy - ful in thine ap - pear - ing.
his in - car - nate Son, And Ho - ly Spirit a - dor - ing.
world doth glo - ri - fy, And shall ex - alt for - ev - er. A - men.

SOURCE OF TEXT: The earliest printed form of this Greek hymn, probably from the third century, is found in Usher's *De Symbolis*, 1647. SOURCE OF TRANSLATION: *The Yattendon Hymnal*, London, 1899. SOURCE OF TUNE: *Genevan Psalter*, 1549. Goudimel included this tune in his harmonizations of psalm tunes published in 1551.

35 **Hope of the World**

Georgia Harkness, 1891-1974

DONNE SECOURS 11.10.11.10.
"Genevan Psalter," 1551

1 Hope of the world, thou Christ of great com-pas-sion,
2 Hope of the world, God's gift from high-est heav-en,
3 Hope of the world, a-foot on dust-y high-ways,
4 Hope of the world, who by thy cross didst save us
5 Hope of the world, O Christ, o'er death vic-to-rious,

Speak to our fear-ful hearts by con-flict rent.
Bring-ing to hun-gry souls the bread of life,
Show-ing to wan-dering souls the path of light,
From death and dark de-spair, from sin and guilt,
Who by this sign didst con-quer grief and pain,

Save us, thy peo-ple, from con-sum-ing pas-sion,
Still let thy Spir-it un-to us be giv-en
Walk thou be-side us lest the tempt-ing by-ways
We ren-der back the love thy mer-cy gave us;
We would be faith-ful to thy gos-pel glo-rious;

Who by our own false hopes and aims are spent.
To heal earth's wounds and end her bit-ter strife.
Lure us a-way from thee to end-less night.
Take thou our lives and use them as thou wilt.
Thou art our Lord! Thou dost for-ev-er reign! A-men.

SOURCE OF TEXT: *Eleven Ecumenical Hymns*, New York, 1954. Used by permission of The Hymn Society of America. SOURCE OF TUNE: *Genevan Psalter*, 1551.

Comfort, Comfort Ye My People 36

Based on Isaiah 40:1-8
Johannes Olearius, 1611-1684
Tr. Catherine Winkworth, 1827-1878, alt.

PSALM 42 8.7.8.7.7.7.8.8.
"Genevan Psalter," 1551

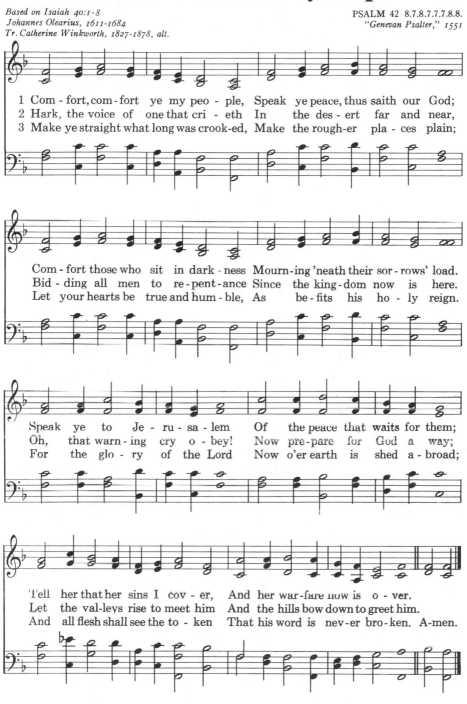

1 Com - fort, com - fort ye my peo - ple, Speak ye peace, thus saith our God;
2 Hark, the voice of one that cri - eth In the des - ert far and near,
3 Make ye straight what long was crook-ed, Make the rough-er pla - ces plain;

Com - fort those who sit in dark - ness Mourn-ing 'neath their sor - rows' load.
Bid - ding all men to re-pent-ance Since the king-dom now is here.
Let your hearts be true and hum - ble, As be - fits his ho - ly reign.

Speak ye to Je - ru - sa - lem Of the peace that waits for them;
Oh, that warn - ing cry o - bey! Now pre-pare for God a way;
For the glo - ry of the Lord Now o'er earth is shed a - broad;

Tell her that her sins I cov - er, And her war-fare now is o - ver.
Let the val-leys rise to meet him And the hills bow down to greet him.
And all flesh shall see the to - ken That his word is nev-er bro-ken. A-men.

SOURCE OF TEXT: *Geistliche Singe-Kunst*, Leipzig, 1671. SOURCE OF TRANSLATION: Winkworth's *Chorale Book for England*, London, 1863. SOURCE OF TUNE: *Genevan Psalter*, 1551.

37 Print Thine Image Pure and Holy

Thomas Hansen Kingo, 1634-1703
Tr. Jens Christian Aaberg, 1877-

PSALM 42 (FREU DICH SEHR) 8.7.8.7.7.7.8.8.
"Genevan Psalter," 1551
Adapted and harmonized by J. S. Bach, 1685-1750

Print Thine im-age pure and ho-ly On my heart, O
So that noth-ing high or low-ly Thy blest like-ness

Lord of Grace;
can ef-face, Let the clear in-scrip-tion be:

Je-sus, cru-ci-fied for me, And the Lord of all cre-a-

tion, Be my ref-uge and sal-va-tion. A-men.

SOURCE OF TEXT: *Danmarks og Norges Kirkers forordnede Salmebog* (The Authorized Hymn Book of the Churches of Denmark and Norway), 1689. SOURCE OF TUNE: *Genevan Psalter*, 1551. Bach's adaptation and harmonization appeared in *Vierstimmige Choralgesänge*, Leipzig, 1769.

168

Lord Jesus, Think on Me

Synesius of Cyrene, c.375-430
Tr. Allen W. Chatfield, 1808-1896, alt.

SOUTHWELL S.M.
Adapted from Damon's "Psalmes" 1579

38

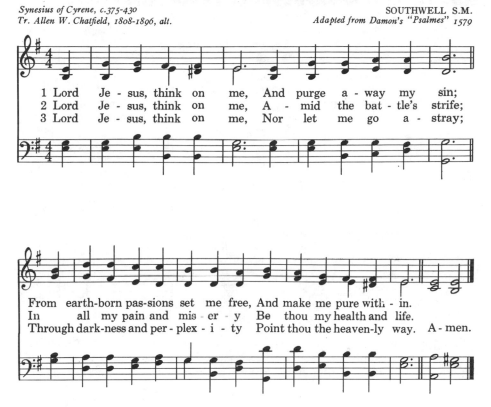

1 Lord Je - sus, think on me, And purge a - way my sin;
2 Lord Je - sus, think on me, A - mid the bat - tle's strife;
3 Lord Je - sus, think on me, Nor let me go a - stray;

From earth-born pas-sions set me free, And make me pure with - in.
In all my pain and mis - er - y Be thou my health and life.
Through dark-ness and per - plex - i - ty Point thou the heaven-ly way. A - men.

4 Lord Jesus, think on me,
That, when this life is past,
I may the eternal brightness see,
And share thy joy at last.

SOURCE OF TEXT: Written early in the fifth century, this is the last of the ten hymns of Synesius, Bishop of Cyrene. SOURCE OF TRANSLATION: Chatfield's *Songs and Hymns of Earliest Greek Christian Poets, Bishops, and others, translated into English verse*, London, 1876. SOURCE OF TUNE: William Damon's *Psalmes*, London, 1579.

39 Lord, Who Throughout These Forty Days

Claudia F. Hernaman, 1838-1898

ST. FLAVIAN C.M.
"Day's Psalter," 1562

1 Lord, who through-out these for - ty days For us didst fast and pray,
2 As thou with Sa - tan didst con - tend, And didst the vic - tory win,
3 And through these days of pen - i - tence, And through thy pas - sion - tide,
4 A - bide with us, that so, this life Of suf-fering o - ver-past,

Teach us with thee to mourn our sins, And close by thee to stay.
O give us strength in thee to fight, In thee to con - quer sin.
Yea, ev - er - more, in life and death, Je - sus! with us a - bide.
An East-er of un - end - ing joy We may at - tain at last! A-men.

SOURCE OF TEXT: Hernaman's *Child's Book of Praise*, London, 1873. SOURCE OF TUNE: Day's *Psalter*, 1562. In its present form it first appeared in Richard Redhead's *Ancient Hymn Melodies*, London, 1853.

40 When All Thy Mercies, O My God

Joseph Addison, 1672-1719

TALLIS' ORDINAL C.M.
Thomas Tallis, d.1585

1 When all thy mer-cies, O my God, My ris - ing soul sur-veys, Trans-
2 Un - num-bered com-forts to my soul Thy ten - der care be-stowed, Be -
3 Ten thou-sand thou-sand pre-cious gifts My dai - ly thanks em-ploy; Nor
4 Through all e - ter - ni - ty to thee A joy - ful song I'll raise; For,

SOURCE OF TEXT: *The Spectator*, London, August 9, 1712. SOURCE OF TUNE: Parker's *Psalter*, London, c.1560.

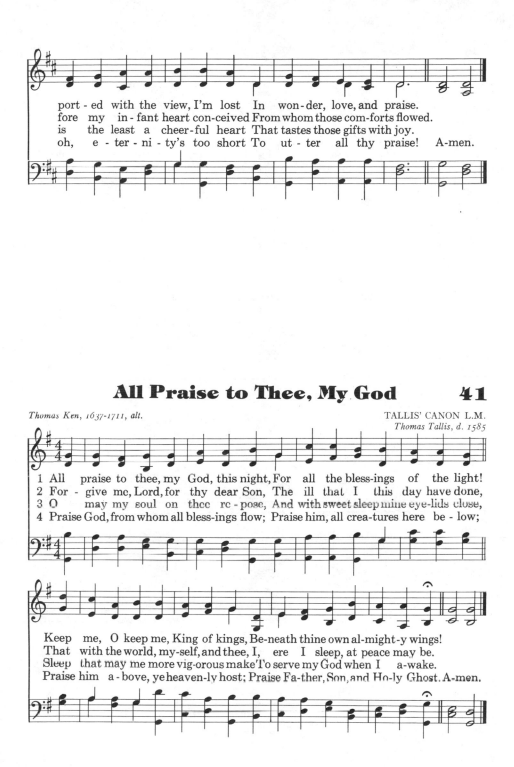

port - ed with the view, I'm lost In won - der, love, and praise.
fore my in - fant heart con-ceived From whom those com-forts flowed.
is the least a cheer-ful heart That tastes those gifts with joy.
oh, e - ter - ni - ty's too short To ut - ter all thy praise! A-men.

All Praise to Thee, My God 41

Thomas Ken, 1637-1711, alt.

TALLIS' CANON L.M.
Thomas Tallis, d. 1585

1 All praise to thee, my God, this night, For all the bless-ings of the light!
2 For - give me, Lord, for thy dear Son, The ill that I this day have done,
3 O may my soul on thee re - pose, And with sweet sleep mine eye-lids close,
4 Praise God, from whom all bless-ings flow; Praise him, all crea-tures here be - low;

Keep me, O keep me, King of kings, Be-neath thine own al-might-y wings!
That with the world, my-self, and thee, I, ere I sleep, at peace may be.
Sleep that may me more vig-orous make To serve my God when I a-wake.
Praise him a - bove, ye heaven-ly host; Praise Fa-ther, Son, and Ho-ly Ghost. A-men.

SOURCE OF TEXT: Ken's *A Manuel of Prayers*, London, 1674. SOURCE OF TUNE: Parker's *Psalter*, London, c.1560.

42   God Moves in a Mysterious Way

William Cowper, 1731-1800

DUNDEE C.M.
"*Scottish Psalter,*" 1615

1 God moves in a mys - te - rious way   His won-ders to per - form;
2 Ye fear - ful saints, fresh cour-age take;   The clouds ye so much dread
3 Judge not the Lord by fee - ble sense,   But trust him for his grace;
4 Blind un - be - lief is sure to err,   And scan his work in vain;

He plants his foot-steps in the sea   And rides up - on the storm.
Are big with mer - cy, and shall break In   bless-ings on your head.
Be - hind a frown-ing prov - i - dence He   hides a smil-ing face.
God is his own in - ter - pret - er,   And he will make it plain. A-men.

SOURCE OF TEXT: Cowper's *Twenty-six Letters on Religious Subjects; to which are added Hymns,* London, 1774. SOURCE OF TUNE: *Scottish Psalter,* 1615.

43   God Moves in a Mysterious Way

William Cowper, 1731-1800

LONDON NEW, C.M.
"*Scottish Psalter*" 1635

1 God moves in a mys - te - rious way   His won-ders to per - form;
2 Ye fear - ful saints, fresh cour - age take;   The clouds ye so much dread
3 Judge not the Lord by fee - ble sense,   But trust him for his grace;
4 Blind un - be - lief is sure to err,   And scan his work in vain;

SOURCE OF TEXT: Cowper's *Twenty-six Letters on Religious Subjects; to which are added Hymns,* London, 1774. SOURCE OF TUNE: *Scottish Psalter,* 1635.

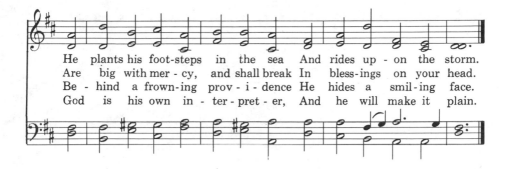

He plants his foot-steps in the sea And rides up-on the storm.
Are big with mer-cy, and shall break In bless-ings on your head.
Be-hind a frown-ing prov-i-dence He hides a smil-ing face.
God is his own in-ter-pret-er, And he will make it plain.

O for a Closer Walk with God   44

William Cowper, 1731-1800

CAITHNESS C.M.
"Scottish Psalter," 1635

1 O   for a clos-er walk with God, A   calm and heaven-ly frame,
2 Where is the bless-ed-ness I   knew When first I   saw the Lord?
3 Re-turn, O ho-ly dove, re-turn, Sweet mes-sen-ger of rest!
4 The dear-est i-dol I have known, What-e'er that i-dol be,
5 So   shall my walk be close with God, Calm and se-rene my frame;

A   light to shine up-on the road That leads me to the Lamb!
Where is the soul-re-fresh-ing view Of Je-sus and his word?
I   hate the sins that made thee mourn And drove thee from my breast.
Help me to tear it from thy throne, And wor-ship on-ly thee.
So   pur-er light shall mark the road That leads me to the Lamb. A-men.

SOURCE OF TEXT: Conyers's *Collection of Psalms and Hymns*, London, 1772. SOURCE OF TUNE: *Scottish Psalter*, 1635.

45 Ye Servants of God, Your Master Proclaim

Charles Wesley, 1707-1788

HANOVER 10.10.11.11.
William Croft, 1678-1727

1 Ye serv-ants of God, your Mas-ter pro-claim,
2 God rul-eth on high, al-might-y to save,
3 Sal-va-tion to God who sits on the throne!
4 Then let us a-dore and give him his right,

And pub-lish a-broad his won-der-ful name.
And still he is nigh, his pres-ence we have;
Let all cry a-loud and hon-or the Son;
All glo-ry and power, all wis-dom and might,

The name, all vic-to-rious, of Je-sus ex-tol;
The great con-gre-ga-tion his tri-umph shall sing,
The prais-es of Je-sus the an-gels pro-claim,
All hon-or and bless-ing with an-gels a-bove,

His king-dom is glo-rious, he rules o-ver all.
As-crib-ing sal-va-tion to Je-sus, our King.
Fall down on their fa-ces and wor-ship the Lamb.
And thanks nev-er ceas-ing and in-fi-nite love. A-men.

SOURCE OF TEXT: *Hymns for Times of Trouble and Persecution*, London, 1744. SOURCE OF TUNE: *Supplement to the New Version*, London, 1708.

174

Thine Arm, O Lord, in Days of Old   46

Edward H. Plumptre, 1821-1891

ST. MATTHEW C.M.D.
William Croft

1 Thine arm, O Lord, in days of old Was strong to heal and save;
2 And lo, Thy touch brought life and health, Gave speech, and strength, and sight;
3 Be Thou our great De - liv - erer still, Thou Lord of life and death;

It tri-umphed o'er dis - ease and death, O'er dark-ness and the grave.
And youth re - newed and fren - zy calmed Owned Thee, the Lord of light.
Re - store and quick-en, soothe and bless With Thine al - might - y breath.

To Thee they went, the blind, the dumb, The pal - sied and the lame,
And now, O Lord, be near to bless, Al - might - y as of yore,
To hands that work and eyes that see, Give wis - dom's heaven-ly lore,

The lep - er with his taint-ed life, The sick with fe - vered frame.
In crowd-ed street, by rest-less couch, As by Gen nes-aret's shore.
That whole and sick, and weak and strong, May praise Thee ev - er - more. A-men.

SOURCE OF TEXT: Written in 1864 and first published in leaflet form. Its first hymnal inclusion was in the Appendix to *Hymns Ancient and Modern*, London, 1868. SOURCE OF TUNE: *Supplement to the New Version*, London, 1708.

Latin, 12th century
Tr. Edward Caswall, 1814-1878, alt.

KING'S NORTON C.M.
Jeremiah Clark, 1670-1707

1 Je - sus, the ver - y thought of thee
2 Nor voice can sing, nor heart can frame,
3 O hope of ev - ery con - trite heart,

With sweet-ness fills my breast; But sweet - er far thy
Nor can the mem - ory find, A sweet - er sound than
O joy of all the meek, To those who fall, how

face to see, And in thy pres - ence rest.
thy blest name, O Sav - iour of man - kind!
kind thou art! How good to those who seek!

SOURCE OF TEXT: Anonymous Latin hymn of the twelfth century, sometimes ascribed to Bernard of Clairvaux. SOURCE OF TRANSLATION: Caswall's *Lyra Catholica*, London, 1849. SOURCE OF TUNE: Playford's *The Divine Companion*, London, 1707.

48 The Head That Once Was Crowned with Thorns

Thomas Kelly, 1769-1855

ST. MAGNUS C.M.
Jeremiah Clark, c.1670-1707

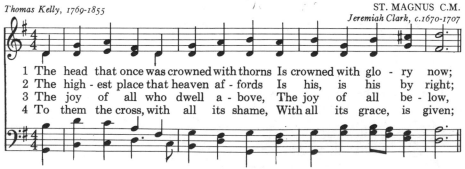

1 The head that once was crowned with thorns Is crowned with glo - ry now;
2 The high - est place that heaven af - fords Is his, is his by right;
3 The joy of all who dwell a - bove, The joy of all be - low,
4 To them the cross, with all its shame, With all its grace, is given;

SOURCE OF TEXT: Kelly's *Hymns on Various Passages of Scripture*, Dublin, fifth edition, 1820. SOURCE OF TUNE: Playford's *The Divine Companion*, London, 1707.

A roy-al di-a-dem a-dorns The might-y vic-tor's brow.
The King of kings, and Lord of lords, And heaven's e-ter-nal light.
To whom he man-i-fests his love, And grants his name to know.
Their name an ev-er-last-ing name, Their joy the joy of heaven. A-men.

Immortal Love, Forever Full 49

John Greenleaf Whittier, 1807-1892

BISHOPTHORPE C.M.
Jeremiah Clark, 1670-1707

1 Im - mor - tal Love, for - ev - er full, For
2 Our out - ward lips con - fess - the Name All

ev - er flow - ing free, For - ev - er shared, for -
oth - er names a - bove; Love on - ly know - eth

ev - er whole, A nev - er - ebb - ing sea!
whence it came, And com - pre - hend - eth love.

3 We may not climb the heavenly steps
    To bring the Lord Christ down;
In vain we search the lowest deeps,
    For him no depths can drown:

4 But warm, sweet, tender, even yet
    A present help is he;
And faith has still its Olivet,
    And love its Galilee.

5 The healing of his seamless dress
    Is by our beds of pain;

We touch him in life's throng and press,
    And we are whole again.

6 Through him the first fond prayers are said
    Our lips of childhood frame;
The last low whispers of our dead
    Are burdened with his Name.

7 O Lord, and Master of us all,
    What'er our name or sign,
We own thy sway, we hear thy call,
    We test our lives by thine.

SOURCE OF TEXT: From the poem, "Our Master,'" which appeared in *Tent on the Beach and other Poems*, 1867. SOURCE OF TUNE: H. Gardner's *Select Portions of the Psalms of David*, c.1780.

50 Eternal Ruler of the Ceaseless Round

John W. Chadwick, 1840-1904

SONG 1 10.10.10.10.10.10.
Orlando Gibbons, 1583-1625

1 E-ter-nal Rul-er of the cease-less round Of cir-cling
2 We are of thee, the chil-dren of thy love, The broth-ers
3 We would be one in ha-tred of all wrong, One in our

plan-ets sing-ing on their way, Guide of the na - tions
of thy well-be-lov-ed Son; De-scend, O Ho - ly
love of all things sweet and fair, One with the joy that

from the night pro-found In - to the glo - ry of the
Spir - it, like a dove In - to our hearts, that we may
break-eth in - to song, One with the grief that trem-bleth

per - fect day, Rule in our hearts, that we may ev - er
be as one: As one with thee, to whom we ev - er
in - to prayer, One in the power that makes the chil - dren

SOURCE OF TEXT: Written 1864, and first published in Chadwick's *A Book of Poems*, 1876. The first hymnal inclusion was Garrett Horder's *Congregational Hymns*, London, 1884. SOURCE OF TUNE: George Wither's *Hymnes and Songs of the Church*, London, 1623.

be Guid-ed and strength-ened and up-held by thee.
tend; As one with him, our broth-er and our friend.
free To fol-low truth, and thus to fol-low thee. A-men.

Forth in Thy Name, O Lord, I Go 51

Charles Wesley, 1707-1788

ANGEL'S SONG (SONG 34) L.M.
Orlando Gibbons, 1583-1625

1 Forth in Thy Name, O Lord, I go, My dai-ly
2 The task thy wis-dom hath as-signed, O, let me
3 Thee may I set at my right hand, Whose eyes my
4 Give Me to bear Thy eas-y yoke, And ev-ery
5 For thee de-light-ful-ly em-ploy What-e'er Thy

la-bor to pur-sue, Thee, on-ly Thee, re-solved to
cheer-ful-ly ful-fill; In all my works Thy pres-ence
in-most sub-stance see, And la-bor on at Thy com-
mo-ment watch and pray, And still to things e-ter-nal
boun-teous grace hath given, And run my course with ev-en

know In all I think, or speak, or do.
find, And prove Thy good and per-fect will.
mand, And of-fer all my works to Thee.
look, And has-ten to Thy glo-rious day;
joy, And close-ly walk with Thee to heaven. A-men.

SOURCE OF TEXT: *Hymns and Sacred Poems*, London, 1749. SOURCE OF TUNE: George Wither's *Hymnes and Songs of the Church*, London, 1623.

52 Before Jehovah's Aweful Throne

Based on Psalm 100
Isaac Watts, 1674-1748
Alt. by John Wesley, 1703-1791

WINCHESTER NEW L.M.
Adapted from
"Musicalisches Handbuch," Hamburg, 1690

1 Be - fore Je - ho - vah's awe - ful throne, Ye na - tions bow with sa - cred joy; Know that the Lord is God a - lone, He can cre - ate, and he de - stroy.

2 His sov - ereign power with - out our aid, Made us of clay, and formed us men; And when, like wan - dering sheep, we strayed, He brought us to his fold a - gain.

3 We are his peo - ple, we his care, Our souls, and all our mor - tal frame; What last - ing hon - ors shall we rear, Al - might - y Mak - er, to thy name?

4 We'll crowd thy gates with thank - ful songs, High as the heavens our voic - es raise; And earth, with her ten thou-sand tongues, Shall fill thy courts with sound - ing praise.

5 Wide as the world is thy com - mand, Vast as e - ter - ni - ty thy love; Firm as a rock thy truth must stand, When roll - ing years shall cease to move. A - men.

SOURCE OF TEXT: Watts's *Psalms of David, Imitated in the Language of the New Testament, and apply'd to the Christian State and Worship,* London, 1719. John Wesley altered this hymn for his *Collection of Psalms and Hymns,* Charlestown, 1737. SOURCE OF TUNE: *Musicalisches Handbuch der geistlichen Melodien,* Hamburg, 1690. It was one of the German tunes adapted for the *Foundery Collection,* 1742, and was first called WINCHESTER in Moore's *Psalm-Singer's Delightful Pocket-Companion,* Glasgow, 1762. The present version is from Havergal's *Old Church Psalmody,* London, 1847.

Rise, My Soul, and Stretch Thy Wings **53**

Robert Seagrave, 1693-1759? alt.

AMSTERDAM 7.6.7.6.7.7.7.6.
German chorale
In The Foundery Collection, 1742

1 Rise, my soul, and stretch thy wings, Thy bet - ter por - tion trace;
2 Riv - ers to the o - cean run, Nor stay in all their course;
3 Cease, my soul, then, cease to mourn, Press on - ward to the prize;

Rise from tran - si - to - ry things Toward heaven, thy des - tined place.
Fire as - cend - ing seeks the sun; Both speed them to their source:
Soon the Sav - iour will re - turn Tri - um - phant in the skies:

Sun and moon and stars de - cay, Time shall soon this earth re - move;
So my soul, de - rived from God, Longs to view His glo - rious face,
Yet a sea - son, and we know Hap - py en - trance will be given,

Rise, my soul, and haste a - way To seats pre - pared a - bove.
For - ward tends to His a - bode, To rest in His em - brace.
All our sor - rows left be - low, And earth ex - changed for heaven. A - men.

SOURCE OF TEXT: Seagrave's *Hymns for Christian Worship*, London, 1742. SOURCE OF TUNE: This is one of six tunes which John Wesley adapted from Freylinghausen's *Geistriches Gesangbuch*, Halle, 1704, for his *Foundery Collection*, London, 1742.

54   Christ the Lord Is Risen Today

Charles Wesley, 1707-1788, alt.

EASTER HYMN 7.7.7.7. *with Alleluias*
Arr. from "Lyra Davidica," 1708

1 Christ the Lord is risen to-day,
2 Lives a-gain our glo-rious King,
3 Love's re-deem-ing work is done, Al — le-lu — ia!
4 Soar we now, where Christ has led,
5 Hail the Lord of earth and heaven!

Sons of men and an-gels say:
Where, O death, is now thy sting?
Fought the fight, the bat-tle won, Al — le-lu — ia!
Fol-lowing our ex-alt-ed Head,
Praise to thee by both be given,

Raise your joys and tri-umphs high,
Dy-ing once, he all doth save,
Death in vain for-bids him rise, Al — le-lu — ia!
Made like him, like him we rise,
Thee we greet tri-um-phant now,

Sing, ye heavens, and earth re — ply:
Where thy vic-to — ry, O grave?
Christ has o-pened Par-a-dise, Al — le-lu — ia!
Ours the cross, the grave, the skies,
Hail, the Res-ur-rec-tion thou!

A-men.

SOURCE OF TEXT: *Hymns and Sacred Poems*, London, 1739. SOURCE OF TUNE: *Lyra Davidica*, London, 1708.

The God of Abraham Praise 55

Revised Version of the Yigdal
Daniel ben Judah, c.1400
Tr. Thomas Olivers, 1725-1799

LEONI 6.6.8.4.D.
Traditional Hebrew Melody
Adapted by Meyer Lyon, 1751-1797

1 The God of A-braham praise, Who reigns en-throned a-bove;
2 He by him-self hath sworn: I on his oath de-pend;
3 There dwells the Lord, our King, The Lord our Right-eous-ness,

An-cient of ev-er-last-ing days, And God of love;
I shall, on ea-gle-wings up-borne, To heav'n as-cend:
Tri-umph-ant o'er the world and sin, The Prince of Peace;

To him up-lift your voice, At whose su-preme com-mand,
I shall be-hold his face, I shall his power a-dore,
On Si-on's sa-cred height His king-dom he main-tains,

From earth we rise, and seek the joys At his right hand.
And sing the won-ders of his grace For ev-er-more.
And, glo-rious with his saints in light, For ev-er reigns. A-men.

4 The God who reigns on high
  The great archangels sing,
And "Holy, Holy, Holy," cry,
  "Almighty King!

Who was, and is, the same,
  And evermore shall be:
Eternal Father, great I AM,
  We worship thee."

SOURCE OF TEXT AND TUNE: First appeared in a tract, *A Hymn to the God of Abraham*, London, c.1770. It is a paraphrase of the Hebrew Yigdal, or doxology, dating from the thirteenth or fourteenth century. The traditional Hebrew melody was transcribed and introduced in London's Great Synagogue by Meyer Lyon (Leoni), 1751–1797. The first hymnal inclusion was John Wesley's *The Pocket Hymn-book*, London, 1785.

56 Alone Thou Goest Forth, O Lord

Peter Abelard, 1079-1142
Tr. F. Bland Tucker, 1895-

BANGOR C.M.
William Tans'ur, 1706?-1783

1 A-lone thou go-est forth, O Lord, In sac-ri-fice to die;
2 Our sins, not thine, thou bear-est, Lord, Make us thy sor-row feel,
3 This is earth's dark-est hour, but thou Dost light and life re-store;
4 Give us com-pas-sion for thee, Lord, That, as we share this hour,

Is this thy sor-row naught to us Who pass un-heed-ing by?
Till through our pit-y and our shame Love an-swers love's ap-peal.
Then let all praise be giv-en thee Who liv-est ev-er-more.
Thy cross may bring us to thy joy And res-ur-rec-tion power. A-men.

SOURCE OF TEXT: Abelard's *Hymnarius Paraclitensis.* SOURCE OF TRANSLATION: *The Hymnal 1940.*
SOURCE OF TUNE: Tans'ur's *A Compleat Harmony of Syon,* London, 1734.

57 Am I a Soldier of the Cross

Issac Watts, 1674-1748

ARLINGTON C.M.
Thomas A. Arne, 1710-1778

1 Am I a sol-dier of the cross, A fol-low-er of the Lamb?
2 Must I be car-ried to the skies On flow-er-y beds of ease,
3 Are there no foes for me to face? Must I not stem the flood?
4 Sure I must fight if I would reign; In-crease my cour-age, Lord;

SOURCE OF TEXT: First appeared in Watts's *Sermons,* 1721–24, at the conclusion of a sermon based on
I Corinthians 16:13. SOURCE OF TUNE: Taken from a theme in the overture to Arne's opera, *Artaxerxes,*
1762. First appeared as a hymn tune in Ralph Harrison's *Sacred Harmony,* Vol. I, London, 1784.

And shall I fear to own His cause, Or blush to speak His name?
While oth - ers fought to win the prize, And sailed through blood-y seas?
Is this vile world a friend to grace, To help me on to God?
I'll bear the toil, en - dure the pain, Sup - port - ed by Thy Word. A-men.

Alas, and Did My Saviour Bleed 58

Issac Watts, 1674-1748

AVON (MARTYRDOM) C.M.
Hugh Wilson, 1764-1824

1 A - las, and did my Sav - iour bleed And did my Sov-'reign die?
2 Was it for crimes that I have done He groaned up - on the tree?
3 Well might the sun in dark-ness hide, And shut his glo - ries in,
4 But drops of grief can ne'er re - pay The debt of love I owe;

Would he de - vote that sa-cred head For sin - ners such as I?
A - maz-ing pit - y, grace unknown, And love be - yond de - gree!
When Christ the might-y Mak-er died For man the crea-ture's sin.
Here, Lord, I give my-self a - way, 'Tis all that I can do. A-men.

SOURCE OF TEXT: Watts's *Hymns and Spiritual Songs*, London, 1707. SOURCE OF TUNE: First printed in leaflets near the end of the eighteenth century for use in music classes. It was originally in duple or common time. In triple time it appeared as an anonymous tune in R. A. Smith's *Sacred Music Sung in St. George's Church, Edinburgh*, second edition, 1825. In Robertson's *The Seraph*, Glasgow, 1827, Wilson is given as composer. However, it is possible that Wilson adapted this from an old Scottish melody.

59 All Hail the Power of Jesus' Name

Edward Perronet, 1726-1792
Alt. by John Rippon, 1751-1836

MILES LANE C.M.
William Shrubsole, 1760-1806

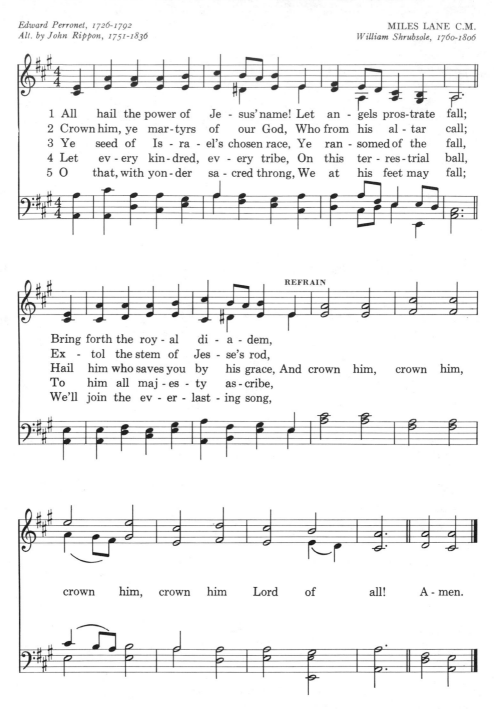

1 All hail the power of Je - sus' name! Let an - gels pros-trate fall;
2 Crown him, ye mar-tyrs of our God, Who from his al - tar call;
3 Ye seed of Is - ra - el's chosen race, Ye ran - somed of the fall,
4 Let ev - ery kin - dred, ev - ery tribe, On this ter - res - trial ball,
5 O that, with yon - der sa - cred throng, We at his feet may fall;

REFRAIN

Bring forth the roy - al di - a - dem,
Ex - tol the stem of Jes - se's rod,
Hail him who saves you by his grace, And crown him, crown him,
To him all maj - es - ty as - cribe,
We'll join the ev - er - last - ing song,

crown him, crown him Lord of all! A - men.

SOURCE OF TEXT: *The Gospel Magazine*, VI, November 1779. Altered by John Rippon for his *Selection of Hymns*, London, 1787. SOURCE OF TUNE: *The Gospel Magazine*, VI, November 1779.

Jesus Shall Reign Where'er the Sun 60

Isaac Watts, 1674-1748

DUKE STREET L.M.
John Hatton, d.1793

1 Je - sus shall reign wher - e'er the sun Doth his suc -
2 For him shall end - less prayer be made, And prais - es
3 Peo - ple and realms of ev - ery tongue Dwell on his

ces - sive jour - neys run; His king - dom stretch from
throng to crown his head; His name like sweet per -
love with sweet - est song, And in - fant voic - es

shore to shore Till moons shall wax and wane no more.
fume shall rise With ev - ery morn - ing sac - ri - fice.
shall pro - claim Their ear - ly bless - ings on his name. A-men.

4 Blessings abound where'er he reigns;
   The prisoner leaps to lose his chains,
   The weary find eternal rest,
   And all the sons of want are blest.

5 Let every creature rise and bring
   Peculiar honors to our King;
   Angels descend with songs again,
   And earth repeat the loud Amen.

SOURCE OF TEXT: Watts's *Psalms of David*, London, 1719. SOURCE OF TUNE: Henry Boyd's *A Select Collection of Psalms and Hymn Tunes*, Glasgow, 1793.

61 Where Cross the Crowded Ways of Life

Frank Mason North, 1850-1935

GERMANY L.M.
Gardiner's "Sacred Melodies," 1815

1 Where cross the crowd-ed ways of life, Where sound the
2 In haunts of wretch-ed - ness and need, On shad-owed
3 From ten-der child-hood's help - less - ness, From wom-an's
4 The cup of wa - ter given for thee Still holds the

cries of race and clan, A-bove the noise of self-ish
thresh-olds dark with fears, From paths where hide the lures of
grief, man's bur - dened toil, From fam-ished souls, from sor-rows'
fresh - ness of thy grace; Yet long these mul - ti-tudes to

strife, We hear thy voice, O Son of man.
greed, We catch the vi - sion of thy tears.
stress, Thy heart has nev - er known re - coil.
see The sweet com - pas - sion of thy face. A - men.

5 O Master, from the mountain side,
    Make haste to heal these hearts of pain;
  Among these restless throngs abide,
    O tread the city's streets again,

6 Till sons of men shall learn thy love,
    And follow where thy feet have trod,
  Till glorious from thy heaven above,
    Shall come the city of our God.

SOURCE OF TEXT: *The Christian City*, XV, June 1903. The first hymnal inclusion was in *The Methodist Hymnal*, 1905. SOURCE OF TUNE: William Gardiner's *Sacred Melodies*, London, 1815.

Glorious Things of Thee Are Spoken 62

John Newton, 1725-1807

AUSTRIAN HYMN 8.7.8.7.D.
Franz J. Haydn, 1732-1809

1 Glo-rious things of thee are spo-ken, Zi - on, cit - y of our God;
2 See, the streams of liv - ing wa - ters, Springing from e - ter - nal love,
3 Round each hab - i - ta - tion hov-ering, See the cloud and fire ap - pear

He whose word can-not be bro - ken Formed thee for his own a - bode.
Well sup-ply thy sons and daughters, And all fear of want re - move.
For a glo - ry and a covering, Show - ing that the Lord is near!

On the Rock of A - ges founded, What can shake thy sure re - pose?
Who can faint, while such a riv - er Ev - er flows their thirst to as-suage?
Thus de - riv - ing from their ban - ner Light by night and shade by day,

With sal-va-tion's walls surrounded, Thou may'st smile at all thy foes.
Grace, which like the Lord, the Giver, Nev - er fails from age to age.
Safe they feed up - on the man-na Which he gives them when they pray. A-men.

SOURCE OF TEXT: *The Olney Hymns*, London, 1779. SOURCE OF TUNE: Haydn composed this tune, based on a Croatian folk song, for the national hymn of Austria, and it was first sung on the birthday of the emperor, Francis II, February 12, 1797. Its first hymnal inclusion was in Edward Miller's *Sacred Music*, London, 1802.

189

63 O Worship the King, All Glorious Above

Based on Psalm 104
Robert Grant, 1779-1838, alt.

LYONS 10.10.11.11.
Arr. from J. Michael Haydn ?, 1737-1806

1 O wor - ship the King, all glo - rious a - bove,
2 O tell of his might, O sing of his grace,
3 The earth with its store of won - ders un - told,
4 Thy boun - ti - ful care, what tongue can re - cite?
5 Frail chil - dren of dust, and fee - ble as frail,

O grate - ful - ly sing his power and his love;
Whose robe is the light, whose can - o - py space;
Al - might - y, thy power hath found - ed of old,
It breathes in the air, it shines in the light;
In thee do we trust, nor find thee to fail;

Our Shield and De - fend - er, the An - cient of Days,
His char - iots of wrath the deep thun - der - clouds form,
Hath stab - lished it fast by a change - less de - cree,
It streams from the hills, it de - scends to the plain,
Thy mer - cies how ten - der, how firm to the end,

Pa - vil - ioned in splen - dor, and gird - ed with praise.
And dark is his path on the wings of the storm.
And round it hath cast, like a man - tle, the sea.
And sweet - ly dis - tills in the dew and the rain.
Our Ma - ker, De - fend - er, Re - deem - er, and Friend! A - men.

SOURCE OF TEXT: Bickersteth's *Christian Psalmody*, London, 1833. SOURCE OF TUNE: William Gardiner's *Sacred Melodies*, London, 1815, where it is attributed to Haydn. Its first appearance in America was in Oliver Shaw's *Sacred Melodies*, Providence, 1818.

The Light of God Is Falling   64

Louis F. Benson, 1855-1930

GREENLAND 7.6.7.6.D.
Ascribed to J. Michael Haydn, 1737-1806

1 The light of God is fall-ing Up-on life's com-mon way;
2 Who shares his life's pure pleas-ures, And walks the hon-est road,
3 Where hu-man lives are throng-ing In toil and pain and sin,
4 Thy ran-somed host in glo-ry, All souls that sin and pray,

The Mas-ter's voice still call-ing, "Come, walk with Me to-day";
Who trades with heap-ing meas-ures, And lifts his broth-er's load,
While clois-tered hearts are long-ing To bring the King-dom in,
Turn toward the cross that bore Thee; "Be-hold the Man!" they say;

No du-ty can seem low-ly To him who lives with Thee,
Who turns the wrong down blunt-ly, And lends the right a hand,
O Christ, the Eld-er Broth-er Of proud and beat-en men,
And while Thy Church is plead-ing For all who would do good,

And all of life grows ho-ly, O Christ of Gal-i-lee!
He dwells in God's own coun-try, He tills the Ho-ly Land.
When they have found each oth-er, Thy King-dom will come then!
We hear Thy true voice lead-ing Our song of broth-er-hood. A-men.

SOURCE OF TEXT: *Westminster Hymnal*, Philadelphia, 1911, and the same year in the Presbyterian *Hymnal*. SOURCE OF TUNE: Ascribed to Haydn in Benjamin Jacob's *National Psalmody*, London, 1819. Jacob apparently took the tune from Latrobe's *Selection of Sacred Music from the Works of the Most Eminent Composers of Germany and Italy*, Vol. I, 1806, where it is noted that this tune is "from one of J. M. Haydn's 'Services for Country Churches.'"

65 All Hail the Power of Jesus' Name

Edward Perronet, 1726-1792
Alt. by John Rippon, 1751-1836

DIADEM C.M.
James Ellor, 1819-1899

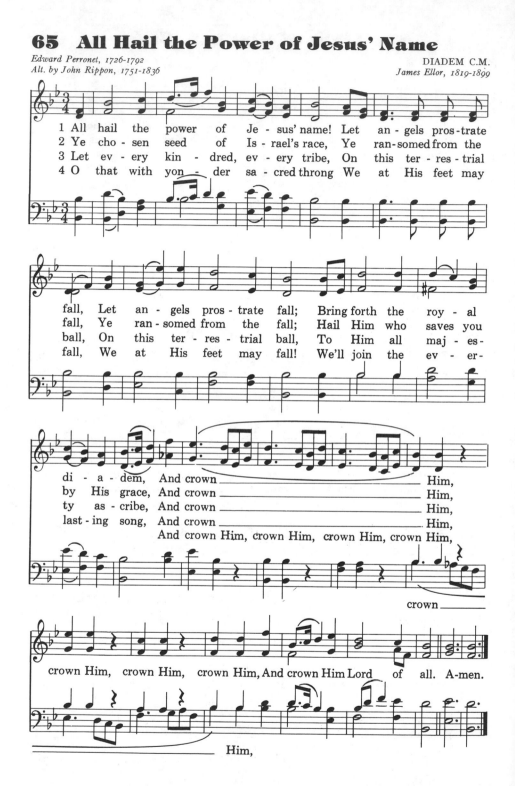

1 All hail the power of Je-sus' name! Let an-gels pros-trate fall, Let an-gels pros-trate fall; Bring forth the roy-al di-a-dem, And crown _____ Him, crown Him, crown Him, crown Him, And crown Him Lord of all. A-men.

2 Ye cho-sen seed of Is-rael's race, Ye ran-somed from the fall, Ye ran-somed from the fall; Hail Him who saves you by His grace, And crown _____ Him,

3 Let ev-ery kin-dred, ev-ery tribe, On this ter-res-trial ball, On this ter-res-trial ball, To Him all maj-es-ty as-cribe, And crown _____ Him,

4 O that with yon-der sa-cred throng We at His feet may fall, We at His feet may fall! We'll join the ev-er-last-ing song, And crown _____ Him,

And crown Him, crown Him, crown Him, crown Him,

crown _____

_____ Him,

SOURCE OF TEXT: *The Gospel Magazine*, VI, November 1779. Altered by John Rippon for his *Selection of Hymns*, London, 1787. SOURCE OF TUNE: Composed for this text in 1838 in England.

Now I Have Found the Ground Wherein 66

Johann Andreas Rothe, 1628-1758
Tr. John Wesley, 1703-1791

MADRID 8.8.8.8.8.8.
William Matthews, 1759-1830

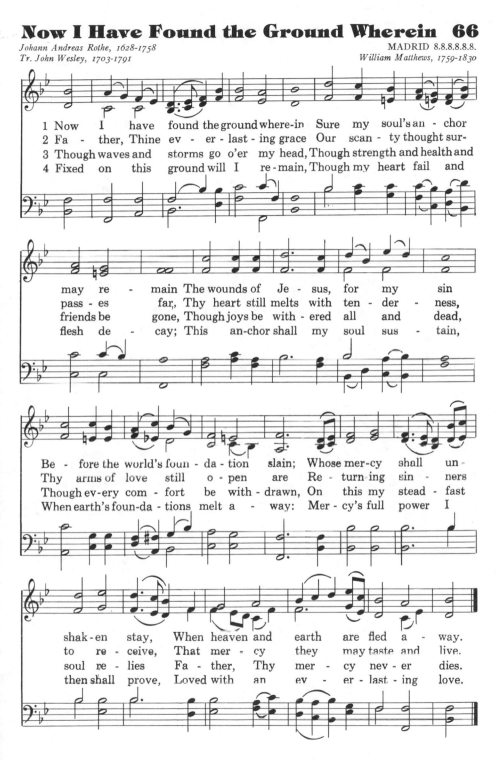

1 Now I have found the ground where-in Sure my soul's an - chor
2 Fa - ther, Thine ev - er - last-ing grace Our scan - ty thought sur-
3 Though waves and storms go o'er my head, Though strength and health and
4 Fixed on this ground will I re-main, Though my heart fail and

may re - main The wounds of Je - sus, for my sin
pass - es far, Thy heart still melts with ten - der - ness,
friends be gone, Though joys be with - ered all and dead,
flesh de - cay; This an-chor shall my soul sus - tain,

Be - fore the world's foun - da - tion slain; Whose mer-cy shall un -
Thy arms of love still o - pen are Re - turn-ing sin - ners
Though ev-ery com - fort be with-drawn, On this my stead - fast
When earth's foun-da - tions melt a - way: Mer - cy's full power I

shak-en stay, When heaven and earth are fled a - way.
to re - ceive, That mer - cy they may taste and live.
soul re - lies Fa - ther, Thy mer - cy nev - er dies.
then shall prove, Loved with an ev - er - last-ing love.

SOURCE OF TEXT: Zinzendorf's *Christ-Catholisches Singe- und Bet Büchlein*, 1727. SOURCE OF TRANS-
LATION: *Hymns and Sacred Poems*, London, 1740. SOURCE OF TUNE: An early nineteenth-century
"Old Methodist" tune.

193

67   "Welcome, Happy Morning!"

Venantius Fortunatus, 530-609
John Ellerton, 1826-1893

FORTUNATUS 11.11.11.11. *with Refrain*
Arthur S. Sullivan, 1842-1900

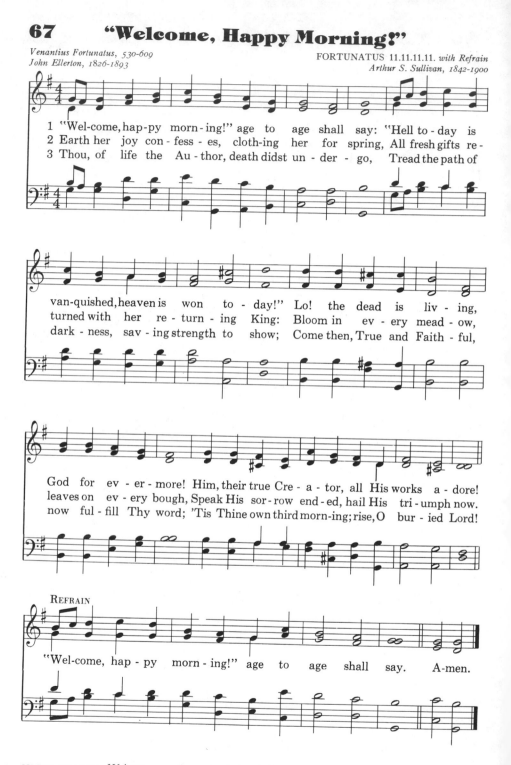

1 "Wel-come, hap-py morn-ing!" age to age shall say: "Hell to-day is
2 Earth her joy con-fess-es, cloth-ing her for spring, All fresh gifts re-
3 Thou, of life the Au-thor, death didst un-der-go, Tread the path of

van-quished, heaven is won to-day!" Lo! the dead is liv-ing,
turned with her re-turn-ing King: Bloom in ev-ery mead-ow,
dark-ness, sav-ing strength to show; Come then, True and Faith-ful,

God for ev-er-more! Him, their true Cre-a-tor, all His works a-dore!
leaves on ev-ery bough, Speak His sor-row end-ed, hail His tri-umph now.
now ful-fill Thy word; 'Tis Thine own third morn-ing; rise, O bur-ied Lord!

REFRAIN

"Wel-come, hap-py morn-ing!" age to age shall say. A-men.

SOURCE OF TEXT: Written near the end of the sixth century. SOURCE OF TRANSLATION: Brown-Borthwick's *Supplemental Hymn and Tune Book*, London, 1869. SOURCE OF TUNE: *The Hymnary*, London, 1872.

O Come, O Come, Emmanuel   68

Latin: c.9th century
Tr. John M. Neale, 1818-1866, Sts. 1,2, alt.
Tr. Henry S. Coffin, 1877-1954, Sts. 3,4

VENI EMMANUEL 8.8.8.8.8.8.
Adapted from Plainsong
Thomas Helmore, 1811-1890

In unison

1 O come, O come, Em-man-u-el, And ran-som cap-tive Is - ra - el, That mourns in lone-ly ex - ile here, Un-til the Son of God ap - pear.

2 O come, thou Day-spring, come and cheer Our spir-its by thine ad - vent here; Dis-perse the gloom-y clouds of night, And death's dark shad-ows put to flight.

3 O come, thou Wis-dom from on high, And or-der all things, far and nigh; To us the path of knowl-edge show, And cause us in her ways to go.

4 O come, De-sire of na - tions, bind All peo-ples in one heart and mind; Bid en-vy, strife and quar-rels cease; Fill the whole world with heav - en's peace.

REFRAIN

Re - joice! Re - joice! Em-man-u-el Shall come to thee, O Is - ra - el! A-men.

SOURCE OF TEXT: Latin, ninth century. SOURCE OF TRANSLATION: Stanzas 1 and 2 — *The Hymnal Noted*, London, 1851. Stanzas 3 and 4 — *Hymns of the Kingdom of God*, New York, 1910. SOURCE OF TUNE: Originally a trope for the *Libera me* from a 15th-century French processional, it first appeared as a hymn tune in Thomas Helmore's musical edition of *The Hymnal Noted*, 1854.

69 Lord of Our Life, and God of Our Salvation

Matthäus von Löwenstern, 1594-1648
Tr. Philip Pusey, 1799-1855

ISTE CONFESSOR (ROUEN) 11.11.11.5.
Poitiers Antiphoner, 1746

1 Lord of our life, and God of our sal - va - tion, Star of our
2 Lord, thou canst help when earth-ly ar - mor fail - eth; Lord, thou canst
3 Peace, in our hearts, our e - vil thoughts as - suag - ing; Peace, in thy

night, and hope of ev - ery na - tion, Hear and re - ceive thy
save when sin it - self as - sail - eth; Lord, o'er thy rock nor
Church, where broth-ers are en - gag - ing; Peace, when the world its

Church's sup - pli - ca - tion, Lord God al - might - y.
death nor hell pre - vail - eth; Grant us thy peace, Lord:
bus - y war is wag - ing; Calm thy foes' rag - ing! A - men.

4 Grant us thy help till backward they are driven;
Grant them thy truth, that they may be forgiven;
Grant peace on earth, or after we have striven,
Peace in thy heaven.

SOURCE OF TEXT: *Geistliche Kirchen- und Haus-Musik*, Breslau, 1644. SOURCE OF TRANSLATION: This free paraphrase was written in 1834, and first published in A. R. Reinagle's *Psalm and Hymn Tunes*, Oxford, 1840. SOURCE OF TUNE: A Rouen church melody found in the *Poitiers Antiphoner*, 1746; not found in English usage prior to *The English Hymnal*, London, 1906.

The Day of Resurrection 70

John of Damascus, c.696-c.754
Tr. John M. Neale, 1818-1866, alt.

LANCASHIRE 7.6.7.6.D.
Henry T. Smart, 1813-1879

1 The day of res-ur-rec-tion! Earth, tell it out a-broad;
2 Our hearts be pure from e-vil, That we may see a-right
3 Now let the heavens be joy-ful, Let earth her song be-gin,

The Pass-o-ver of glad-ness, The Pass-o-ver of God.
The Lord in rays e-ter-nal Of res-ur-rec-tion light;
The round world keep high tri-umph, And all that is there-in;

From death to life e-ter-nal, From earth un-to the sky,
And, lis-tening to his ac-cents, May hear so calm and plain
Let all things seen and un-seen Their notes of glad-ness blend,

Our Christ hath brought us o-ver With hymns of vic-to-ry.
His own "All hail," and, hear-ing, May raise the vic-tor strain.
For Christ the Lord is ris-en, Our joy that hath no end. A-men.

SOURCE OF TEXT: Written about 750. SOURCE OF TRANSLATION: Neale's *Hymns of the Eastern Church*, London, 1862. SOURCE OF TUNE: *Psalms and Hymns for Divine Worship*, London, 1867.

197

71　The Church's One Foundation

Samuel J. Stone, 1839-1900

AURELIA 7.6.7.6.D.
Samuel S. Wesley, 1810-1876

1 The Church's one foun-da-tion Is Je-sus Christ her Lord;
2 E-lect from ev-ery na-tion, Yet one o'er all the earth,
3 'Mid toil and trib-u-la-tion, And tu-mult of her war,
4 Yet she on earth hath un-ion With God, the Three in One,

She is his new cre-a-tion By wa-ter and the word;
Her char-ter of sal-va-tion, One Lord, one faith, one birth,
She waits the con-sum-ma-tion Of peace for ev-er-more;
And mys-tic sweet com-mun-ion With those whose rest is won.

From heaven he came and sought her To be his ho-ly bride;
One ho-ly name she bless-es, Par-takes one ho-ly food,
Till with the vi-sion glo-rious, Her long-ing eyes are blest,
O hap-py ones and ho-ly! Lord, give us grace that we

With his own blood he bought her, And for her life he died.
And to one hope she press-es, With ev-ery grace en-dued.
And the great Church vic-to-rious Shall be the Church at rest.
Like them, the meek and low-ly, On high may dwell with thee. A-men.

SOURCE OF TEXT: Stone's *Lyra Fidelium; Twelve Hymns on the Twelve Articles of the Apostles' Creed*, 1866. In the 1868 edition of *Hymns Ancient and Modern*, it appeared with this tune. SOURCE OF TUNE: Kemble's *Selection of Psalms and Hymns*, London, 1864, of which Wesley was musical editor.

Jerusalem the Golden

St. Bernard of Cluny, 12th century
Tr. John M. Neale, 1818-1866, alt.

EWING 7.6.7.6.D.
Alexander Ewing, 1830-1895

1 Je - ru - sa - lem the gold - en, With milk and hon - ey blest,
2 They stand, those halls of Zi - on, All ju - bi - lant with song,
3 There is the throne of Da - vid, And there, from care re - leased,
4 O sweet and bless - ed coun - try, The home of God's e - lect!

Be - neath thy con - tem - pla - tion Sink heart and voice op - pressed.
And bright with man - y an an - gel, And all the mar - tyr throng.
The shout of them that tri - umph, The song of them that feast,
O sweet and bless - ed coun - try, That ea - ger hearts ex - pect!

I know not, O I know not, What joys a - wait us there,
The Prince is ev - er in them; The day - light is se - rene;
And they, who with their lead - er, Have con - quered in the fight,
Je - sus, in mer - cy bring us To that dear land of rest,

What ra - dian - cy of glo - ry, What bliss be - yond com - pare!
The pas - tures of the bless - ed Are decked in glo - rious sheen.
For - ev - er and for - ev - er Are clad in robes of white.
Who art, with God the Fa - ther And Spir - it, ev - er blest! A - men.

SOURCE OF TEXT: Taken from *De Contemptu Mundi*. SOURCE OF TRANSLATION: Neale's *Rhythm of Bernard de Morlaix, Monk of Cluny, on the Celestial Country, London*, 1858. SOURCE OF TUNE: First printed in leaflet form in 1853, in triple rhythm, and published in John Grey's *A Manual of Psalm and Hymn Tunes*, London, 1857. It was altered to its present form in *Hymns Ancient and Modern*, London, 1861.

73 Hark! The Herald Angels Sing

Charles Wesley, 1707-1788, alt.

MENDELSSOHN 7.7.7.7.D. *with Refrain*
Felix Mendelssohn, 1809-1847
Arr. by William H. Cummings, 1831-1915

1 Hark! the her - ald an - gels sing, "Glo - ry to the new-born King;
2 Christ, by high - est heaven a - dored; Christ, the ev - er - last - ing Lord!
3 Hail the heaven-born Prince of peace! Hail the Sun of right-eous-ness!

Peace on earth, and mer - cy mild, God and sin - ners rec - on-ciled!"
Late in time be - hold him come, Off - spring of the Vir-gin's womb.
Light and life to all he brings, Risen with heal - ing in his wings,

Joy - ful, all ye na - tions, rise, Join the tri - umph of the skies;
Veiled in flesh the God-head see; Hail the in-car - nate De - i - ty,
Mild he lays his glo - ry by, Born that man no more may die,

With the an-gel - ic host pro - claim, "Christ is born in Beth - le - hem!"
Pleased as man with men to dwell, Je - sus, our Em-man - u - el.
Born to raise the sons of earth, Born to give them sec - ond birth.

SOURCE OF TEXT: *Hymns and Sacred Poems*, London, 1739. SOURCE OF TUNE: Adapted from Mendelssohn's *Festgesange*, 1840, by Cummings in 1855, and published by him the following year. The first hymnal inclusion was Richard Chope's *Congregational Hymn and Tune Book*, London, 1857.

REFRAIN

Hark! the her-ald an-gels sing, "Glo - ry to the new-born King!" A-men.

From Heaven Above to Earth I Come   74

Martin Luther, 1483-1546
Tr. Catherine Winkworth, 1827-1878

VOM HIMMEL HOCH L.M.
"Geistliche Lieder," Leipzig, 1539

1 From heaven a - bove to earth I come To bear good news to
2 To you, this night, is born a child Of Mar - y, chos - en
3 Ah, dear - est Je - sus, ho - ly child, Make thee a bed, soft,
4 Glo - ry to God in high - est heaven, Who un - to man his

ev - ery home; Glad tid - ings of great joy I bring,
moth - er mild; This lit - tle child, of low - ly birth,
un - de - filed With - in my heart, that it may be
son hath given, While an - gels sing with pi - ous mirth,

Where - of I now will say and sing.
Shall be the joy of all your earth.
A qui - et cham - ber kept for thee.
A glad new year to all the earth.

SOURCE OF TEXT: Klug's *Geistliche Lieder*, Wittenberg, 1535. SOURCE OF TUNE: Schumann's *Geistliche Lieder*, Leipzig, 1539.

75   Come, Ye Thankful People, Come

Henry Alford, 1810-1871

ST. GEORGE'S WINDSOR 7.7.7.7.D.
George J. Elvey, 1816-1893

1 Come, ye thank-ful peo-ple, come, Raise the song of har-vest home;
2 All the world is God's own field, Fruit un-to his praise to yield;
3 For the Lord our God shall come, And shall take his har-vest home;
4 E - ven so, Lord, quick-ly come To thy fi - nal har-vest home;

All is safe-ly gath-ered in, Ere the win-ter storms be-gin;
Wheat and tares to-geth-er sown, Un-to joy or sor-row grown;
From his field shall in that day All of-fens-es purge a-way,
Gath-er thou thy peo-ple in, Free from sor-row, free from sin;

God, our Mak-er, doth pro-vide For our wants to be sup-plied;
First the blade, and then the ear, Then the full corn shall ap-pear;
Give his an-gels charge at last In the fire the tares to cast,
There for-ev-er pu-ri-fied, In thy pres-ence to a-bide;

Come to God's own tem-ple, come, Raise the song of har-vest home.
Lord of har-vest, grant that we Whole-some grain and pure may be.
But the fruit-ful ears to store In his gar-ner ev-er-more.
Come, with all thine an-gels, come, Raise the glo-rious har-vest home. A-men.

SOURCE OF TEXT: Alford's *Psalms and Hymns*, London, 1844. SOURCE OF TUNE: *Hymns Ancient and Modern*, London, 1861.

Come, Ye Faithful, Raise the Strain 76

Attr. to John of Damascus, c.696-c.754
Tr. John M. Neale, 1818-1866

ST. KEVIN 7.6.7.6.D.
Arthur S. Sullivan, 1842-1900

1 Come, ye faith - ful, raise the strain Of tri - umph - ant glad - ness;
2 'Tis the spring of souls to - day; Christ hath burst his pris - on,
3 Now the queen of sea - sons, bright With the day of splen - dor,
4 Neith - er might the gates of death, Nor the tomb's dark por - tal,

God hath brought his Is - ra - el In - to joy from sad - ness;
And from three days' sleep in death As a sun hath ris - en;
With the roy - al feast of feasts, Comes its joy to ren - der;
Nor the watch - ers, nor the seal Hold thee as a mor - tal;

Loosed from Pha - raoh's bit - ter yoke Ja - cob's sons and daugh - ters;
All the win - ter of our sins, Long and dark, is fly - ing
Comes to glad Je - ru - sa - lem Who with true af - fec - tion
But to - day a - midst the twelve Thou didst stand, be - stow - ing

Led them with un-moist-ened foot Through the Red Sea wa - ters.
From his light, to whom we give Laud and praise un - dy - ing.
Wel-comes in un - wea-ried strains Je - sus' res - ur - rec - tion.
That thy peace which ev - er - more Pass - eth hu - man know - ing. A-men.

SOURCE OF TEXT: Written about 750. SOURCE OF TRANSLATION: *The Christian Remembrancer*, XXXVII, April 1859, and in Neale's *Hymns of the Eastern Church*, London, 1862. SOURCE OF TUNE: *The Hymnary*, London, 1872.

77 How Sweet the Name of Jesus Sounds

John Newton, 1725-1807, alt.

ST. PETER C.M.
Alexander R. Reinagle, 1799-1877

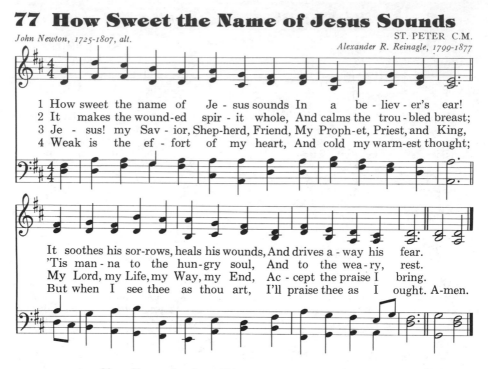

1 How sweet the name of   Je - sus sounds In   a   be - liev - er's ear!
2 It   makes the wound-ed   spir - it whole, And calms the trou - bled breast;
3 Je - sus! my Sav - ior, Shep-herd, Friend, My Proph-et, Priest, and King,
4 Weak is   the   ef - fort   of   my heart, And cold my warm-est thought;

It soothes his sor-rows, heals his wounds, And drives a - way his   fear.
'Tis man - na to the hun-gry soul, And to the wea - ry,   rest.
My Lord, my Life, my Way, my End,   Ac - cept the praise I   bring.
But when I   see thee as thou art, I'll praise thee as   I   ought. A-men.

SOURCE OF TEXT: *Olney Hymns*, London, 1779. SOURCE OF TUNE: Reinagle's *Psalm Tunes for the Voice and Pianoforte*, Oxford, 1830. It was first used with this text in *Hymns Ancient and Modern*, London, 1861.

78 Jesus, Thou Joy of Loving Hearts

Bernard of Clairvaux, 1091-1153
Tr. Ray Palmer, 1808-1887

QUEBEC L.M.
Henry Baker, 1835-1910

1 Je - sus, Thou joy   of lov-ing hearts, Thou fount of   life, Thou light of men,
2 Thy truth un-changed hath ev - er stood; Thou sav - est those who   on Thee call;
3 Our rest-less spir - its yearn for Thee, Wher-e'er our change-ful   lot   is cast;
4 O   Je - sus, ev - er with us stay, Make all our mo-ments calm and bright;

SOURCE OF TEXT: This Latin hymn was probably written about 1150. Palmer's translation was made for the *Sabbath Hymn Book*, 1858. SOURCE OF TUNE: Written for Keble's "Sun of my soul," in 1854, it was first published in John Grey's *A Hymnal for Use in the English Church*, London, 1866.

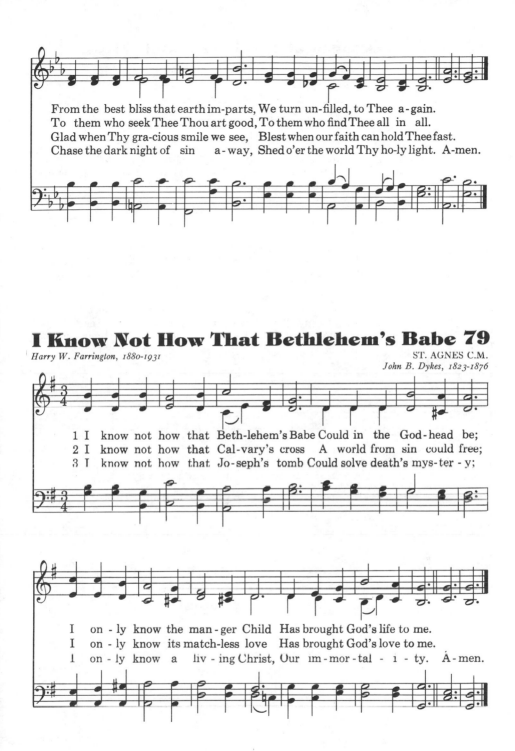

From the best bliss that earth im-parts, We turn un-filled, to Thee a-gain.
To them who seek Thee Thou art good, To them who find Thee all in all.
Glad when Thy gra-cious smile we see, Blest when our faith can hold Thee fast.
Chase the dark night of sin a-way, Shed o'er the world Thy ho-ly light. A-men.

I Know Not How That Bethlehem's Babe 79

Harry W. Farrington, 1880-1931

ST. AGNES C.M.
John B. Dykes, 1823-1876

1 I know not how that Beth-lehem's Babe Could in the God-head be;
2 I know not how that Cal-vary's cross A world from sin could free;
3 I know not how that Jo-seph's tomb Could solve death's mys-ter-y;

I on-ly know the man-ger Child Has brought God's life to me.
I on-ly know its match-less love Has brought God's love to me.
I on-ly know a liv-ing Christ, Our im-mor-tal-i-ty. A-men.

SOURCE OF TEXT: Written in 1910, this hymn was submitted in a competition for a Christmas hymn sponsored by Harvard University. It was first published in Farrington's collection of poems, *Rough and Brown*, 1921. Its first hymnal inclusion seems to be *The Abingdon Hymnal*, New York, 1928, compiled by Earl E. Harper. SOURCE OF TUNE: John Grey's *A Hymnal for Use in the English Church*, London, 1866.

Washington Gladden, 1836-1918

MARYTON L.M.
H. Percy Smith, 1825-1898

1 O   Mas - ter,   let   me   walk   with   thee   In   low - ly
2 Help me   the   slow   of   heart   to   move   By   some clear,
3 Teach me   thy   pa - tience; still   with   thee   In   clos - er,
4 In   hope that   sends   a   shin - ing   ray   Far   down the

paths   of   serv - ice   free;   Tell   me   thy   se - cret,   help   me
win - ning   word   of   love;   Teach   me   the   way - ward   feet   to
dear - er   com - pa - ny,   In   work that   keeps faith   sweet   and
fu - ture's   broad-ening way,   In   peace that   on - ly   thou   canst

bear   The   strain   of   toil,   the   fret   of   care.
stay,   And   guide   them   in   the   home - ward   way.
strong, In   trust   that   tri - umphs   o - ver   wrong.
give,   With thee,   O   Mas - ter,   let   me   live.   A - men.

SOURCE OF TEXT: First appeared as a poem, entitled, "Walking with God," in Gladden's magazine, *Sunday Afternoon*, III, 1879, while Gladden was pastor of North Church, Springfield, Massachusetts. Charles H. Richards recognized its value as a hymn and first used it in his *Christian Praise* (later called *Songs of Christian Praise*), New York, 1880. SOURCE OF TUNE: Arthur S. Sullivan's *Church Hymns with Tunes*, London, 1874.

Christ, Whose Glory Fills the Skies 81

Charles Wesley, 1707-1788

RATISBON 7.7.7.7.7.7.
Johann Werner's "Choralbuch," 1815

1 Christ, whose glo - ry fills the skies, Christ, the true, the on - ly Light,
2 Dark and cheer - less is the morn Un - ac - com - pa - nied by thee;

Sun of right-eous-ness, a - rise, Tri-umph o'er the shades of night;
Joy - less is the day's re - turn, Till thy mer - cy's beams I see,

Day-spring from on high, be near; Day-star, in my heart ap - pear.
Till they in-ward light im - part, Glad my eyes, and warm my heart. A-men.

3 Visit, then, this soul of mine;
   Pierce the gloom of sin and grief;
Fill me, Radiancy divine,
   Scatter all my unbelief;
More and more thyself display,
   Shining to the perfect day.

SOURCE OF TEXT: *Hymns and Sacred Poems*, London, 1740. SOURCE OF TUNE: Johann Werner's *Choralbuch zu den neuern Protestantischen Gesangbüchern*, Berlin, 1815. First used with this text in *Hymns Ancient and Modern*, London, 1861.

82   Angels, from the Realms of Glory

James Montgomery, 1771-1854

REGENT SQUARE 8.7.8.7.8.7.
Henry T. Smart, 1813-1879

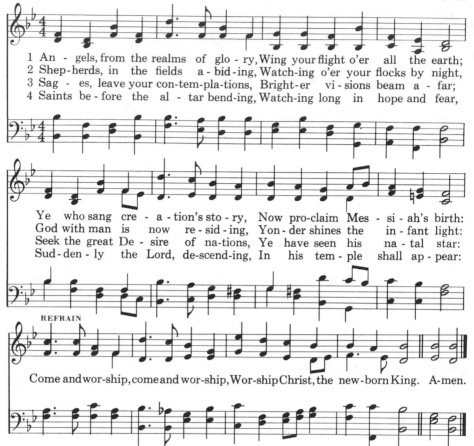

1 An - gels, from the realms of glo - ry, Wing your flight o'er all the earth;
2 Shep-herds, in the fields a - bid - ing, Watch-ing o'er your flocks by night,
3 Sag - es, leave your con-tem-pla-tions, Bright-er vi - sions beam a - far;
4 Saints be - fore the al - tar bend-ing, Watch-ing long in hope and fear,

Ye who sang cre - a - tion's sto - ry, Now pro-claim Mes - si - ah's birth:
God with man is now re - sid - ing, Yon - der shines the in - fant light:
Seek the great De - sire of na-tions, Ye have seen his na - tal star:
Sud - den - ly the Lord, de-scend-ing, In his tem - ple shall ap - pear:

REFRAIN

Come and wor-ship, come and wor-ship, Wor-ship Christ, the new-born King. A-men.

SOURCE OF TEXT: First appeared in *Iris*, December 24, 1816. The text was slightly altered for Mont-gomery's *Christian Psalmist*, Glasgow, 1825. SOURCE OF TUNE: *Psalms and Hymns for Divine Worship*, London, 1867.

83   The Lord's My Shepherd

Based on Psalm 23
"Scottish Psalter," 1650, alt.

CRIMOND C.M.
Melody by Jessie S. Irvine, 1836-1887

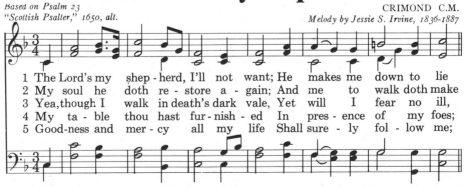

1 The Lord's my shep - herd, I'll not want; He makes me down to lie
2 My soul he doth re - store a - gain; And me to walk doth make
3 Yea, though I walk in death's dark vale, Yet will I fear no ill,
4 My ta - ble thou hast fur - nish - ed In pres - ence of my foes;
5 Good-ness and mer - cy all my life Shall sure - ly fol - low me;

SOURCE OF TEXT: *The Scottish Psalter*, 1650. SOURCE OF TUNE: William Carnie's *Northern Psalter*, Aberdeen, 1872.

In pas-tures green; he lead-eth me The qui-et wa-ters by.
With-in the paths of right-eous-ness, E'en for his own name's sake.
For thou art with me, and thy rod And staff me com-fort still.
My head thou dost with oil a-noint, And my cup o-ver-flows.
And in God's house for ev-er-more My dwell-ing-place shall be. A-men.

As with Gladness Men of Old 84

William C. Dix, 1837-1898, alt.

DIX 7.7.7.7.7.7.
Adapted from a chorale by Conrad Kocher, 1786-1872

1 As with glad-ness men of old Did the guid-ing star be-hold;
2 As with joy-ful steps they sped To that low-ly man-ger-bed,
3 As they of-fered gifts most rare, At the man-ger rude and bare,
4 Ho-ly Je-sus, ev-ery day Keep us in the nar-row way;

As with joy they hailed its light, Lead-ing on-ward, beam-ing bright;
There to bend the knee be-fore Him whom heaven and earth a-dore;
So may we with ho-ly joy, Pure and free from sin's al-loy,
And, when earth-ly things are past, Bring our ran-somed souls at last

So, most gra-cious Lord, may we Ev-er-more be led to thee.
So may we with will-ing feet Ev-er seek thy mer-cy seat.
All our cost-liest treas-ures bring, Christ, to thee, our heaven-ly King.
Where they need no star to guide, Where no clouds thy glo-ry hide. A-men.

SOURCE OF TEXT: Written *c.* 1858, first appeared in a privately circulated collection, *Hymns of Love and Joy*, 1861, and later in *Hymns Ancient and Modern*. SOURCE OF TUNE: Adapted from a chorale in Kocher's *Stimmen aus dem Reiche Gottes*, Stuttgart, 1838, by W. H. Monk for this text for *Hymns Ancient and Modern*, London, 1861.

85   O God of Earth and Altar

Gilbert K. Chesterton, 1874-1936

LLANGLOFFAN 7.6.7.6.D.
Traditional Welsh Melody

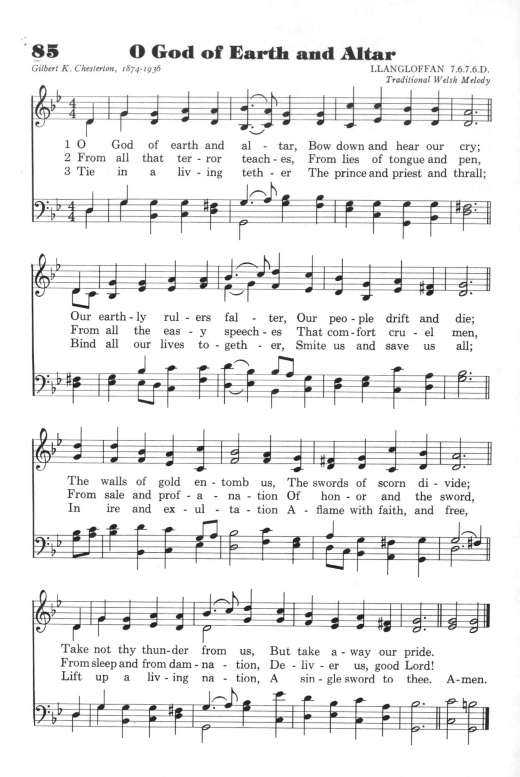

1 O God of earth and al - tar, Bow down and hear our cry,
2 From all that ter - ror teach - es, From lies of tongue and pen,
3 Tie in a liv - ing teth - er The prince and priest and thrall;

Our earth - ly rul - ers fal - ter, Our peo - ple drift and die;
From all the eas - y speech - es That com - fort cru - el men,
Bind all our lives to - geth - er, Smite us and save us all;

The walls of gold en - tomb us, The swords of scorn di - vide;
From sale and prof - a - na - tion Of hon - or and the sword,
In ire and ex - ul - ta - tion A - flame with faith, and free,

Take not thy thun - der from us, But take a - way our pride.
From sleep and from dam - na - tion, De - liv - er us, good Lord!
Lift up a liv - ing na - tion, A sin - gle sword to thee. A - men.

SOURCE OF TEXT: First published in *The Commonwealth;* first hymnal inclusion was in *The English Hymnal,* London, 1906, by permission of Oxford University Press. SOURCE OF TUNE: D. Evans's *Hymnau a Thonau,* Wales, 1865.

Jesus, Lover of My Soul

86

Charles Wesley, 1707-1788

ABERYSTWYTH 7.7.7.7.D.
Joseph Parry, 1841-1903

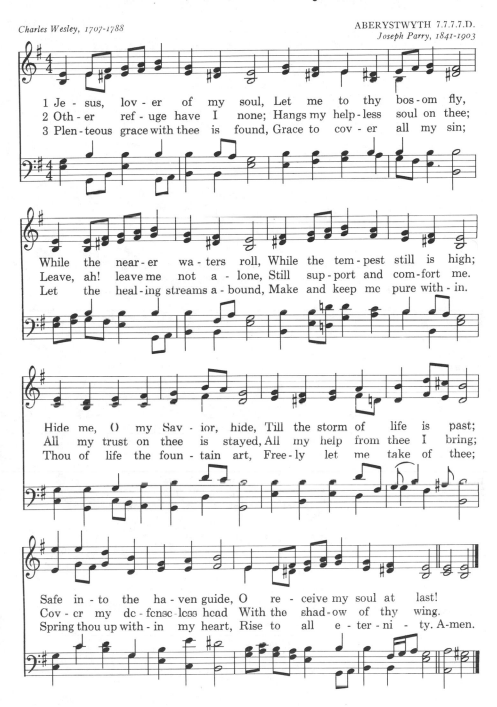

1 Je - sus, lov - er of my soul, Let me to thy bos - om fly,
2 Oth - er ref - uge have I none; Hangs my help - less soul on thee;
3 Plen - teous grace with thee is found, Grace to cov - er all my sin;

While the near - er wa - ters roll, While the tem - pest still is high;
Leave, ah! leave me not a - lone, Still sup - port and com - fort me.
Let the heal - ing streams a - bound, Make and keep me pure with - in.

Hide me, O my Sav - ior, hide, Till the storm of life is past;
All my trust on thee is stayed, All my help from thee I bring;
Thou of life the foun - tain art, Free - ly let me take of thee;

Safe in - to the ha - ven guide, O re - ceive my soul at last!
Cov - er my de - fense - less head With the shad - ow of thy wing.
Spring thou up with - in my heart, Rise to all e - ter - ni - ty. A - men.

SOURCE OF TEXT: *Hymns and Sacred Poems*, London, 1740. SOURCE OF TUNE: Stephen and Jones's
Ail Llyfr Tonau ac Emynau, Wales, 1879.

God of Grace and God of Glory

Harry Emerson Fosdick, 1878-1969

CWM RHONDDA 8.7.8.7.8.7.7.
John Hughes, 1873-1932

1 God of grace and God of glo - ry, On thy peo - ple
2 Lo! the hosts of e - vil round us Scorn thy Christ, as -
3 Cure thy chil - dren's war - ring mad - ness; Bend our pride to
4 Set our feet on loft - y pla - ces; Gird our lives that
5 Save us from weak res - ig - na - tion To the e - vils

pour thy power; Crown thine an - cient church's sto - ry; Bring her bud to
sail his ways! From the fears that long have bound us, Free our hearts to
thy con - trol; Shame our wan - ton, self - ish glad - ness, Rich in things and
they may be Arm - ored with all Christ-like gra - ces In the fight to
we de - plore; Let the search for thy sal - va - tion Be our glo - ry

glo - rious flower. Grant us wis - dom, Grant us cour - age,
faith and praise. Grant us wis - dom, Grant us cour - age,
poor in soul. Grant us wis - dom, Grant us cour - age,
set men free. Grant us wis - dom, Grant us cour - age,
ev - er - more. Grant us wis - dom, Grant us cour - age,

For the fac - ing of this hour, For the fac - ing of this hour.
For the liv - ing of these days, For the liv - ing of these days.
Lest we miss thy king-dom's goal, Lest we miss thy king-dom's goal.
That we fail not man nor thee, That we fail not man nor thee.
Serv - ing thee whom we a - dore, Serv - ing thee whom we a - dore. A-men.

SOURCE OF TEXT: Written for the dedication of Riverside Church, New York City, 1930. First hymn
inclusion was in *Praise and Service*, New York, 1932. SOURCE OF TUNE: Written in 1907 for a singing
festival in Wales, and first appeared in the *Fellowship Hymn Book*, revised, London, 1933, and in
the *Methodist Hymn Book*, London, the same year. The first American inclusion was *The Methodist
Hymnal*, 1935. Copyright 1957, W. Paxton & Co., Ltd. Used by permission Mills Music, Inc.

Be Thou My Vision

Ancient Irish
Tr. by Mary E. Byrne, 1880-1931
Versified by Eleanor H. Hull, 1860-1935

SLANE 10.10.9.10.
Traditional Irish Melody
Harm. by David Evans, 1874-1948

88

1 Be thou my vi-sion, O Lord of my heart;
2 Be thou my wis-dom, and thou my true word;
3 Rich-es I heed not, nor man's emp-ty praise,
4 High King of heav-en, my vic-to-ry won,

Nought be all else to me save that thou art.
I ev-er with thee and thou with me, Lord;
Thou mine in-her-it-ance, now and al-ways:
May I reach heaven's joys, O bright heav-en's Sun!

Thou my best thought, by day or by night,
Thou my great Fa-ther, I thy true son;
Thou and thou on-ly, first in my heart,
Heart of my own heart, what-ev-er be-fall,

Wak-ing or sleep-ing, thy pres-ence my light.
Thou in me dwell-ing, and I with thee one.
High King of heav-en, my treas-ure thou art.
Still be my vi-sion, O Rul-er of all. A-men.

SOURCE OF TEXT: An old Irish poem dating from about the eighth century. The literal translation appeared in Miss Byrne's *Erin*, Vol. II, Dublin, 1905, and the versification appeared in Miss Hull's *Poem-book of the Gael*, London, 1912. Used by permission of Chatto & Windus Ltd., London.
SOURCE OF TUNE: A traditional Irish melody given in Patrick W. Joyce's *Old Irish Folk Music and Songs*, Dublin, 1909. Harmonized by David Evans in *The Revised Church Hymnary*, 1927, used by permission of Oxford University Press, London.

O Brother Man

John Greenleaf Whittier, 1807-1892

INTERCESSOR 11.10.11.10.

Charles H. H. Parry, 1848-1918

1 O Broth-er man, fold to thy heart thy broth-er:
2 Fol-low with rev-erent steps the great ex - am - ple
3 Then shall all shack-les fall: the storm-y clang - our

Where pit - y dwells, the peace of God is there;
Of Him whose ho - ly work was do - ing good:
Of wild war mu - sic o'er the earth shall cease;

To wor - ship right - ly is to love each oth - er,
So shall the wide earth seem our Fa - ther's tem - ple,
Love shall tread out the bale - ful fire of an - ger,

Each smile a hymn, each kind - ly deed a prayer.
Each lov - ing life a psalm of grat - i - tude.
And in its ash - es plant the tree of peace.

SOURCE OF TEXT: Taken from Whittier's poem "Worship," written in 1848 and published in his *Labor and Other Poems*, 1850. SOURCE OF TUNE: *Hymns Ancient and Modern*, London, 1904. Music used by permission of the Proprietors of *Hymns Ancient and Modern*.

Come Down, O Love Divine

90

Bianco da Siena, c. 1367
Tr. Richard F. Littledale, 1833-1890

DOWN AMPNEY 6.6.11.D.
R. Vaughan Williams, 1872-1958

1 Come down, O Love divine, Seek thou this soul of
2 O let it free-ly burn, Till earth-ly pas-sions
3 And so the yearn-ing strong With which the soul will

mine, And vis-it it with thine own ar-dor glow-ing;
turn To dust and ash-es in its heat con-sum-ing;
long, Shall far out-pass the power of hu-man tell-ing;

O Com-fort-er, draw near, With-in my heart ap-pear,
And let thy glo-rious light Shine ev-er on my sight,
For none can guess its grace, Till he be-come the place

And kin-dle it, thy ho-ly flame be-stow-ing.
And clothe me round, the while my path il-lum-ing.
Where-in the Ho-ly Spir-it makes his dwell-ing. A-men.

SOURCE OF TEXT: *Laudi Spirituali*, edited by Telesforo Bini in 1851. SOURCE OF TRANSLATION: Little-dale's *People's Hymnal*, London, 1867. SOURCE OF TUNE: Composed for this text for *The English Hymnal*, London, 1906, used by permission of Oxford University Press, London.

For All the Saints

William W. How, 1823-1897, alt.

SINE NOMINE 10.10.10.4..
R. Vaughan Williams, 1872-1958

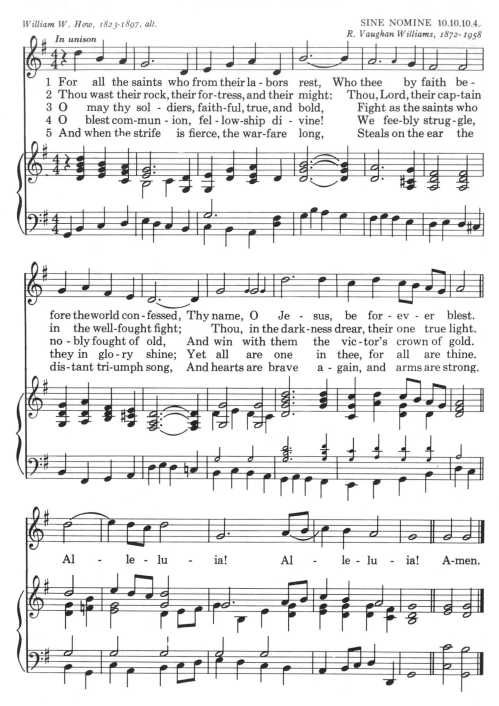

In unison

1 For all the saints who from their la-bors rest, Who thee by faith be-
2 Thou wast their rock, their for-tress, and their might: Thou, Lord, their cap-tain
3 O may thy sol-diers, faith-ful, true, and bold, Fight as the saints who
4 O blest com-mun-ion, fel-low-ship di-vine! We fee-bly strug-gle,
5 And when the strife is fierce, the war-fare long, Steals on the ear the

fore the world con-fessed, Thy name, O Je-sus, be for-ev-er blest.
in the well-fought fight; Thou, in the dark-ness drear, their one true light.
no-bly fought of old, And win with them the vic-tor's crown of gold.
they in glo-ry shine; Yet all are one in thee, for all are thine.
dis-tant tri-umph song, And hearts are brave a-gain, and arms are strong.

Al - le-lu - ia! Al - le-lu - ia! A-men.

SOURCE OF TEXT: Earl Nelson's *Hymns for Saints' Days, and Other Days*, London, 1864. SOURCE OF TUNE: From *The English Hymnal*, London, 1906, by permission of Oxford University Press, London.

He Who Would Valiant Be 92

John Bunyan, 1628-1688
Alt. Percy Dearmer, 1867-1836

MONKS GATE 6.5.6.5.6.6.6.5.
English Traditional Melody
Harm. Ralph Vaughan Williams, 1872-1958

1 He who would val-iant be 'Gainst all dis-as-ter,
2 Who so be set him round With dis-mal sto-ries,

Let him in con-stan-cy Fol-low the Mas-ter.
Do but them-selves con-found, His strength the more is.

There's no dis-cour-age-ment Shall make him once re-lent
No foes shall stay his might, Though he with gi-ants fight;

His first a-vowed in-tent To be a pil-grim.
He will make good his right To be a pil-grim.

3 Since, Lord, thou dost defend
    Us with thy Spirit,
We know we at the end
    Shall life inherit.

Then fancies flee away!
I'll fear not what men say,
I'll labor night and day
    To be a pilgrim.

SOURCE OF TEXT: *Pilgrim's Progress*, London, 1684. This adaptation made by Dearmer for *The English Hymnal*, London, 1906, used by permission of Oxford University Press, London. SOURCE OF TUNE: Vaughan Williams' arrangement of a traditional English melody noted at the village near Horsham, Sussex, for which it is named, and used with this text in *The English Hymnal*, London, 1906. Used by permission of Oxford University Press, London.

217

93   O Master Workman of the Race

Jay T. Stocking, 1870-1936

KINGSFOLD C.M.D.
Traditional English Melody
Arr. by R. Vaughan Williams, 1872-1958

1 O Mas-ter Work-man of the race, Thou Man of Gal - i - lee,
2 O Car-pen-ter of Naz-a-reth, Build-er of life di - vine,
3 O thou who didst the vi-sion send And gives to each his task,

Who with the eyes of ear - ly youth E - ter - nal things did see,
Who shap-est man to God's own law, Thy - self the fair de - sign,
And with the task suf - fi-cient strength, Show us thy will, we ask.

We thank thee for thy boy - hood faith That shone thy whole life through;
Build us a tower of Christ-like height, That we the land may view,
Give us a con-science bold and good, Give us a pur - pose true,

"Did ye not know it is my work My Fa-ther's work to do?"
And see like thee our no - blest work Our Fa-ther's work to do.
That it may be our high - est joy Our Fa-ther's work to do. A-men.

SOURCE OF TEXT: Written in 1911; first published in *The Pilgrim Hymnal*, Boston, 1912. SOURCE OF TUNE: Traditional English melody which appeared in Lucy E. Broadwood's *English County Songs*, 1893. Harmonization by Ralph Vaughan Williams from *The English Hymnal*, London, 1906. Used by permission of Oxford University Press, London.

Lift Up Your Voice, Ye Christian Folk　94

P. H. B. Lyon, 1893-

LADYWELL C.M.D.
William H. Ferguson, 1874-1950

1 Lift up your voice, ye Chris-tian folk, To praise the Ho - ly
2 Lift up your voice! with shout and song Ex - tol his maj - es -

One, Who ran-soms us from Sa - tan's yoke Through
ty, Whose power hath made the fee - ble strong And

Christ, his bless - ed Son. Lo, we who were in
caused the blind to see. And when the sound of

griev - ous state By rea - son of our sin, Our
praise grows dim Still may our lives forth tell, In

heads look up, our fears a - bate, Our tri - umphs now be - gin.
all we do, our love of him Who do - eth all things well.

SOURCE OF TEXT: *The Rugby School Hymn Book*, London, 1932. Words used by permission of the author. SOURCE OF TUNE: *The Public School Hymn Book*, London, 1919. Music copyright by the Royal School of Church Music, Addington Palace, Croydon, England. Used by permission.

Lead, Kindly Light

John Henry Newman, 1801-1890

ALBERTA 10.4.10.4.10.10.
William H. Harris, 1883-

Unison

1 Lead, kind-ly Light, a - mid the en-cir-cling gloom, Lead Thou me
2 I was not ev - er thus, nor prayed that Thou Shouldst lead me
3 So long Thy power hath blest me, sure it still Will lead me

on; The night is dark, and I am far from home, Lead
on; I loved to choose and see my path; but now Lead
on O'er moor and fen, o'er crag and tor - rent, till The

Thou me on. Keep Thou my feet; I do not ask to see
Thou me on. I loved the gar - ish day, and, spite of fears,
night is gone, And with the morn those an-gel fa - ces smile,

The dis - tant scene. one step e - nough for me.
Pride ruled my will: re-mem-ber not past years.
Which I have loved long since, and lost a - while.

SOURCE OF TEXT: Written June 16, 1833, and first published in the *British Magazine*, V, February 1834.
SOURCE OF TUNE: From *Enlarged Songs of Praise*, Oxford, 1932, used by permission of Oxford University Press, London.

God of Love and Truth and Beauty 96

Timothy Rees, 1874-1939

CAROLYN 8.5.8.5.8.8.8.5.
Herbert Murrill, 1909-1952

1 God of love and truth and beau-ty, Hal-lowed be thy name;
2 Lord, re-move our guil-ty blind-ness, Hal-lowed be thy name;
3 In our wor-ship, Lord most ho-ly, Hal-lowed be thy name;

Fount of or-der, law, and du-ty, Hal-lowed be thy name.
Show thy heart of lov-ing-kind-ness, Hal-lowed be thy name.
In our work, how-ev-er low-ly, Hal-lowed be thy name.

As in heaven thy hosts a-dore thee, And their fa-ces veil be-fore thee,
By our heart's deep-felt con-tri-tion, By our mind's en-light-ened vi-sion,
In each heart's im-ag-i-na-tion, In the Chur-ch's ad-o-ra-tion,

So on earth, Lord, we im-plore thee, Hal-lowed be thy name.
By our will's com-plete sub-mis-sion, Hal-lowed be thy name.
In the con-science of the na-tion, Hal-lowed be thy name.

SOURCE OF TEXT: Timothy Rees's *Sermons and Hymns*, London. Words copyright, A. R. Mowbray & Co., Ltd., London. Used by permission. SOURCE OF TUNE: *The BBC Hymn Book*, London, 1951. Used by permission.

97 Glorious Things of Thee Are Spoken

John Newton, 1725-1807

ABBOT'S LEIGH 8.7.8.7.D.
Cyril V. Taylor, 1907-

1 Glo - rious things of thee are spok-en, Zi - on, cit - y of our God! He whose word can-not be brok-en Formed thee for His own a - bode. On the Rock of A - ges found-ed, What can shake thy sure re - pose? With sal - va - tion's

2 See, the streams of liv - ing wa-ters, Spring-ing from e - ter - nal love, Well sup - ply thy sons and daugh-ters, And all fear of want re - move. Who can faint while such a riv - er Ev - er flows their thirst to assuage — Grace, which, like the

3 Sav - iour, if of Zi - on's cit - y I, through grace, a mem-ber am, Let the world de - ride or pit - y, I will glo - ry in Thy name: Fad - ing is the word - ling's pleas - ure, All his boast - ed pomp and show, Sol - id joys and

SOURCE OF TEXT: *Olney Hymns,* London, 1779. **SOURCE OF TUNE:** Written in 1941 and first published in leaflet form. From *The BBC Hymn Book* by permission of Oxford University Press, London.

walls sur-round-ed, Thou mayst smile at all thy foes.
Lord the Giv - er, Nev - er fails from age to age?
last - ing treas - ure None but Zi - on's chil - dren know.

Jesus, Thy Blood and Righteousness 98

Nicolaus L. von Zinzendorf, 1700-1760
Tr. John Wesley, 1703-1791

LLEDROD L.M.
Welsh Hymn Melody

In unison

1 Je - sus, thy blood and right-eous-ness My beau-ty are, my
2 Lord, I be - lieve thy pre-cious blood, Which at the mer - cy-
3 Je - sus, be end - less praise to thee, Whose bound-less mer - cy

glo-rious dress; Midst flam ing worlds, in these ar - rayed,
seat of God For - ev - er doth for sin-ners plead,
hath for me, For me and all thy hands have made,

With joy shall I lift up my head.
For me — e'en for my soul — was shed.
An ev - er - last - ing ran - som paid.

SOURCE OF TEXT: *Appendix VIII* to the *Herrnhut Gesangbuch*, 1739. Wesley's translation appeared in his *Hymns and Sacred Poems*, London, 1740. SOURCE OF TUNE: John Roberts's *Caniadau y Cysegr*, Wales, 1839.

99 **Now Thank We All Our God**

Martin Rinkart, 1586-1649
Tr. Catherine Winkworth, 1827-1878

GRACIAS 6.7.6.7.6.6.6.6.
Geoffrey Beaumont, 1903-

1 Now thank we all our God, With hearts and hands and
2 may this boun-teous God Through all our life be
3 praise and thanks to God The Fa-ther now be

voic - es, Who won-drous things hath done, In
near us, With ev - er - joy - ful hearts And
giv - en, The Son, and Him who reigns With

whom His world re - joic - es; Who, from our
bless - ed peace to cheer us; And keep us
them in high - est heav - en; The one e -

SOURCE OF TEXT: Probably in Rinkart's *Jesu Hertz-Buchlein*, Leipzig, 1636. SOURCE OF TRANSLATION: Winkworth's *Lyra Germanica*, second series, London, 1858. SOURCE OF TUNE: Beaumont's *Twentieth Century Folk Mass*, London, 1957. The first hymnal inclusion was *The Baptist Hymn Book*, London, 1961. Copyright 1957, W. Paxton & Co., Ltd. Used by permission of Mills Music, Inc.

224

mo - thers' arms, Hath blessed us on our way With
in His grace, And guide us when per - plexed, And
ter - nal God, Whom earth and heaven a - dore; For

count - less gifts of love, And still is ours to -
free us from all ills In this world and the
thus it was, is now, And shall be ev - er -

1 & 2

Last time

day.
next.

2 O
3 All

more.

Ped.

100 Let All the Multitudes of Light

F. B. Macnutt, 1873-1949

CONQUERING LOVE 8.7.8.7.8.8.7.
David Willcocks, 1919—

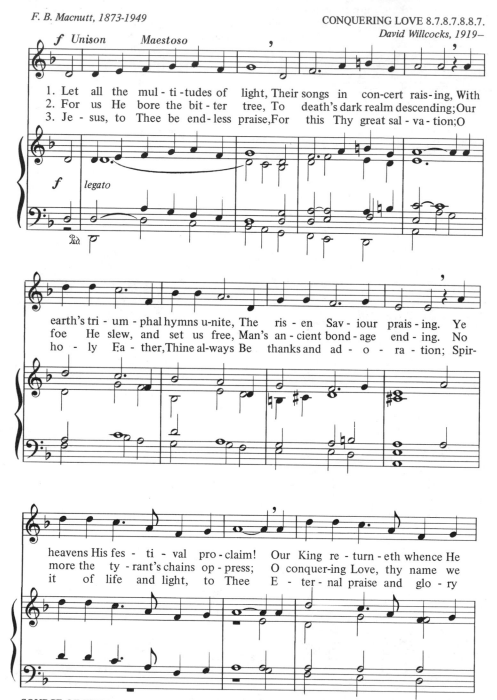

1. Let all the mul-ti-tudes of light, Their songs in con-cert rais-ing, With
2. For us He bore the bit-ter tree, To death's dark realm descending; Our
3. Je-sus, to Thee be end-less praise, For this Thy great sal-va-tion; O

earth's tri-um-phal hymns u-nite, The ris-en Sav-iour prais-ing. Ye
foe He slew, and set us free, Man's an-cient bond-age end-ing. No
ho-ly Fa-ther, Thine al-ways Be thanks and ad-o-ra-tion; Spir-

heavens His fes-ti-val pro-claim! Our King re-turn-eth whence He
more the ty-rant's chains op-press; O conquer-ing Love, thy name we
it of life and light, to Thee E-ter-nal praise and glo-ry

SOURCE OF TEXT: *Anglican Hymn Book*, 1965. Used by permission of Mrs. F.B.Macnutt.
SOURCE OF TUNE: *Anglican Hymn Book*, 1965. © David Willcocks. Reprinted by permission of the composer.

came,   With   vic - to - ry a - maz - ing.
bless,   With   Thee   to heaven as - cend - ing.
be: One   God   of   all cre - a - tion!

When in Our Music God Is Glorified 101

Frederick Pratt Green, 1903–

ENGELBERG 10.10.10.4
Charles V. Stanford, 1852–1924

♩=116

All   1. When   in   our   mu - sic   God   is   glo - ri - fied,
Woman 2. How   oft - en,   mak - ing   mu - sic,   we   have   found
All   3. So   has   the   Church,   in   lit - ur - gy   and   song,
Men   4. And   did   not   Je - sus   sing   a   psalm   that   night
All   5. Let   ev - 'ry   in - stru - ment   be   tuned   for   praise!

and   a - do - ra - tion leaves   no   room   for   pride,
a   new   di - men - sion   in   the   world   of   sound,
in   faith   and   love, through cen - tu - ries   of   wrong,
when   ut - most   e - vil strove   a - gainst   the   Light?
Let   all   re - joice   who have   a   voice   to   raise!

SOURCE OF TEXT: *26 Hymns*, 1971; written to be used with Stanford's tune. Used by permission of Oxford University Press. SOURCE OF TUNE: Written in 1904 by Stanford for William W. How's "For all the saints."

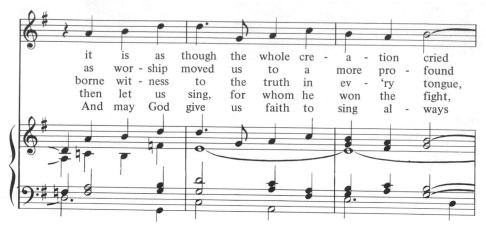

it   is   as though the whole cre - a - tion   cried
as   wor - ship moved   us   to   a   more pro - found
borne wit - ness   to   the   truth in   ev - 'ry   tongue,
then   let   us   sing,   for whom   he   won   the   fight,
And   may God give   us   faith   to   sing   al - ways

St. 1-4   St. 5

All: Al - le - lu - ia!

                              Al - le - lu - ia!

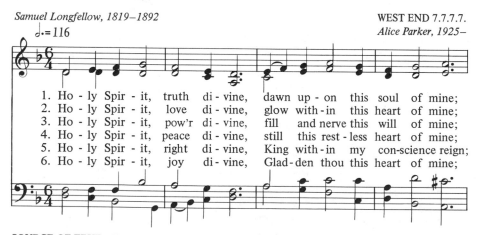

102   Holy Spirit, Truth Divine

Samuel Longfellow, 1819–1892

WEST END 7.7.7.7.
Alice Parker, 1925–

♩.=116

1. Ho - ly Spir - it, truth di - vine, dawn up - on this soul of mine;
2. Ho - ly Spir - it, love di - vine, glow with - in this heart of mine;
3. Ho - ly Spir - it, pow'r di - vine, fill and nerve this will of mine;
4. Ho - ly Spir - it, peace di - vine, still this rest - less heart of mine;
5. Ho - ly Spir - it, right di - vine, King with - in my con - science reign;
6. Ho - ly Spir - it, joy di - vine, Glad - den thou this heart of mine;

SOURCE OF TEXT: *Hymns of the Spirit,* 1864, edited by Longfellow and Samuel Johnson.
SOURCE OF TUNE: *Mennonite Hymnal,* 1969. Copyright 1976 by Hinshaw Music, Inc. Used by permission.

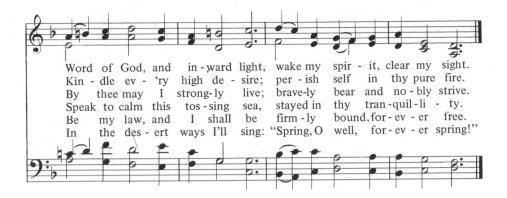

Word of God, and in-ward light, wake my spir-it, clear my sight.
Kin-dle ev-'ry high de-sire; per-ish self in thy pure fire.
By thee may I strong-ly live; brave-ly bear and no-bly strive.
Speak to calm this tos-sing sea, stayed in thy tran-quil-li-ty.
Be my law, and I shall be firm-ly bound, for-ev-er free.
In the des-ert ways I'll sing: "Spring, O well, for-ev-er spring!"

God Who Spoke in the Beginning 103

Fred Kaan, 1929–

VERBUM DEI 8.7.8.7.8.7.
Geoffrey Laycock, 1927-

($\downarrow$ = c. 70)

1. God who spoke in the be-
2. God who spoke through men and
3. God whose speech be-comes in-

gin-ning, form-ing rock and shap-ing spar, set all
na-tions, through e-vents long past and gone, show-ing
car-nate Christ is ser-vant, Christ is Lord! calls us

life and growth in mo - tion, earth - ly world and dis - tant
still to - day his pur - pose, speaks su - preme - ly through his
to a life of ser - vice, heart and will to ac - tion

star; He who calls the earth to or - der is the
Son; He who calls the earth to or - der gives his
stirred; He who u - ses man's o - be - dience has the

Verses 1 and 2 | Verse 3

ground of what we are.
word and it is done.
first and fi - nal word.

104   **In Babylon Town**

Hamish Swanston, 1933-

IN BABYLON TOWN 5.6.5.6. with Refrain
Ian Copley, 1926-

(♩. = c. 120)

1. In Ba - by - lon
3. Old Ba - by - lon

No Pedal

SOURCE OF TEXT AND TUNE: *New Catholic Hymnal*, 1971. Reprinted by permission of
Faber Music Ltd.

230

town By an a - li – en stream We had sad - ly sat
town By an a - li – en stream May be tum - bled all

down and slept with a dream. *Can you hear the pipe and*
down, We've no need to dream.

cresc.

drums? *Now he comes, now he comes.*

f

2. In Beth - le - hem town There's no room at the
4. Here now in our town There is room at the

No Pedal *Pedal*

inn,   so she cra-dles him down   And won-ders be-
inn,   where we all may sit down   His meal to be-

gin.
gin.   *Can you   hear   the pipe and drums?   Now he*

comes,   now he comes.   *comes.*

105   **Blow Ye the Trumpet, Blow**

Charles Wesley, 1707-1788   LENOX 6.6.6.6.8.8.
Lewis Edson, 1748-1820

1 Blow ye the trum-pet, blow! The glad-ly sol-emn sound Let all the na-tions know,
2 Je-sus, our great High Priest, Hath full atonement made; Ye wea-ry spir-its, rest;
3 The gospel trumpet hear, The news of heav'nly grace; And, saved from earth, appear

SOURCE OF TEXT: *Hymns for New Year's Day*, London, 1750, a collection of seven hymns published by Charles Wesley. SOURCE OF TUNE: Simeon Jocelyn's *The Chorister's Companion*, New Haven, Connecticut, 1782 or 1783.

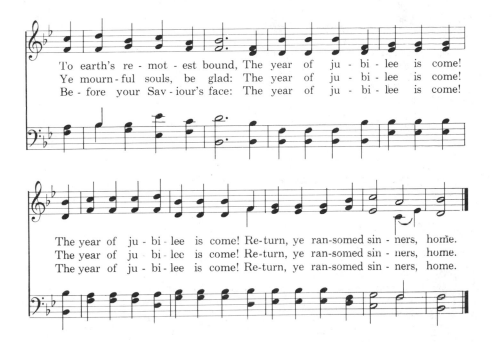

To earth's re - mot - est bound, The year of ju - bi - lee is come!
Ye mourn - ful souls, be glad: The year of ju - bi - lee is come!
Be - fore your Sav - iour's face: The year of ju - bi - lee is come!

The year of ju - bi - lee is come! Re-turn, ye ran-somed sin - ners, home.
The year of ju - bi - lee is come! Re-turn, ye ran-somed sin - ners, home.
The year of ju - bi - lee is come! Re-turn, ye ran-somed sin - ners, home.

How Beauteous Were the Marks Divine 106

A. Cleveland Coxe, 1818–1896

WINDHAM, L.M.
Daniel Read, 1757–1836

1. How   beau - teous were   the   marks di - vine,   That
2. O   who   like   thee,   so   mild,   so   bright,   Thou
3. O   who   like   thee   so   hum - bly   bore   The
4. O   won - drous Lord,   my   soul would   be   Still

in   thy meek - ness used   to   shine, That   lit   thy lone - ly
Son   of   man, thou Light   of   light? O   who   like thee   did
scorn,   the scoffs   of   men,   be - fore? So   meek,   so   low - ly,
more   and more   con - formed to   thee, And   learn   of   thee, the

SOURCE OF TEXT: Part of a poem entitled *"Hymn to the Redeemer"* first published in Coxe's
Christian Ballads, 1840. SOURCE OF TUNE: *The American Singing Book*, 1785.

path - way, trod In won - drous love, O Son of God!
ev - er go, So pa - tient through a world of woe?
yet so high, So glo - rious in hu - mil - i - ty?
low - ly one, And like thee, all my jour - ny run. A - men.

107 All Hail the Power of Jesus' Name

Edward Perronet, *1726-1792*
Alt. by John Rippon, *1751-1836*

CORONATION C.M.
Oliver Holden, *1765-1844*

1 All hail the power of Je - sus' name! Let an - gels pros - trate fall;
2 Crown him, ye mar - tyrs of our God, Who from his al - tar call;
3 Ye seed of Is - ra - el's chosen race, Ye ran - somed of the fall,
4 Let ev - ery kin - dred, ev - ery tribe, On this ter - res - trial ball,
5 O that, with yon - der sa - cred throng, We at his feet may fall;

Bring forth the roy - al di - a - dem, And crown him Lord of all.
Ex - tol the stem of Jes - se's rod, And crown him Lord of all.
Hail him who saves you by his grace, And crown him Lord of all.
To him all maj - es - ty as - cribe, And crown him Lord of all.
We'll join the ev - er - last - ing song, And crown him Lord of all.

Bring forth the roy - al di - a - dem, And crown him Lord of all.
Ex - tol the stem of Jes - se's rod, And crown him Lord of all.
Hail him who saves you by his grace, And crown him Lord of all.
To him all maj - es - ty as - cribe; And crown him Lord of all.
We'll join the ev - er - last - ing song, And crown him Lord of all. A - men.

SOURCE OF TEXT: *The Gospel Magazine*, VI, November 1779. Altered by John Rippon for his *Selection of Hymns*, London, 1787. SOURCE OF TUNE: Holden's *Union Harmony, or Universal Collection of Sacred Music*, Boston, 1793.

I Love Thee

108

I LOVE THEE 11.11.11.11.

Anonymous

Ingall's "Christian Harmony," 1805

1 I love Thee, I love Thee, I love Thee, my Lord;
2 I'm hap - py, I'm hap - py, oh, won - drous ac - count!
3 O Je - sus, my Sav - iour, with Thee I am blest,
4 Oh, who's like my Sav - iour? He's Sa - lem's bright King;

I love Thee, my Sav - iour, I love Thee, my God:
My joys are im - mor - tal, I stand on the mount:
My life and sal - va - tion, my joy and my rest:
He smiles and He loves me and helps me to sing:

I love Thee, I love Thee, and that Thou dost know;
I gaze on my treas - ure and long to be there,
Thy name be my theme, and Thy love be my song;
I'll praise Him I'll praise Him with notes loud and clear,

But how much I love Thee my ac - tions will show.
With Je - sus and an - gels and kin - dred so dear.
Thy grace shall in - spire both my heart and my tongue.
While riv - ers of pleas - ure my spir - it shall cheer. A - men.

SOURCE OF TEXT AND TUNE: Jeremiah Ingall's *Christian Harmony*, Exeter, New Hampshire, 1805.

109 Hail, Thou Once Despised Jesus

John Bakewell, 1721-1819

PLEADING SAVIOUR 8.7.8.7.D.
"Christian Lyre," 1831

1 Hail, Thou once de - spis - ed Je - sus, Crowned in mock - er - y a King!
2 Je - sus, hail! en-throned in glo - ry, There for - ev - er to a - bide;
3 Wor - ship, hon - or, power, and bless - ing Thou art wor - thy to re-ceive;

Thou didst suf - fer to re - lease us; Thou didst free sal - va - tion bring.
All the heaven-ly hosts a - dore Thee, Seat - ed at Thy Fa - ther's side:
Loud - est prais - es, with - out ceas - ing, Meet it is for us to give.

Hail, Thou ag - o - niz - ing Sav - iour, Bear - er of our sin and shame!
There for sin - ners Thou art plead-ing; There Thou dost our place pre - pare:
Help, ye bright an - gel - ic spir - its, Bring your sweet-est, no - blest lays;

By Thy mer - its we find fa - vor; Life is giv - en through Thy name.
Ev - er for us in - ter - ced - ing, Till in glo - ry we ap - pear.
Help to sing our Sav-iour's mer-its; Help to chant Im - man-uel's praise. A-men.

SOURCE OF TEXT: *A Collection of Hymns addressed to The Holy, Holy, Holy Triune God, in the Person of Christ Jesus, our Mediator and Advocate*, London, 1757. It was altered and expanded in Martin Madan's *Collection of Psalms and Hymns*, 1760. SOURCE OF TUNE: Joshua Leavitt's *Christian Lyre*, New York, 1831.

Saviour, When in Dust to Thee　110

Robert Grant, 1779-1838

SPANISH HYMN 7.7.7.7.D.
Arr. by Benjamin Carr, 1769–1831

Quietly

1 Sa-viour, when in dust to thee Low we bow the a-dor-ing knee;
2 By thy help-less in-fant years, By thy life of want and tears,
3 By thine hour of dire de-spair, By thine ag-o-ny of prayer,
4 By thy deep ex-pir-ing groan, By the sad se-pul-chral stone,

When, re-pent-ant, to the skies Scarce we dare to lift our eyes;
By thy days of sore dis-tress In the sav-age wil-der-ness,
By the cross, the nail, the thorn, Pierc-ing spear and taunt and scorn;
By the vault, whose dark a-bode Held in vain the ris-ing God;

O by all thy pains and woe Suf-fer'd once for man be-low,
By the dread mys-te-rious hour Of the in-sult-ing temp-ter's power;
By the gloom that veiled the skies O'er the dread-ful sac-ri-fice;
O from earth to heav'n re-stored, Might-y, re-as-cend-ed Lord,

Bend-ing from thy throne on high, Hear our sol-emn lit-a-ny!
Turn, O turn a fa-vor-ing eye, Hear our sol-emn lit-a-ny!
Lis-ten to our hum-ble cry, Hear our sol-emn lit-a-ny!
Lis-ten, lis-ten to the cry Of our sol-emn lit-a-ny! A-men.

SOURCE OF TEXT: *The Christian Observer*, XIV (London), November 1815. SOURCE OF TUNE: Unknown. Benjamin Carr published a version of this melody with variations for the piano in 1825, and the next year an arrangement for vocal solo and quartet with the notice, "an ancient Spanish melody." As a hymn tune it appeared in M. Burgoyne's *A Collection of Metrical Versions*, London, 1827. The 6.6.6.6.D. version of this tune is known as MADRID. Cf. *The Hymnbook*, no. 131.

O Come, All Ye Faithful

Latin: *John F. Wade, 1711-1786*
Tr. Frederick Oakeley, 1802-1880, and others

ADESTE FIDELES *Irregular*
John F. Wade's "Cantus Diversi," 1751

1 O come, all ye faith - ful, joy - ful and tri - um - phant, O
2 Sing, choirs of an - gels, sing in ex - ul - ta - tion,
3 Child, for us sin - ners poor and in the man - ger,
4 Yea, Lord, we greet thee, born this hap - py morn - ing,

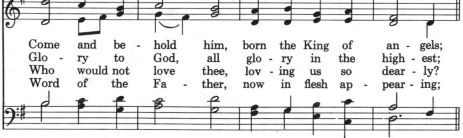

come ye, O come ye to Beth - le - hem;
Sing, all ye cit - i - zens of heaven a - bove!
We would em - brace thee, with love and awe;
Je - sus, to thee be all glo - ry given;

Come and be - hold him, born the King of an - gels;
Glo - ry to God, all glo - ry in the high - est;
Who would not love thee, lov - ing us so dear - ly?
Word of the Fa - ther, now in flesh ap - pear - ing;

SOURCE OF TEXT AND TUNE: Words and music believed to have been written about 1740, found in seven known manuscript copybooks dating mid-eighteenth century, which show the tune in triple time. First appeared in duple time in Samuel Webbe's *Essay on the Church Plain Chant,* London, 1782. First American appearance was in Benjamin Carr's *Musical Journal,* II (Philadelphia), December 29, 1800. SOURCE OF TRANSLATION: Oakeley's translation, made in 1841, was altered to its present form in F. H. Murray's *A Hymnal for Use in the English Church,* London, 1852.

O come, let us a-dore him, O come, let us a-dore him,

O come, let us a-dore him, Christ, the Lord! A-men.

Children of the Heavenly King 112

John Cennick, 1718-1755

PLEYEL'S HYMN 7.7.7.7.
Arr. from Ignaz J. Pleyel, 1757-1831

1 Chil-dren of the Heaven-ly King, As we jour-ney, sweet-ly sing;
2 We are trav-eling home to God In the way the fa-thers trod;
3 Fear not, breth-ren; joy-ful stand On the bor-ders of your land;
4 Lord, o-be-dient-ly we go, Glad-ly leav-ing all be-low;

Sing our Sav-iour's wor-thy praise, Glo-rious in His works and ways.
They are hap-py now, and we Soon their hap-pi-ness shall see.
Je-sus Christ, your Fa-ther's Son, Bids you un-dis-mayed go on.
On-ly Thou our Lead-er be, And we still will fol-low Thee. A-men.

SOURCE OF TEXT: Cennick's *Sacred Hymns for the Children of God*, London, 1742. SOURCE OF TUNE: This tune is the theme of a set of variations in Pleyel's *String Quartet*, Op. 7, No. 4, *c*.1782. It first appeared as a hymn tune in Arnold and Callcott's *Psalms of David for the Use of Parish Churches*, London, 1791. First published in America in Benjamin Carr's *Masses, Vespers, Litanies, Hymns*, Baltimore, 1805, where it was used with this text.

113 From Greenland's Icy Mountains

Reginald Heber, 1783-1826

MISSIONARY HYMN 7.6.7.6.D.
Lowell Mason, 1792-1872

1 From Green-land's i - cy moun-tains, From In - dia's cor - al strand,
2 What though the spi - cy breez - es Blow soft o'er Cey-lon's isle;
3 Shall we, whose souls are light - ed With wis-dom from on high,
4 Waft, waft, ye winds, His sto - ry, And you, ye wa - ters, roll,

Where Af - ric's sun - ny foun-tains Roll down their gold - en sand,
Though ev - ery pros-pect pleas - es, And on - ly man is vile;
Shall we to men be-night - ed The lamp of life de - ny?
Till, like a sea of glo - ry, It spreads from pole to pole;

From man-y an an-cient riv - er, From man-y a palm - y plain,
In vain with lav - ish kind-ness The gifts of God are strown;
Sal - va - tion! O sal - va - tion! The joy - ful sound pro-claim,
Till o'er our ran-somed na - ture The Lamb for sin - ners slain,

They call us to de - liv - er Their land from er - ror's chain.
The hea-then in his blind - ness Bows down to wood and stone.
Till earth's re - mot - est na - tion Has learned Mes-si - ah's name.
Re - deem - er, King, Cre - a - tor, In bliss re - turns to reign. A - men.

SOURCE OF TEXT: *Evangelical Magazine*, XXIX, July 1821, and later in Heber's *Hymns*, 1827. Its first American inclusion was in Nettleton's *Village Hymns*, New York, 1824. SOURCE OF TUNE: Written in Savannah, Georgia, 1824, and first published as a soprano solo in Boston, n.d. It first appeared as a hymn tune in the *Boston Handel and Haydn Society Collection of Church Music*, seventh edition, Boston, 1829.

Joy to the World! the Lord Is Come 114

Isaac Watts, 1674-1748

ANTIOCH C.M.
Attr. to Georg F. Handel, 1685-1759
Arr. by Lowell Mason, 1792-1872

1 Joy to the world! the Lord is come: Let earth re-
2 Joy to the earth! the Sav - ior reigns: Let men their
3 He rules the world with truth and grace, And makes the

ceive her King; Let ev - ery heart pre - pare him room,
songs em - ploy; While fields and floods, rocks, hills, and plains
na - tions prove The glo - ries of his right - eous - ness,

And heaven and na - ture sing, And heaven and na - ture
Re - peat the sound - ing joy, Re - peat the sound - ing
And won - ders of his love, And won - ders of his

And heaven and na - ture sing, And
Re - peat the sound-ing joy, Re -
And won-ders of his love, And

sing, And heaven, and heaven and na - ture sing.
joy, Re - peat, re - peat the sound - ing joy.
love, And won - ders, won - ders of his love. A-men.

heaven and na - ture sing.
peat the sound-ing joy,
won - ders of his love,

SOURCE OF TEXT: Watts's *Psalms of David Imitated in the Language of the New Testament*, 1719.
SOURCE OF TUNE: Appeared in Lowell Mason's *The Modern Psalmist*, Boston, 1839, with the notation: "from Handel."

115 When I Survey the Wondrous Cross

Isaac Watts, 1674-1748

HAMBURG L.M.
Arr. by Lowell Mason, 1792-1872

1 When I sur-vey the won-drous cross On which the
2 For-bid it, Lord, that I should boast, Save in the
3 See, from his head, his hands, his feet, Sor-row and

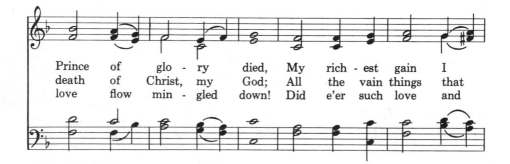

Prince of glo-ry died, My rich-est gain I
death of Christ, my God; All the vain things that
love flow min-gled down! Did e'er such love and

count but loss, And pour con-tempt on all my pride.
charm me most I sac-ri-fice them to his blood.
sor-row meet, Or thorns com-pose so rich a crown? A-men.

4 Were the whole realm of nature mine,
   That were a present far too small;
Love so amazing, so divine,
   Demands my soul, my life, my all.

SOURCE OF TEXT: *Hymns and Spiritual Songs*, London, 1707. SOURCE OF TUNE: *Boston Handel and Haydn Society Collection of Church Music*, third edition, Boston, 1825, where the compiler, Lowell Mason, indicated that it was arranged from a Gregorian chant.

Rock of Ages

Augustus M. Toplady, 1740-1778, alt.

TOPLADY 7.7.7.7.7.7.
Thomas Hastings, 1784-1872

1 Rock of a - ges, cleft for me, Let me hide my-self in thee;
2 Not the la - bors of my hands Can ful - fill thy law's de-mands;
3 Noth-ing in my hand I bring, Sim-ply to thy cross I cling;

Let the wa - ter and the blood, From thy riv - en side which flowed,
Could my zeal no res - pite know, Could my tears for - ev - er flow,
Na - ked, come to thee for dress; Help-less, look to thee for grace;

Be of sin the dou - ble cure, Cleanse me from its guilt and power.
All for sin could not a - tone; Thou must save, and thou a - lone.
Foul, I to the foun-tain fly; Wash me, Sav-ior, or I die! A-men.

4 While I draw this fleeting breath,
　When mine eyes shall close in death,
When I soar to worlds unknown,
　See thee on thy judgment throne,
Rock of ages, cleft for me,
　Let me hide myself in thee!

SOURCE OF TEXT: *Gospel Magazine*, III, March 1776, and in Toplady's *Psalms and Hymns*, London, the same year. SOURCE OF TUNE: *Spiritual Songs for Social Worship*, Boston, 1832.

117 Amazing Grace! How Sweet the Sound

John Newton, 1725-1807

AMAZING GRACE C.M.
Early American Melody
Arr. by Edwin O. Excell, 1851-1921

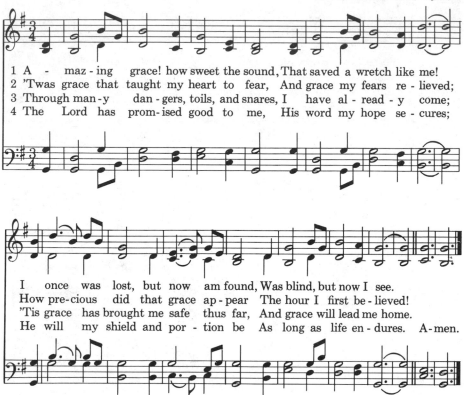

1 A - maz - ing grace! how sweet the sound, That saved a wretch like me!
2 'Twas grace that taught my heart to fear, And grace my fears re - lieved;
3 Through man - y dan - gers, toils, and snares, I have al - read - y come;
4 The Lord has prom-ised good to me, His word my hope se - cures;

I once was lost, but now am found, Was blind, but now I see.
How pre-cious did that grace ap - pear The hour I first be - lieved!
'Tis grace has brought me safe thus far, And grace will lead me home.
He will my shield and por - tion be As long as life en - dures. A - men.

5 Yes, when this heart and flesh shall fail,
   And mortal life shall cease,
I shall possess within the veil,
   A life of joy and peace.

6 The earth shall soon dissolve like snow,
   The sun forbear to shine;
But God, who called me here below,
   Will be for ever mine.

SOURCE OF TEXT: *Olney Hymns*, London, 1779. SOURCE OF TUNE: An early American folk melody of unknown origin. It reappeared in the South during the nineteenth century in many of the oblong tune books under such names as NEW BRITAIN, REDEMPTION, HARMONY GROVE, SYMPHONY, and SOLON. The earliest known collection containing it (found by George Pullen Jackson) is the *Virginia Harmony*, printed 1831 in Winchester, Virginia — compiled by James P. Carrell and David S. Clayton (Lebanon, Virginia). This arrangement by E. O. Excell, a Chicago gospel-songbook publisher, was included in his *Make His Praise Glorious*, 1900, no. 235.

How Firm a Foundation   118

"K" in Rippon's "Selection," 1787

FOUNDATION 11.11.11.11.
Early American Melody

1 How firm a foun-da tion, ye saints of the Lord,
2 "Fear not, I am with thee; O be not dis-mayed,
3 "When through fier-y tri-als thy path-way shall lie,
4 "The soul that on Je-sus hath leaned for re-pose

Is laid for your faith in His ex-cel-lent Word!
For I am thy God, and will still give thee aid;
My grace, all-suf-fi-cient, shall be thy sup-ply:
I will not, I will not de-sert to his foes;

What more can He say than to you He hath said,
I'll strength-en thee, help thee, and cause thee to stand,
The flame shall not hurt thee; I on-ly de-sign
That soul, though all hell should en-deav-or to shake,

To you who for ref-uge to Je-sus have fled?
Up-held by my right-eous, om-nip-o-tent hand.
Thy dross to con-sume, and thy gold to re-fine.
I'll nev-er, no, nev-er, no, nev-er for-sake!"

SOURCE OF TEXT: John Rippon's *Selection of Hymns*, London, 1787. SOURCE OF TUNE: An early American melody which appears in William Caldwell's *Union Harmony*, Maryville, Tennessee, 1837, and in the *Sacred Harp*, 1844, in which it is called BELLEVUE and credited to "Z. Chambless."

119 Awake, Awake to Love and Work

Geoffrey A. Studdert-Kennedy, 1883-1929

MORNING SONG 8.6.8.6.8.6.
Melody, "Kentucky Harmony," 1816
Harm. by C. Winfred Douglas, 1867-1944

1 A - wake, a - wake to love and work! The lark is in the sky;
2 Come, let thy voice be one with theirs, Shout with their shout of praise;
3 To give and give, and give a - gain, What God hath giv - en thee;

The fields are wet with dia-mond dew; The worlds a - wake to cry
See how the gi - ant sun soars up, Great lord of years and days!
To spend thy - self nor count the cost; To serve right glo - rious - ly

Their bless-ings on the Lord of life, As he goes meek-ly by.
So let the love of Je - sus come And set thy soul a - blaze.
The God who gave all worlds that are, And all that are to be.

source of text: This hymn is the last half of a poem, "At a Harvest Festival," included in Studdert-Kennedy's *Sorrows of God, and other Poems,* London, 1921. It also appears in *The Unutterable Beauty*. Used by permission Hodder & Stoughton Ltd., London. source of tune: Named CONSOLATION and credited to "Dean," this tune is first found in the *Kentucky Harmony*, 1816, compiled by Ananias Davisson. The harmonization given here was made by Douglas for *The Hymnal 1940*. Used by permission The Church Pension Fund.

Jerusalem, My Happy Home   120

F. B. P., c.16th century, alt.

LAND OF REST C.M.
Traditional American Melody
Harm. by Annabel Morris Buchanan, 1888-

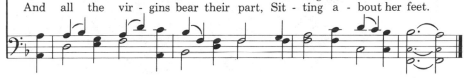

1 Je - ru - sa - lem, my hap - py home, When shall I come to thee?
2 Thy saints are crowned with glo - ry great; They see God face to face;
3 There Da - vid stands with harp in hand As mas - ter of the choir;
4 There Mar - y sings Mag - nif - i - cat With tune sur - pass - ing sweet;

When shall my sor - rows have an end? Thy joys, when shall I see?
They tri - umph still, they still re - joice; Most hap - py is their case.
Ten thou - sand times that man were blest That might this mu - sic hear.
And all the vir - gins bear their part, Sit - ting a - bout her feet.

5 There Magdalen hath left her moan,
   And cheerfully doth sing
   With blessèd saints, whose harmony
   In every street doth ring.

6 Jerusalem, Jerusalem,
   God grant that I may see
   Thine endless joy, and of the same
   Partaker ever be!

SOURCE OF TEXT: Attempts to identify the author of this sixteenth-century sacred ballad, entitled *A Song made by F. B. P.*, have been unsuccessful (cf. Julian, *A Dictionary of Hymnology*, pp. 580–582). SOURCE OF TUNE: A traditional American folk melody adapted by Mrs. Buchanan in her *Folk Hymns of America*, New York, 1938. Reprinted with the permission of the copyright owners, J. Fischer & Bro.

121 Brethren, We Have Met to Worship

George Atkins ?

HOLY MANNA 8.7.8.7.D.
William Moore

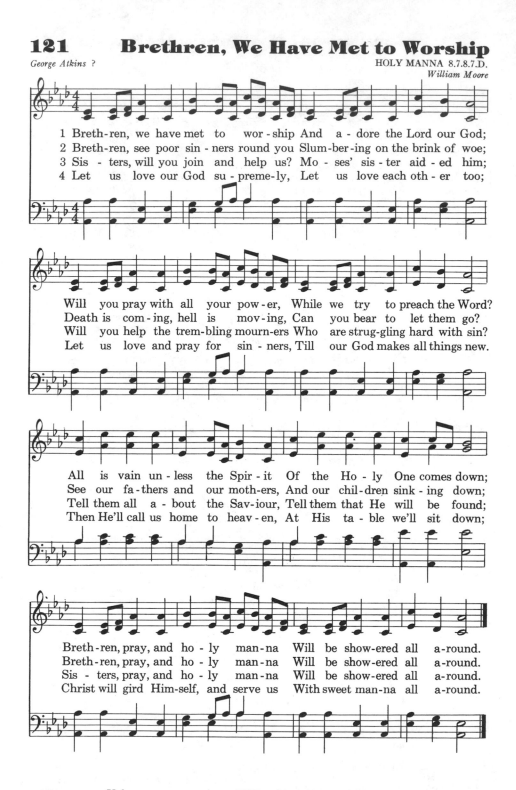

1 Breth-ren, we have met to wor-ship And a-dore the Lord our God;
2 Breth-ren, see poor sin-ners round you Slum-ber-ing on the brink of woe;
3 Sis-ters, will you join and help us? Mo-ses' sis-ter aid-ed him;
4 Let us love our God su-preme-ly, Let us love each oth-er too;

Will you pray with all your pow-er, While we try to preach the Word?
Death is com-ing, hell is mov-ing, Can you bear to let them go?
Will you help the trem-bling mourn-ers Who are strug-gling hard with sin?
Let us love and pray for sin-ners, Till our God makes all things new.

All is vain un-less the Spir-it Of the Ho-ly One comes down;
See our fa-thers and our moth-ers, And our chil-dren sink-ing down;
Tell them all a-bout the Sav-iour, Tell them that He will be found;
Then He'll call us home to heav-en, At His ta-ble we'll sit down;

Breth-ren, pray, and ho-ly man-na Will be show-ered all a-round.
Breth-ren, pray, and ho-ly man-na Will be show-ered all a-round.
Sis-ters, pray, and ho-ly man-na Will be show-ered all a-round.
Christ will gird Him-self, and serve us With sweet man-na all a-round.

SOURCE OF TEXT: Unknown. SOURCE OF TUNE: William Moore's *Columbian Harmony*, Knoxville, Tennessee, 1825.

248

When I Can Read My Title Clear 122

Isaac Watts, 1674-1748

PISGAH 8.6.8.6.6.6.8 6.
"Tennessee Harmony," c. 1819

1 When I can read my ti - tle clear To man-sions in the skies,
2 Should earth a-gainst my soul en - gage, And fier - y darts be hurled,
3 Let cares, like a wild del - uge come, And storms of sor-row fall!
4 There shall I bathe my wea - ry soul In seas of heav'n-ly rest,

I'll bid fare-well to ev - 'ry fear, And wipe my weep - ing eyes;
Then I can smile at Sa - tan's rage, And face a frown-ing world;
May I but safe - ly reach my home, My God, my heav'n, my all;
And not a wave of trou - ble roll A - cross my peace-ful breast;

And wipe my weep - ing eyes, And wipe my weep - ing eyes,
And face a frown-ing world, And face a frown-ing world,
My God, my heav'n, my all, My God, my heav'n, my all,
A - cross my peace-ful breast, A - cross my peace-ful breast,

I'll bid fare-well to ev - 'ry fear, And wipe my weep-ing eyes.
Then I can smile at Sa-tan's rage, And face a frown-ing world.
May I but safe - ly reach my home, My God, my heav'n, my all.
And not a wave of trou-ble roll A - cross my peace-ful breast.

SOURCE OF TEXT: *Hymns and Spiritual Songs*, London, 1707. SOURCE OF TUNE: This tune appears in Alexander Johnson's *Tennessee Harmony*, c. 1819. It is called CHRISTIAN TRIUMPH, and in the index is credited to Johnson. In Leavitt's *Christian Lyre*, 1831, it is credited to J. C. Lowry. Another version of this tune, called COVENANTERS, is found in *The Hymmbook*, 1955, no. 153.

123 Come, Come, Ye Saints

William Clayton
Alt. by Joseph F. Green, 1924-

ALL IS WELL 10.6.10.6 8.8.8.6.
Adapted from J. T. White
"The Sacred Harp," 1844

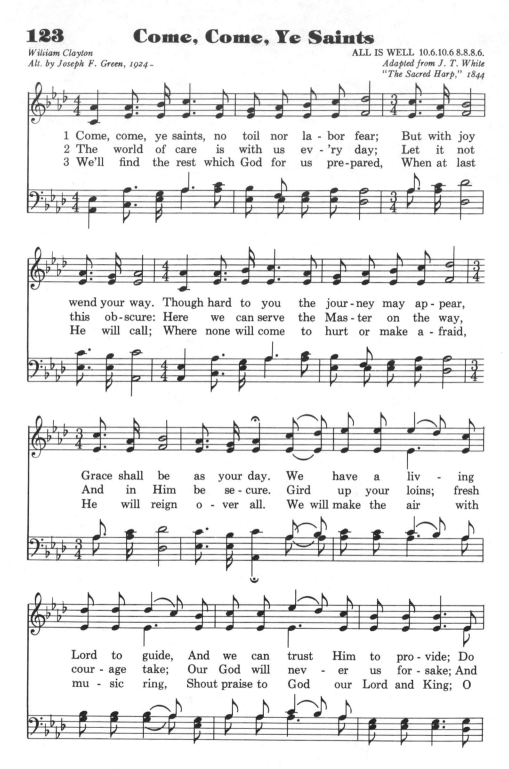

1 Come, come, ye saints, no toil nor la-bor fear; But with joy wend your way. Though hard to you the jour-ney may ap-pear, Grace shall be as your day. We have a liv-ing Lord to guide, And we can trust Him to pro-vide; Do

2 The world of care is with us ev-'ry day; Let it not this ob-scure: Here we can serve the Mas-ter on the way, And in Him be se-cure. Gird up your loins; fresh cour-age take; Our God will nev-er us for-sake; And

3 We'll find the rest which God for us pre-pared, When at last He will call; Where none will come to hurt or make a-fraid, He will reign o-ver all. We will make the air with mu-sic ring, Shout praise to God our Lord and King; O

SOURCE OF TEXT: First written in 1846. The altered version copyright, 1960, Broadman Press, first appeared in *Broadman Songs for Men No. 2*, 1960. Used by permission. SOURCE OF TUNE: *The Sacred Harp*, 1844, where it is credited to J. T. White.

this, and joy your hearts will swell: All is well! All is well!
so our song no fear can quell; All is well! All is well!
how we'll make the cho - rus swell: All is well! All is well!

Sunset to Sunrise Changes Now 124

Clement of Alexandria, c.170-220
Para. by Howard C. Robbins, 1876-1952

KEDRON L.M.
"Tennessee Harmony," c.1819

In unison

1 Sun - set to sun - rise chang - es now, For
2 E'en though the sun with - holds its light, Lo!
3 Here in o'er - whelm - ing fi - nal strife The

God doth make his world a - new; On the Re - deem - er's
a more heaven - ly lamp shines here, And from the cross on
Lord of life hath vic - to - ry; And sin is slain, and

thorn-crowned brow The won - ders of that dawn we view.
Cal - vary's height Gleams of e - ter - ni - ty ap - pear.
death brings life, And sons of earth hold heaven in fee.

SOURCE OF TEXT: Robbins' paraphrase first appeared in his *Preaching the Gospel*, 1939. The first hymnal inclusion was *The Hymnal 1940*. Used by permission of Mrs. Howard C. Robbins. SOURCE OF TUNE: Alexander Johnson's *Tennessee Harmony*, c. 1819, with this tune credited to "Dare." Also found in William Walker's *Southern Harmony*, 1835.

125 Love Divine, All Loves Excelling

Charles Wesley, 1707-1788, alt.

BEECHER 8.7.8.7.D.
John Zundel, 1815-1882

1 Love di - vine, all loves ex - cel - ling, Joy of heaven, to earth come down,
2 Breathe, O breathe thy lov - ing Spir - it In - to ev - ery trou - bled breast;
3 Come, al - might - y to de - liv - er, Let us all thy life re - ceive;
4 Fin - ish, then, thy new cre - a - tion; Pure and spot-less let us be;

Fix in us thy hum - ble dwell - ing, All thy faith-ful mer - cies crown!
Let us all in thee in - her - it, Let us find thy prom - ised rest;
Sud-den - ly re - turn, and nev - er, Nev-er - more thy tem - ples leave.
Let us see thy great sal - va - tion Per-fect - ly re - stored in thee;

Je - sus, thou art all com - pas - sion, Pure, un-bound-ed love thou art;
Take a - way the love of sin - ning; Al - pha and O - me - ga be;
Thee we would be al - ways bless-ing, Serve thee as thy hosts a - bove,
Changed from glo - ry in - to glo - ry, Till in heaven we take our place,

Vis - it us with thy sal - va - tion, En - ter ev - ery trem - bling heart.
End of faith, as its be - gin-ning, Set our hearts at lib - er - ty.
Pray, and praise thee with-out ceas-ing, Glo - ry in thy per - fect love.
Till we cast our crowns be-fore thee, Lost in won-der, love, and praise. A-men.

SOURCE OF TEXT: *Hymns for those that seek and those that have Redemption in the Blood of Jesus Christ,* London, 1747. SOURCE OF TUNE: *Christian Heart Songs,* New York, 1870.

What a Friend We Have in Jesus 126

Joseph Scriven, 1819-1886

ERIE 8.7.8.7.D.
Charles C. Converse, 1832-1918

1 What a friend we have in Je - sus, All our sins and griefs to bear!
2 Have we tri - als and temp-ta - tions? Is there trou-ble an - y - where?
3 Are we weak and heav - y lad - en, Cum-bered with a load of care?

What a priv - i - lege to car - ry Ev - ery-thing to God in prayer!
We should nev - er be dis - cour - aged; Take it to the Lord in prayer!
Pre - cious Sav - ior, still our ref - uge, Take it to the Lord in prayer!

Oh, what peace we of - ten for - feit, Oh, what need-less pain we bear,
Can we find a friend so faith - ful, Who will all our sor - rows share?
Do thy friends de-spise, for - sake thee? Take it to the Lord in prayer!

All be-cause we do not car - ry Ev - ery-thing to God in prayer.
Je - sus knows our ev - ery weak-ness; Take it to the Lord in prayer!
In his arms he'll take and shield thee, Thou wilt find a sol - ace there. A-men.

SOURCE OF TEXT: Horace L. Hastings's *Social Hymns, Original and Selected*, Richmond, Virginia, 1865.
SOURCE OF TUNE: *Silver Wings*, 1870, a small Sunday school collection, in which the tune is signed "Karl Reden," pseudonym of Converse.

127   He Leadeth Me, O Blessed Thought

Joseph H. Gilmore, 1834-1918

HE LEADETH ME L.M. *with Refrain*
William B. Bradbury, 1816-1868

1 He lead-eth me, oh bless-ed thought! O words with heaven-ly com-fort fraught!
2 Lord, I would clasp thy hand in mine, Nor ev - er mur - mur nor re - pine;
3 And when my task on earth is done, When, by thy grace, the vic-tory's won,

What-e'er I do, wher-e'er I be, Still 'tis God's hand that lead-eth me.
Con-tent, what-ev - er lot I see, Since 'tis my God that lead-eth me.
E'en death's cold wave I will not flee, Since God through Jor-dan lead-eth me.

REFRAIN

He lead-eth me, he lead - eth me, By his own hand he lead-eth me;

His faith-ful fol-lower I would be, For by his hand he lead-eth me. A-men.

SOURCE OF TEXT: *The Christian Watchman and Reflector*, XLIII (New York), December 4, 1862.
SOURCE OF TUNE: Bradbury's *The Golden Censer: a Musical Offering to the Sabbath Schools of Children's Hosannas to the Son of David*, New York, 1864, and in the same year in the *Devotional Hymn and Tune Book*, Philadelphia.

All the Way My Saviour Leads Me 128

Fanny J. Crosby, 1820-1915

ALL THE WAY 8.7.8.7.D.
Robert Lowry, 1826-1899

1 All the way my Sav-iour leads me; What have I to ask be-side?
2 All the way my Sav-iour leads me, Cheers each wind-ing path I tread,
3 All the way my Sav-iour leads me; Oh, the ful - ness of His love!

Can I doubt His ten - der mer - cy, Who thro' life has been my guide?
Gives me grace for ev - 'ry tri - al, Feeds me with the liv - ing bread:
Per - fect rest to me is prom - is'd In my Fa-ther's house a - bove:

Heav'n-ly peace, di - vin - est com - fort, Here by faith in Him to dwell!
Tho' my wea - ry steps may fal - ter, And my soul a - thirst may be,
When my spir - it, cloth'd im-mor - tal, Wings its flight to realms of day,

For I know what-e'er be - fall me, Je - sus do - eth all things well;
Gush-ing from the Rock be - fore me, Lo! a spring of joy I see;
This my song thro' end - less a - ges: Je - sus led me all the way;

For I know what-e'er be - fall me, Je - sus do - eth all things well.
Gush-ing from the Rock be - fore me, Lo! a spring of joy I see.
This my song thro' end - less a - ges: Je - sus led me all the way.

SOURCE OF TEXT AND TUNE: Doane and Lowry's *Brightest and Best*, Chicago, 1875, a collection of songs for Sunday schools.

129   To God Be the Glory

Fanny J. Crosby, *1820-1915*

TO GOD BE THE GLORY 11.11.11.11. *with Refrain*
William H. Doane, *1832-1915*

1 To God be the glo - ry, great things He hath done; So loved He the
2 O per - fect re - demp - tion, the pur - chase of blood, To ev - 'ry be -
3 Great things He hath taught us, great things He hath done, And great our re -

world that He gave us His Son, Who yield - ed His life an a -
liev - er the prom - ise of God; The vil - est of - fend - er who
joic - ing thro' Je - sus the Son; But pur - er, and high - er, and

tone-ment for sin, And o - pened the life - gate that all may go in.
tru - ly be - lieves, That mo - ment from Je - sus a par - don re - ceives.
great-er will be Our won - der, our trans-port, when Je - sus we see.

REFRAIN

Praise the Lord, praise the Lord, Let the earth hear His voice! Praise the Lord,

SOURCE OF TEXT AND TUNE: Doane and Lowry's *Brightest and Best*, Chicago, 1875, a collection of songs for Sunday schools. Ironically, this American gospel song had long been forgotten in the United States. It became immensely popular during the Billy Graham crusades in Great Britain in 1954, and was "imported" back across the Atlantic. Through Graham's crusades it has now become widely known throughout America.

praise the Lord, Let the peo-ple re-joice! O come to the Fa-ther, thro'

Je-sus the Son, And give Him the glo-ry, great things He hath done. A-men.

O for a Thousand Tongues to Sing 130

Charles Wesley, 1707-1788

AZMON C.M.
Carl G. Gläser, 1784-1829
Mason's "Modern Psalmodist," 1839

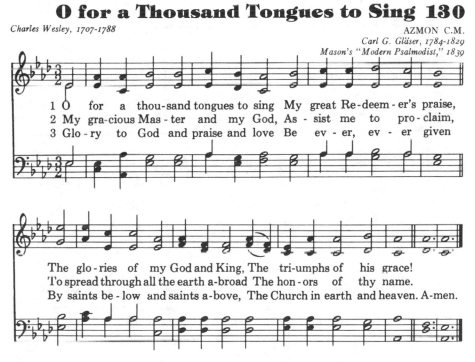

1 O for a thou-sand tongues to sing My great Re-deem-er's praise,
2 My gra-cious Mas-ter and my God, As-sist me to pro-claim,
3 Glo-ry to God and praise and love Be ev-er, ev-er given

The glo-ries of my God and King, The tri-umphs of his grace!
To spread through all the earth a-broad The hon-ors of thy name.
By saints be-low and saints a-bove, The Church in earth and heaven. A-men.

SOURCE OF TEXT: *Hymns and Sacred Poems*, London, 1740. SOURCE OF TUNE: Lowell Mason's *The Modern Psalmodist*, 1839.

131 Sing Them Over Again to Me

Philip P. Bliss, 1838-1876

WORDS OF LIFE 8.6.8.6.6.6. *with Refrain*
Philip P. Bliss. 1838-1876

1 Sing them o-ver a-gain to me, Won-der-ful words of life;
2 Christ, the bless-ed One, gives to all Won-der-ful words of life;
3 Sweet-ly ech-o the gos-pel call, Won-der-ful words of life;

Let me more of their beau-ty see, Won-der-ful words of life;
Sin-ner, list to the lov-ing call, Won-der-ful words of life;
Of-fer par-don and peace to all, Won-der-ful words of life;

Words of life and beau-ty, Teach me faith and du-ty:
All so free-ly giv-en, Woo-ing us to heav-en:
Je-sus, on-ly Sav-iour, Sanc-ti-fy for-ev-er,

REFRAIN

Beau-ti-ful words, won-der-ful words, Won-der-ful words of life;

Beau-ti-ful words, won-der-ful words, Won-der-ful words of life.

SOURCE OF TEXT AND TUNE: Written especially for the first issue of *Words of Life*, 1874, a Sunday school paper published by Fleming H. Revell Company, New York. First hymnal inclusion was in *Gospel Hymns No. 3*, 1878.

My Hope Is Built on Nothing Less 132

Edward Mote, 1797-1874

SOLID ROCK L.M. *with Refrain*
William B. Bradbury, 1816-1868

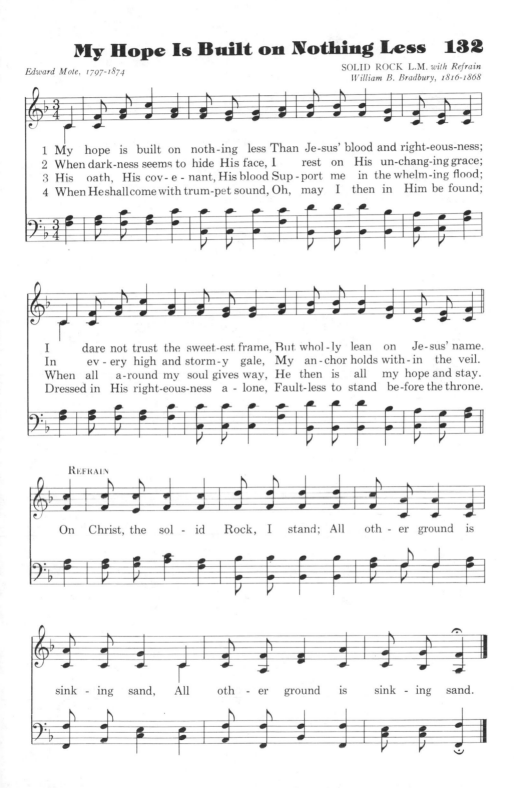

1 My hope is built on noth-ing less Than Je-sus' blood and right-eous-ness;
2 When dark-ness seems to hide His face, I rest on His un-chang-ing grace;
3 His oath, His cov-e-nant, His blood Sup-port me in the whelm-ing flood;
4 When He shall come with trum-pet sound, Oh, may I then in Him be found;

I dare not trust the sweet-est frame, But whol-ly lean on Je-sus' name.
In ev-ery high and storm-y gale, My an-chor holds with-in the veil.
When all a-round my soul gives way, He then is all my hope and stay.
Dressed in His right-eous-ness a-lone, Fault-less to stand be-fore the throne.

REFRAIN

On Christ, the sol-id Rock, I stand; All oth-er ground is

sink-ing sand, All oth-er ground is sink-ing sand.

SOURCE OF TEXT: *Hymns of Praise, A New Selection of Gospel Hymns*, London, 1836. SOURCE OF TUNE: Bradbury's *The Devotional Hymn and Tune Book*, Philadelphia, 1864.

133 Farther Along

W. B. Stevens

Rev. W. B. Stevens
Arr. J. R. Baxter, Jr., 1887-1960

1. Tempt-ed and tried we're oft made to won-der Why it should be thus
2. When death has come and tak-en our loved ones, It leaves our home so
3. Faith-ful till death said our lov-ing Mas-ter, A few more days to
4. When we see Je-sus com-ing in glo-ry, When He comes from His

all the day long, While there are oth-ers liv-ing a-bout us,
lone-ly and drear; Then do we won-der why oth-ers pros-per,
la-bor and wait; Toils of the road will then seem as noth-ing,
home in the sky; Then we shall meet Him in that bright mansion,

Chorus

Nev-er mo-lest-ed tho in the wrong.
Liv-ing so wick-ed year af-ter year.
As we sweep thru the beau-ti-ful gate. Far-ther a-long we'll
We'll un-der-stand it all by and by.

know all a-bout it, Farther a-long we'll un-derstand why; Cheer up, my

broth-er, live in the sunshine, We'll un-derstand it all by and by.

SOURCE OF TEXT AND TUNE: First appeared in *Starlit Crown*, Dallas, Texas, copyright 1937 by The Stamps-Baxter Music Co. Used by permission.

O God of Light, Thy Word, a Lamp Unfailing 134

Sarah E Taylor, 1883-1954

ANCIENT OF DAYS 11.10.11.10.
J. Albert Jeffery, 1855-1929

1 O God of light, Thy Word, a lamp un-fail-ing,
2 From days of old, through swift-ly roll-ing a-ges,
3 Un-dimmed by time, the Word is still re-veal-ing
4 To all the world the mes-sage Thou art send-ing,

Shines through the dark-ness of our earth-ly way,
Thou hast re-vealed Thy will to mor-tal men,
To sin-ful men Thy jus-tice and Thy grace;
To ev-'ry land, to ev-'ry race and clan;

O'er fear and doubt, o'er black de-spair pre-vail-ing,
Speak-ing to saints, to proph-ets, kings, and sag-es,
And quest-ing hearts that long for peace and heal-ing,
And myr-iad tongues, in one great an-them blend-ing,

Guid-ing our steps to Thine e-ter-nal day.
Who wrote the mes-sage with im-mor-tal pen.
See Thy com-pas-sion in the Sav-iour's face.
Ac-claim with joy Thy won-drous gift to man. A-men.

SOURCE OF TEXT: *Ten New Hymns on the Bible*, New York, 1952. Used by permission of The Hymn Society of America. SOURCE OF TUNE: Composed in 1886, and first appeared in Charles L. Hutchins's musical edition of the Episcopal *Hymnal*, 1894.

135 O Zion, Haste, Thy Mission High Fulfilling

Mary A. Thomson, 1834-1923

TIDINGS 11.10.11.10. *with Refrain*
James Walch, 1837-1901

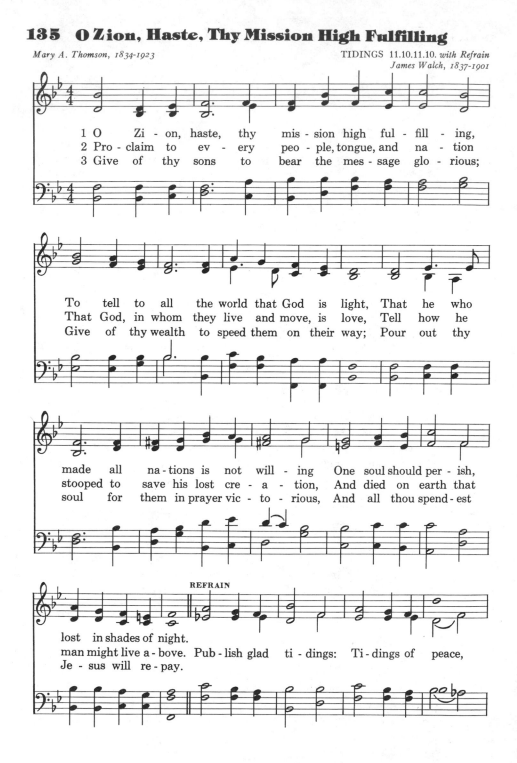

1 O Zi - on, haste, thy mis - sion high ful - fill - ing,
2 Pro - claim to ev - ery peo - ple, tongue, and na - tion
3 Give of thy sons to bear the mes - sage glo - rious;

To tell to all the world that God is light, That he who
That God, in whom they live and move, is love, Tell how he
Give of thy wealth to speed them on their way; Pour out thy

made all na - tions is not will - ing One soul should per - ish,
stooped to save his lost cre - a - tion, And died on earth that
soul for them in prayer vic - to - rious, And all thou spend - est

REFRAIN

lost in shades of night.
man might live a - bove. Pub - lish glad ti - dings: Ti - dings of peace,
Je - sus will re - pay.

SOURCE OF TEXT: Written 1868–1871, the first hymnal inclusion seems to be the Episcopal *Hymnal*,
New York, 1892. SOURCE OF TUNE: Written in 1875, it was included in Charles L. Hutchins's musical
edition of the Episcopal *Hymnal*, 1894.

Ti - dings of Je - sus, Re - demp-tion and re - lease. A - men.

Creation's Lord, We Give Thee Thanks 136

William De Witt Hyde, 1858-1917, alt.

RAMWOLD L.M.
Richard Warner, 1908-

1 Cre - a - tion's Lord, we give thee thanks   That this thy world is
2 That thou hast not yet fin - ished man,   That we are in the
3 Be - yond the pres - ent sin and shame,   Wrong's bit - ter, cru - el,
4 What though the king-dom long de - lay,   And still with haugh-ty

in - com - plete,   That bat - tle calls our mar-shaled ranks,
mak - ing still,   As friends who share the Mak - er's plan,
scorch-ing blight,   We see the beck-oning 'vi - sion flame,
foes must cope?   It gives us that for which to pray,

In unison

That work a - waits our hands and feet,
As sons who know the Fa - ther's will.
The bless - ed king - dom of the right.
A field for toil and faith and hope. A - men.

SOURCE OF TEXT: *The Outlook*, LXXIV, May 1903. The first hymnal inclusion was Hosmer's *Unity Hymns and Carols*, New York, 1911. SOURCE OF TUNE: *The Pilgrim Hymnal*, Boston, 1958, copyright The Pilgrim Press. Used by permission.

137 We Praise Thee, O God, Our Redeemer

Julia C. Cory, 1882-1963

KREMSER 12.11.12.11.
Netherlands Folk Song, 1626
Arr. by Edward Kremser, 1838-1914

1 We praise Thee, O God, our Re-deem-er, Cre-a-tor,
2 We wor-ship Thee, God of our fa-thers, we bless Thee;
3 With voic-es u-nit-ed our prais-es we of-fer,

In grate-ful de-vo-tion our trib-ute we bring.
Through life's storm and tem-pest our Guide hast Thou been.
And glad-ly our song of true wor-ship we raise;

We lay it be-fore Thee, we kneel and a-dore Thee,
When per-ils o'er-take us, es-cape Thou wilt make us,
Our sins now con-fess-ing, we pray for Thy bless-ing,

We bless Thy ho-ly name, glad prais-es we sing.
And with Thy help, O Lord, life's bat-tles we win.
To Thee, our great Re-deem-er, ev-er be praise. A-men.

SOURCE OF TEXT: Written in 1902. Used by permission of the author. SOURCE OF TUNE: A Dutch folk song which appeared in Valerius' *Neder-landtsch Gedenckclanck*, Haarlem, 1626. Kremser's version appeared in his *Sechs Altniederlandische Volkslieder*, Leipzig, 1877.

My Song Is Love Unknown 138

Samuel Crossman, 1624-1684

ROBERTSON 6.6 6.6.4.4.4.4.
James Bigelow, 1920-

1 My song is love un - known, My Sav - iour's love to
2 He came from His blest throne, Sal - va - tion to be -
3 Some-times they strew His way, And His sweet prais - es
4 In life, no house, no home My Lord on earth might
5 Here might I stay and sing, No sto - ry so di -

me, Love to the love - less shown, That
stow: But men made strange, and none The
sing; Re - sound - ing all the day Ho -
have; In death, no friend - ly tomb But
vine; Nev - er was love, dear King, Ne -

they might love - ly be. O who am I, That
longed - for Christ would know. But O, my friend, My
san - nas to their King. Then "Cru - ci - fy!" Is
what a strang - er gave. What may I say? Heav'n
ver was grief like thine! This is my friend, In

for my sake My Lord should take Frail flesh and die.
friend in - deed, Who at my need His life did spend!
all their breath, And for His death They thirst and cry.
was His home: But mine the tomb Where - in he lay.
whose sweet praise I all my days Could glad - ly spend.

SOURCE OF TEXT: *The Young Man's Meditation, or some few Sacred Poems upon Select Subjects, and Scriptures*, London, 1664. SOURCE OF TUNE: Copyright 1962 by the composer. Used by permission.

139 Let All the World in Every Corner Sing

George Herbert, *1593-1633*

ALL THE WORLD 10.4.6.6.6.6.10.4.
Robert G. McCutchan, 1877-1959

1 Let all the world in ev-ery cor-ner sing: My God and
2 Let all the world in ev-ery cor-ner sing: My God and

King! The heavens are not too high, His praise may thith-er fly; The
King! The Church with psalms must shout, No door can keep them out: But,

earth is not too low, His prais-es there may grow. Let all the world in
more than all, the heart Must bear the long-est part. Let all the world in

ev - ery cor - ner sing: My God and King! God and King!

SOURCE OF TEXT: First published posthumously in Herbert's *The Temple*, London, 1633. SOURCE OF TUNE: *The Methodist Hymnal*, 1935. McCutchan, editor of this hymnal, submitted this tune in manuscript to the Hymnal Commission. It was accepted without the Commission knowing it was McCutchan's tune, and appeared with the pseudonym "John Porter." Music copyright renewal 1962, Abingdon Press. Used by permission.

Were You There?

Negro Spiritual

WERE YOU THERE *Irregular*
Negro Melody

1 Were you there when they cru-ci-fied my Lord? Were you
2 Were you there when they nailed him to the tree? Were you
3 Were you there when they laid him in the tomb? Were you

there when they cru-ci-fied my Lord?
there when hey hailed him to the tree? Oh!
there when they laid him in the tomb?

Some-times it caus-es me to trem-ble, trem-ble, trem-ble.

Were you there when they cru-ci-fied my Lord?
Were you there when they nailed him to the tree?
Were you there when they laid him in the tomb?

SOURCE OF TEXT AND TUNE: The first published appearance of this traditional negro spiritual was in William E. Barton's *Old Plantation Hymns*, Boston, 1899, with some difference in the first phrase of the melody. The present version first appeared in *Folk Songs of the American Negro*, by John W. Work and Frederick J. Work, Nashville, Tennessee, 1907.

141   Rise Up, O Men of God!

William P. Merrill, 1867-1954

FESTAL SONG S.M.
William H. Walter, 1825-1893

1 Rise up, O men of God! Have done with less-er things;
2 Rise up, O men of God! His king-dom tar-ries long;
3 Rise up, O men of God! The Church for you doth wait,
4 Lift high the cross of Christ; Tread where his feet have trod;

Give heart and soul and mind and strength To serve the King of kings.
Bring in the day of broth-er-hood, And end the night of wrong.
Her strength un-e-qual to her task; Rise up and make her great.
As broth-ers of the Son of man Rise up, O men of God! A-men.

SOURCE OF TEXT: The Presbyterian *Continent*, XLII, February 16, 1911. First hymnal inclusion was in *The Pilgrim Hymnal*, 1912. SOURCE OF TUNE: J. Ireland Tucker's *Hymnal Revised and Enlarged*, 1894.

142   Let Us with a Gladsome Mind

Based on Psalm 136
John Milton, 1608-1674, alt.

CHINESE MELODY 7.7.7.7.
Arr. by Bliss Wiant, 1895-

1 Let us with a glad-some mind Praise the Lord, for he is kind;
2 He, with all-com-mand-ing might, Filled the new-made world with light;
3 He the gold-en-tress-èd sun Caused all day his course to run;
4 The hornèd moon to shine by night, 'Mid her span-gled sis-ters bright;
5 All things liv-ing he doth feed; His full hand sup-plies their need;
6 Let us with a glad-some mind Praise the Lord, for he is kind;

SOURCE OF TEXT: John Milton's *Poems in English and Latin*, 1645. SOURCE OF TUNE: This tune, also known as P'u T'o, is based on a Buddhist chant. It was adapted as a hymn tune by Bliss Wiant and first appeared in *Hymns of Universal Praise (P'u T'ien Sung Tsan)*, Shanghai, 1936, for which Wiant was music editor.

For his mer-cies aye en-dure, Ev - er faith-ful, ev - er sure.

In Christ There Is No East or West 143

John Oxenham, 1852-1941

ST. PETER C.M.
Alexander R. Reinagle, 1799-1877

1 In Christ there is no East or West, In him no South or North;
2 In him shall true hearts ev - ery-where Their high com-mun-ion find;
3 Join hands, then, broth-ers of the faith, What-e'er your race may be!
4 In Christ now meet both East and West, In him meet South and North;

But one great fel-low-ship of love Through-out the whole wide earth.
His serv-ice is the gold-en cord Close-bind-ing all man-kind.
Who serves my Fa-ther as a son Is sure-ly kin to me.
All Christ-ly souls are one in him Through-out the whole wide earth. A-men.

SOURCE OF TEXT: Written in 1908 and first published in *Bees in Amber*, 1913. Used by permission.
SOURCE OF TUNE: Reinagle's *Psalm Tunes for the Voice and Pianoforte*, Oxford, 1830.

144 Lord, I Want to Be a Christian

Negro Spiritual

I WANT TO BE A CHRISTIAN *Irregular.*
Negro Melody

1 Lord, I want to be a Chris-tian In my heart, in my heart;
2 Lord, I want to be more lov-ing In my heart, in my heart;
3 Lord, I want to be more ho-ly In my heart, in my heart;
4 Lord, I want to be like Je-sus In my heart, in my heart;

Lord, I want to be a Chris-tian In my heart.
Lord, I want to be more lov-ing In my heart.
Lord, I want to be more ho-ly In my heart.
Lord, I want to be like Je-sus In my heart.

In my heart, In my heart,
In my heart, In my heart,

Lord, I want to be a Chris-tian In my heart.
Lord, I want to be more lov-ing In my heart.
Lord, I want to be more ho-ly In my heart.
Lord, I want to be like Je-sus In my heart.

SOURCE OF TEXT AND TUNE: The first published appearance of this traditional Negro spiritual was in *Folk Songs of the American Negro*, by John W. Work and Frederick J. Work, Nashville, Tennessee, 1907.

270

I Know Not Where the Road Will Lead 145

Evelyn Atwater Cummins, 1891-

LARAMIE C.M.D.
Arnold G. H. Bode, 1866-

1 I know not where the road will lead I fol - low day by day,
2 And some I love have reached the end, But some with me may stay,
3 The count-less hosts lead on be -fore, I must not fear nor stray;

Or where it ends: I on - ly know I walk the King's high - way.
Their faith and hope still guid - ing me: I walk the King's high - way.
With them, the pil - grims of the faith, I walk the King's high - way.

2 I know not if the way is long, And no one else can say;
4 The way is truth, the way is love, For light and strength I pray,
6 Through light and dark the road leads on Till dawns the end - less day,

But rough or smooth, up hill or down, I walk the King's high-way,
And through the years of life, to God, I walk the King's high-way.
When I shall know why in this life I walk the King's high-way.

SOURCE OF TEXT: Written 1922. First hymnal inclusion was in *The Hymnal 1940*. SOURCE OF TUNE: Composed for this text in 1941 and published in *The Hymnal 1940*. Music copyright. Used by permission The Church Pension Fund.

146   Peace in Our Time, O Lord

John Oxenham, 1852-1941

TAYLOR HALL S.M.D.
Leo Sowerby, 1895-

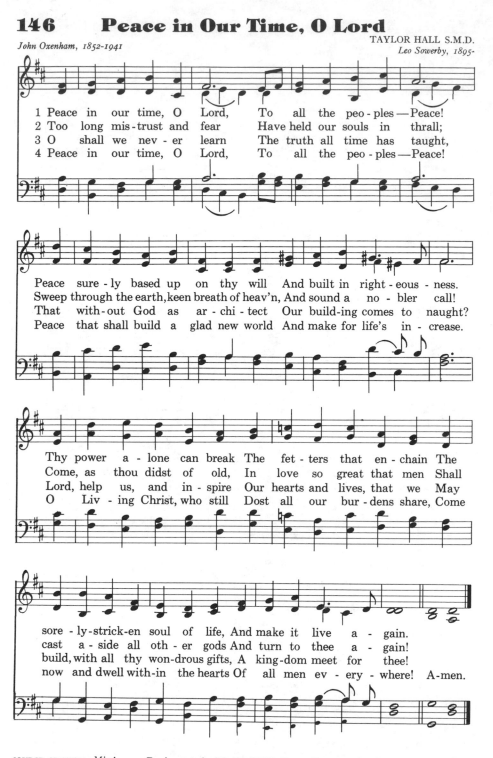

1 Peace in our time, O Lord, To all the peo-ples—Peace!
2 Too long mis-trust and fear Have held our souls in thrall;
3 O shall we nev-er learn The truth all time has taught,
4 Peace in our time, O Lord, To all the peo-ples—Peace!

Peace sure-ly based up on thy will And built in right-eous-ness.
Sweep through the earth, keen breath of heav'n, And sound a no-bler call!
That with-out God as ar-chi-tect Our build-ing comes to naught?
Peace that shall build a glad new world And make for life's in-crease.

Thy power a-lone can break The fet-ters that en-chain The
Come, as thou didst of old, In love so great that men Shall
Lord, help us, and in-spire Our hearts and lives, that we May
O Liv-ing Christ, who still Dost all our bur-dens share, Come

sore-ly-strick-en soul of life, And make it live a-gain.
cast a-side all oth-er gods And turn to thee a-gain!
build, with all thy won-drous gifts, A king-dom meet for thee!
now and dwell with-in the hearts Of all men ev-ery-where! A-men.

SOURCE OF TEXT: *Missionary Review of the World*, LXII, December 1938. Its first hymnal inclusion was in *The Hymnal 1940*. Used by permission. SOURCE OF TUNE: Composed in 1941 and first published in *The Hymnal 1940*. Music copyright. Used by permission of The Church Pension Fund.

The Lord Is Rich and Merciful 147

Thomas T. Lynch, 1818-1871

SHEPHERDS' PIPES C.M.D.
Annabeth McClelland Gay, 1925-

1 The Lord is rich and mer - ci - ful; The Lord is ver - y kind;
2 The Lord is glo - ri - ous and strong; Our God is ver - y high;
3 The Lord is won - der - ful and wise, As all the a - ges tell;

O come to him, come now to him With a be - liev - ing mind.
O trust in him, trust now in him, And have se - cur - i - ty.
O learn of him, learn now of him, Then with thee it is well,

His com - forts, they shall strengthen thee, Like flow - ing wa - ters cool,
He shall be to thee like the sea, And thou shalt sure - ly feel
And with his light thou shalt be blest, There - in to work and live,

And he shall for thy spir - it be A foun - tain ev - er full.
His wind, that blow - eth health - i - ly, Thy sick - ness - es to heal.
And he shall be to thee a rest When eve - ning hours ar - rive.

SOURCE OF TEXT: *The Rivulet*, third edition, London, 1868. SOURCE OF TUNE: *The Pilgrim Hymnal*, Boston, 1958, copyright by The Pilgrim Press. Used by permission.

Ascribed to Clement of Alexandria, 170-220
Trans. by Henry M. Dexter, 1821-1890

HINMAN 6.6.4.6.6.6.4.
Austin C. Lovelace, 1919-

In unison

1 Shep-herd of ea-ger youth, Guid-ing in love and truth Through de-vious ways,
2 Thou art our ho-ly Lord, The all-sub-du-ing Word, Heal-er of strife;
3 Ev-er be Thou our Guide, Our Shep-herd and our Pride, Our Staff and Song;
4 So now, and till we die, Sound we Thy prais-es high, And joy-ful sing;

Christ, our tri-um-phant King, We come Thy name to sing,
Thou didst Thy-self a-base, That from sin's deep dis-grace
Je-sus, Thou Christ of God, By Thy per-en-nial Word,
Let all the ho-ly throng Who to Thy Church be-long

Hith-er our chil-dren bring To shout Thy praise.
Thou might-est save our race, And give us life.
Lead us where Thou hast trod, Make our faith strong.
U-nite and swell the song To Christ our King! A-men.

SOURCE OF TEXT: This hymn was appended to *The Instructor* (or *The Tutor*), written in the second century. SOURCE OF TRANSLATION: *The Congregationalist*, December 21, 1849. The first hymnal publication was in Hedge and Huntington's *Hymns for the Church of Christ*, Boston, 1853. SOURCE OF TUNE: *The Hymnbook*, 1955. Music copyright, 1955, by John Ribble; used by permission.

O Jesus Christ, to Thee May Hymns Be Rising. 149

Bradford Gray Webster

CITY OF GOD 11.10.11.10.
Daniel Moe, 1926–

1. O Jesus Christ, to thee may hymns be ris - ing,
2. Grant us new cour - age, sac - ri - fi - cial, hum - ble,
3. Show us thy Spir - it, brood - ing o'er each cit - y,

In ev - 'ry cit - y for thy love and care;
Strong in thy strength to ven - ture and to dare;
As thou didst weep a - bove Je - ru - sa - lem,

In - spire our wor - ship, grant the glad sur - pris - ing
To lift the fall - en, guide the feet that stum - ble,
Seek - ing to gath - er all in love and pit - y,

That thy blest Spir - it brings men ev - 'ry where.
Seek out the lone - ly and God's mer - cy share.
And heal - ing those who touch thy gar - ment's hem.

SOURCE OF TEXT: *Five New Hymns on the City*, 1954. Copyright 1954 by the Hymn Society of America. Used by permission. SOURCE OF TUNE: Music copyright 1957 Augsburg Publishing House. Used by permission.

150   Jesus, Name All Names Above

Theoctistus of the Studium, c.890
Tr. John M, Neale, 1818-1866, alt.

NAME OF JESUS 7.6.7.6.8.8.7.6.
Ralph Alvin Strom, 1909-

1 Je - sus, Name all names a - bove;   Je - sus, best and dear - est;
2 Je - sus, crowned with bit - ter thorn,   By man - kind for - sak - en,
3 Je - sus, o - pen me the gate   That of old he en - tered

Je - sus, fount of per - fect love,   Ho - liest, ten - derest, near - est;
Je - sus, who through scourge and scorn   Held thy faith un - shak - en,
Who, in that most lost es - tate,   Whol - ly on thee ven - tured;

Thou the source of grace com - plet - est, Thou the pur - est, thou the sweet - est,
Je - sus, clad in pur - ple rai - ment, For man's e - vils mak - ing pay - ment:
Je - sus, leave me not to lan - guish: Help - less, hope - less, full of an - guish!

Thou the well of power di - vine,   Make me, keep me, seal me thine!
Let not all thy woe and pain,   Let not Cal - vary be in vain!
Je - sus, let me hear thee say,   'Thou shalt be with me to - day!' A - men.

SOURCE OF TEXT: From Theoctistus's "Suppliant Canon to Jesus" in the *Paracletice* or *Great Octoechus* of the Eastern Orthodox Church. SOURCE OF TRANSLATION: *Hymns of the Eastern Church*, London, 1862. SOURCE OF TUNE: Lutheran *Service Book and Hymnal*, 1958. Used by permission.

The Bread of Life for All Men Broken 151

Timothy T'ing-fang Lew, *1892-1947*
Tr. Walter R. O. Taylor, *1890-*

SHENG EN 9.8.9.9.
Su Yin-lan, 1915-1937
Arr. by Bliss Wiant, 1895-

1 The bread of life for all men broken! He drank the cup
2 With god-ly fear we seek thy pre-sence; Our hearts are sad,
3 O Lord, we pray, come thou a-mong us, Light-en our eyes,

on Gol-go-tha. His grace we trust, and spread with rev-er-ence
peo-ple dis-tressed. Thy ho-ly face is stained with bit-ter tears,
bright-ly ap-pear! Im-man-u-el, heav'n's joy un-end-ing,

This ho-ly feast, and thus re-mem-ber.
Our hu-man pain still bear-est thou with us.
Our life with thine for-ev-er blend-ing. A-men.

SOURCE OF TEXT AND TUNE: The Chinese text with this arrangement of the tune first appeared in *Hymns of Universal Praise* (*P'u T'ien Sung Tsan*), Shanghai, 1936, with the author as editor and Wiant as music editor. The tune name means "Holy Grace."

Rise to Greet the Sun

SOURCE OF TEXT AND TUNE: The Chinese text, a paraphase of Psalm 19:1–6, together with this arrangement of the tune, first appeared in *Hymns of Universal Praise* (*P'u T'ien Sung Tsan*), Shanghai, 1936. The translation first appeared in *The Pagoda*, 1946, a small collection of Chinese songs with English translations, compiled by Bliss Wiant. Used by permission.

Deep Were His Wounds, and Red 153

William Johnson, 1906-

MARLEE 6.6.6.6.8.8.
Leland B. Sateren, 1913-

1 Deep were his wounds, and red, On cru - el Cal - va - ry,
2 He suf - fered shame and scorn, And wretch - ed, dire dis - grace;
3 His life, his all, he gave When he was cru - ci - fied;

As on the Cross he bled In bit - ter ag - o - ny; But they, whom
For - sak - en and for - lorn, He hung there in our place. But such as
Our bur - dened souls to save, What fear - ful death he died! But each of

sin has wound - ed sore, Find heal - ing in the wounds he bore.
would from sin be free Look to his Cross for vic - to - ry.
us, though dead in sin, Through him e - ter - nal life may win.

SOURCE OF TEXT AND TUNE: Lutheran *Service Book and Hymnal*, 1958. Used by permission.

Lord Christ, When First Thou Cam'st to Men

W. Russell Bowie, 1882-

KIRKEN DEN ER ET 8.7.8.7.8.8.7.
Ludvig M. Lindeman, 1812-1887

1 Lord Christ, when first thou cam'st to men, Up-on a cross they bound thee,
2 O awe-ful love, which found no room In life where sin de-nied thee,
3 New ad-vent of the love of Christ, Shall we a-gain re-fuse thee
4 O wound-ed hands of Je-sus, build In us thy new cre-a-tion;

And mocked thy sav-ing king-ship then By thorns with which they crowned thee;
And, doomed to death, must bring to doom The power which cru-ci-fied thee,
Till in the night of hate and war We per-ish as we lose thee?
Our pride is dust; our vaunt is stilled; We wait thy rev-e-la-tion.

And still our wrongs may weave thee now New thorns to pierce that
Till not a stone was left on stone, And all a na-tion's
From old un-faith our souls re-lease To seek the king-dom
O love that tri-umphs o-ver loss, We bring our hearts be-

stead-y brow, And robe of sor-row round thee.
pride o'erthrown, Went down to dust be-side thee!
of thy peace, By which a-lone we choose thee.
fore thy cross, To fin-ish thy sal-va-tion. A-men.

SOURCE OF TEXT: Written in 1928, its first hymnal inclusion was in *Enlarged Songs of Praise*, London, 1931. It is from Bowie's *Lift Up Your Hearts*, used by permission of Abingdon Press. SOURCE OF TUNE: Composed for Grundtvig's "Kirken den er et gammelt Hus" (Built on the Rock the Church doth stand), it first appeared in W. A. Wexel's *Christelige Psalmer*, Norway, 1840. First used with this text in *Congregational Praise*, London, 1951.

From Thee All Skill and Science Flow 155

Charles Kingsley, 1819–1875

MASSACHUSETTS C.M.D.
Katherine K. Davis, 1892–

Unison

1. From thee all skill and sci-ence flow, All pit-y, care, and love,
2. And has-ten, Lord, that per-fect day When pain and death shall cease,

All calm and cour-age, faith and hope: O pour them from a-bove;
And thy just rule shall fill the earth With health and light and peace,

And part them, Lord, to each and all, As each and all shall need,
When-ev-er blue the sky shall gleam, And ev-er green the sod,

To rise like in-cense, each to thee, In no-ble thought and deed.
And man's rude work de-face no more The par-a-dise of God. A-men.

SOURCE OF TEXT: Purportedly written by Kingsley upon request for a ceremony laying the foundation stone for a section of Queen's Hospital, Birmingham, England, 1871. SOURCE OF TUNE: *The Methodist Hymnal*, 1966. Music copyright © 1964 by Abingdon Press. Used by permission.

156 Christian, Dost Thou See Them

Andrew of Crete (?), 660–732
Tr. John M. Neale, 1818–1866

WALDA 6.5.6.5.D.
Lloyd Pfautsch, 1921–

Unison

1. Chris - tian, dost thou see them On the ho - ly ground,
2. Chris - tian, dost thou feel them, How they work with - in,
3. Chris - tian, dost thou hear them, How they speak thee fair?
4. Well I know thy trou - ble, O my ser - vant true;

How the powers of dark - ness Rage thy steps a - round?
Striv - ing, tempt - ing, lur - ing, Goad - ing in - to sin?
"Al - ways fast and vi - gil? Al - ways watch and prayer?"
Thou art ver - y wea - ry; I was wea - ry too;

Chris - tian, up and smite them, Count - ing gain but loss,
Chris - tian, nev - er trem - ble; Nev - er be down - cast;
Chris - tian, an - swer bold - ly, "While I breathe I pray!"
But that toil shall make thee Some day all mine own,

SOURCE OF TEXT: Attributed by Neale to St. Andrew, as one of the "Stichera for the Second Week of the Great Fast." SOURCE OF TRANSLATION: Neale's *Hymns of the Eastern Church*, 1862. SOURCE OF TUNE: Written in 1960–61, it was published for the first time in *The Methodist Hymnal*, 1966. Music copyright © 1962 by Abingdon Press. Used by permission.

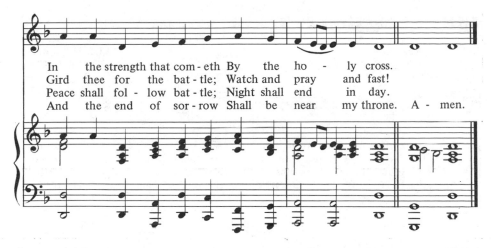

In the strength that com - eth By the ho - ly cross.
Gird thee for the bat - tle; Watch and pray and fast!
Peace shall fol - low bat - tle; Night shall end in day.
And the end of sor - row Shall be near my throne. A - men.

Thou, Whose Purpose Is to Kindle 157

David Elton Trueblood, 1900–

LIBERTY 8.7.8.7.
American Folk Tune
arr. Don Riddle, 1930–

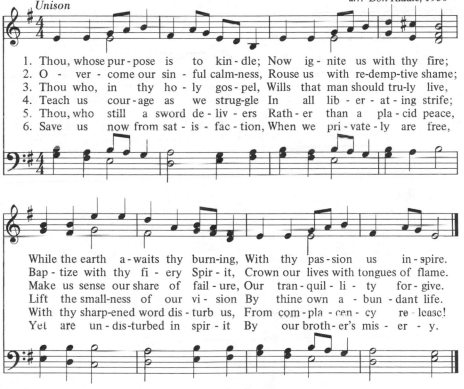

1. Thou, whose pur - pose is to kin - dle; Now ig - nite us with thy fire;
2. O - ver - come our sin - ful calm-ness, Rouse us with re-demp-tive shame;
3. Thou who, in thy ho - ly gos - pel, Wills that man should tru - ly live,
4. Teach us cour - age as we strug-gle In all lib - er - at - ing strife;
5. Thou, who still a sword de - liv - ers Rath - er than a pla - cid peace,
6. Save us now from sat - is - fac - tion, When we pri - vate - ly are free,

While the earth a - waits thy burn-ing, With thy pas - sion us in - spire.
Bap - tize with thy fi - ery Spir - it, Crown our lives with tongues of flame.
Make us sense our share of fail - ure, Our tran - quil - li - ty for - give.
Lift the small-ness of our vi - sion By thine own a - bun - dant life.
With thy sharp-ened word dis - turb us, From com - pla - cen - cy re - lease!
Yet are un - dis-turbed in spir - it By our broth - er's mis - er - y.

158 My God Is There, Controlling

William W. Reid, 1890–

ROBIN 8.8.8.7.
J. R. Tipton, 1942–

1. We search the star - lit Milk - y Way, A mil - ion worlds in rhyth - mic sway, Yet in our blind - ness some will say, "There is no God con - trol - ling, con - trol - ling!"

2. But as I grope from sphere to sphere, New won - ders crowd the eye, the ear, And faith grows firm - er ev - 'ry year: "My God is there, con - trol - ling, con - trol - ling!"

3. We probe the at - oms for their cause, Ex - plore the earth for na - ture's laws, Yet sel - dom in our search - ing pause To think of God con - trol - ling, con - trol - ling.

4. Each flash of fact from out the night, Each burst of truth up - on my sight That quick - ens awe or adds de - light, Re - veals my God con - trol - ling, con - trol - ling.

SOURCE OF TEXT: Reid's *My God Is There, Controlling, and other Hymns and Poems.* Copyright 1965 by The Hymn Society of America. Used by permission. SOURCE OF TUNE: *Baptist Hymnal,* 1975. © Copyright 1975 Broadman Press. All rights reserved. Used by permission.

Praise the Lord 159

Psalm 113:1–2 (st. 1)
Marjorie Jillson (st. 2-4), 1931–

CARPENTER 1970, Irregular
Heinz Werner Zimmermann, 1930–

Unison

1. Praise the Lord! Praise, O ser-vants of the Lord! Praise the
2. Praise the Lord! Thanks and prais-es sing to God! Day by
3. Praise the Lord! Praise and glo-ry give to God! Who is
4. Praise the Lord! Praise, O ser-vants of the Lord! Praise the

name of the Lord! Bless-ed be the name of the Lord!
day to the Lord! High a-bove the na-tions is God,
like un-to Him? Rais-ing up the poor from the dust,
love of the Lord! Giv-ing to the home-less a home,

Bless-ed be the name of the Lord From this time
High a-bove the na-tions is God, His glo-ry
Rais-ing up the poor from the dust, He makes them
Giv-ing to the home-less a home, He fills their

forth and for-ev-er-more! Praise the Lord! Praise the Lord!
high o-ver earth and sky! Praise the Lord! Praise the Lord!
dwell in his heart and home. Praise the Lord! Praise the Lord!
hearts with new hope and joy! Praise the Lord! Praise the Lord!

SOURCE OF TEXT AND TUNE: From *Five Hymns* by Heinz Werner Zimmermann, copyright 1973 by Concordia Publishing House. Used by permission.

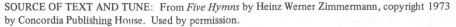

Index of Illustrative Hymns

First column lists hymn title; second, hymn number; third, name of corresponding tune.

Index of Illustrative Tunes

Numbers refer to hymns for which tunes are used.

General Index

First lines of hymns are given in quotes. Tune names appear in capitals and small capitals. All numbers refer to pages. Illustrative hymns and tunes are indexed under separate Indexes—Illustrative Hymns and Illustrative Tunes.